Leaving Your Mark

The Political Career of Nebraska State Senator Jerome Warner

Charlyne Berens

Leaving Your Mark

The Political Career of Nebraska State Senator Jerome Warner

Charlyne Berens

T**imes** Nebraska

"Timeless thoughts from thoughtful Nebraskans."
Sharing Nebraska with the world.

Nebraska Times
1160 Eastridge, Seward, NE 68434

5 4 3 2 1

ISBN 0-9643353-5-2

Photo Credits:

Cover photo and photo of Warner in committee meeting: courtesy of the Unicameral Information Office.

Photo of Senator Warner, his brother Charlie and his children Liz and Jamie (pg. 140): courtesy of the Lower Platte South Natural Resources District.

All other photos are from the Warner family collection.

TABLE OF CONTENTS

Part Four: Committing to Legislative Leadership

Part Five: Practicing Statesmanship

Part Six: Perfecting Statesmanship

This book is dedicated to Senator Jerome Warner, who has left the indelible and beneficial mark of his intelligence and integrity upon the State of Nebraska.

ACKNOWLEDGMENTS

Senator Jerome Warner is, of course, the reason for this book. A modest man, he never would have suggested that someone set down the story of his legislative career. He agreed to allow me to do so not because he wanted his own accomplishments trumpeted about but because of his belief in the importance of the Nebraska Legislature's institutional memory. He realized he is himself the repository of hundreds of megabytes of that memory, and he realized it was worth committing it to paper.

"Yeah, I suppose somebody ought to get some of this stuff down" was his response to my request that I be allowed to write his biography.

He has been enormously generous with his time, spending hours recollecting the high points—and some of the low points—of his career. He has remembered and discussed people and events, programs and plans. In the process, he has talked political theory and philosophy. Sometimes it is overt; sometimes it simply informs his analysis, giving credence to the fact that he has, indeed, been politically educated during his 34 years in the Legislature.

I thank him for his time, his patience and his insights. It has been an honor and pleasure to work with him.

Several other people also deserve thanks for their contributions to this project. Will Norton, Jr., agreed to be my primary editor. The dean of the College of Journalism and Mass Communications at the University of Nebraska-Lincoln, Dr. Norton is a good friend and a good editor. His suggestions have been enormously helpful and have made this book far better than it would otherwise have been. I will always be grateful.

Corliss Young, a long-time member of Senator Warner's staff, has been an invaluable help. She checked dates and names and spellings. She caught discrepancies and errors of fact. She tracked down information and photographs. She put up with endless questions—and all with patience and good humor.

Brian Humes, political science professor at UNL, also read the manuscript and offered helpful criticisms. Daryl Frazell, journalism professor at UNL, applied his outstanding copy editing skills to the final draft. And Jennifer Bartels, journalism student at UNL, was a fine proof reader.

Of course, I would never have made it through this project without the encouragement of my husband, Dennis, who never gave up on me and never let me give up on myself.

PREFACE

Three friends waited out a snowstorm in Omaha in 1984, sharing observations and philosophies at a hotel bar. One of the three was a trade association executive who had done a lot of lobbying in the Nebraska Unicameral Legislature. The other two were avid political on-lookers. I was one of the latter.

Much of the conversation centered on the machinations—for good or ill—of the state legislature and its members. We talked about how it seemed that legislators of questionable character were often the most influential while the rock-bottom honest ones seldom played much of a role in the action.

I asked my friend the lobbyist whether he thought it were possible for a politician to be powerful and still maintain his integrity.

"No, I don't think so," he said, but then he interrupted himself.

"No, wait. There is one exception: Jerome Warner."

I never forgot that comment. In fact, I heard it echoed more than just occasionally in various forms and settings in subsequent years. It seemed everyone respected Jerome Warner, the senator from Waverly. And it seemed everyone turned to Warner when major legislative work needed to be done.

Then in 1994, I began research for my political science master's thesis. The paper focused on the committee system in the Nebraska Unicameral with special attention to the Appropriations Committee. Warner had been Appropriations chairman from 1977 to 1990, so I interviewed him at some length. That experience reinforced my belief that all those comments I had heard were right: Warner was a powerful politician who had maintained his integrity throughout a long legislative career.

I decided someone ought to tell his story. I asked him whether he would allow me to be that someone, and he agreed. This book is the result.

It is, without question, a sympathetic portrait. I did not set out to dig dirt, and as I went along, I became thoroughly convinced there was no dirt to dig anyway. Jerome Warner is not perfect. He is not without political detractors. But the testimony of friends, colleagues and political observers and his own recollections of his 34 years in public life have led me overwhelmingly to conclude that Senator Warner has done great good for Nebraska. It has been a privilege to know him and to set down his story for his fellow citizens to read.

Charlyne Berens
November 1996

PART ONE
THE PATH TO THE LEGISLATURE

Introduction

State Senator Jerome Warner says he always knew he would go into politics. It was, he says, "like knowing I'd get my driver's license when I turned 16 or knowing I'd go to the university." It was a foregone conclusion.

It was a conclusion learned from his father, Charles Warner, himself a state senator and speaker of the Nebraska Legislature when it became a one-house chamber in 1937. Politics and public service were in the Warner blood and in the family's dinner table conversation and in their everyday lives.

"I remember going to town with my dad when I was a kid," Warner recalls. "Almost every time, somebody would stop Dad on the street and say, 'Charlie, have you got a minute?'

"'I'd better have,' Dad would say. 'I work for you.'" Father and son would stop and hear out the constituent and, more often than not, talk to several more along the way before they finished their business and went home to the farm. Charles Warner took seriously the needs of the people he represented. Politics, in the Warner book, meant service. To Jerome Warner, it still does.

Take the office, for instance. One might expect a plush office in the state Capitol for a senator who has spent 34 years in the legislature and has been the speaker and the chairman of the body's most powerful committees.

Instead, Jerome Warner works out of a cavernous office with no windows. Voices raised above a modulated murmur echo off the ceiling, and fluorescent bulbs provide stark white light. Visitors and occupant alike enter the office down a long hall that further separates the room from daylight. The seasons could change and the occupant of this office would have no way of knowing.

Why this office? The senator looks toward the ceiling out of the corners of his eyes and smiles a small smile. "Nobody else wanted it," he says.

He moved to Room 1401 in 1991, when he was chairman of the Executive Board and in charge of assigning offices for all the senators. "This was space no one else wanted," Warner says. "I tend not to ask someone else to do something I'm not willing to do myself."

The work Warner has been willing to do himself has been considerable. Through it, he has made an impact on Nebraska's present and future, sometimes in short-term ways whose effects are felt almost at once and, just as often, by laying the groundwork for long-term change whose effects may stretch over years or even decades.

Warner managed to accomplish both kinds of change during his 14 years as chairman of the Nebraska Legislature's Appropriations Committee and over the span of his legislative career as a leader in state aid to schools. The emphasis is on the long-term side when it comes to Warner's influence on the state's highway system and the way it is financed. And his concern for the state's university system has been obvious year in and year out during Warner's 34 years in office.

Of course, those 34 years in office have an impact in and of themselves. Warner has developed an institutional memory that has increased his value to the Legislature and to the state. "He was there at the creation," says Henry Cordes, an Omaha World-Herald reporter. "He remembers the original purpose (or programs and legislation) and tries to make sure it doesn't get lost" when the legislature decides to revisit issues.

But it is probably as chairman of the Appropriations Committee from 1977-90 that the senator made the news most often. Warner smiles as he remembers that newspapers often referred to him as "the powerful chairman of the powerful Appropriations Committee."

"He *was* the Appropriations Committee," says Senator Don Wesely of Lincoln, who still serves in the Unicameral.[1] "He forged alliances that were blocks of granite, and he could build what he wanted with those blocks."

What he built was the state's budget. To the Appropriations Commit-

[1] While the word "unicameral" is an adjective, Nebraskans often refer to their unicameral legislature as the Unicameral. The word will be used as a noun throughout this book.

tee is given the power of the purse—a great deal of power. Scott Moore, who succeeded Warner as chair of Appropriations in 1990, describes it as a new take on the Golden Rule: "He who has the gold makes the rules."

Being chairman of Appropriations made Warner one of the most powerful people in the state, probably as powerful as the governor. Warner told the Lincoln Journal in 1987 that "governors can propose, and they can veto, but their input between the two—its very practical effect—is limited. ... They can help set the stage for change, but only the Legislature can cause it."

Although most Nebraskans probably still associate Warner with the Appropriations Committee, his service there is only part of the picture. Long before he was elected to chair that committee, Warner had already fought major campaigns that changed some of the fundamental undergirdings of the state.

For example, Nebraska's system of state aid to schools has Warner's fingerprints all over it. The new senator introduced a bill to provide such aid in 1963, during his first session in the Unicameral, and again 1965. He finally saw a measure passed in 1967.

Dick Herman, then a reporter for the Lincoln Journal, points out that Warner's bill was the first educational reform proposal that held the double-edged sword. It included both property tax relief and a way to improve educational opportunities for children in property-poor districts.

Don Walton, who covered the Legislature for the Lincoln Star in the 1960s, says he remembers how doggedly Warner fought for state aid to schools. When the bill finally passed, "there were tears in his eyes," Walton says.

Warner's impact on state aid to schools is legendary, even among those who came to the Unicameral years after the first battles were fought and won. "Warner was a major force in writing state aid to schools legislation in the 1960s," says Sandy Scofield, who served in the Legislature from 1983-90. While he may not have been the point man in succeeding campaigns for state aid to schools, Warner's interest in the topic and the fairness he saw it providing to the children of the state has never wavered.

But the Warner contribution that has probably had the biggest day-to-day impact on Nebraska's citizens is not directly connected to the

Appropriations Committee and has nothing to do with aid to schools. Instead, it can be summed up in one word: roads.

"He totally revised the way highways are financed in Nebraska," says Jim Joyce. Joyce is a reporter who has covered the Statehouse for 22 years, the last 17 for the Lincoln Star (now the Journal Star). As a result of Warner's efforts, Joyce says, "We have one of the finer systems of public roads in the nation."

Ben Nelson, governor of Nebraska from 1991 to the present, also cites Warner's role in Nebraska's highway system. "He elevated the whole area of roads generally above politics—and certainly above partisanship," Nelson says.

Warner is widely acknowledged as the force behind the package of 16 highway bills that passed the Legislature in 1967, establishing a system that is still largely intact. That move established a system to assure future decisions will be based on long-term planning and real need, not on political games and power.

Warner is also responsible for the 1980 legislation that created a formula for setting the state's variable gasoline tax rates. That, too, takes politics out of the process, Nelson points out.

As Scofield says, "We're pretty fortunate not to have political roads."

Nearly three decades after presiding over the birth of Nebraska's highway plan, Warner is still interested in roads. But his career also reflects his interest in lots of other big issues; higher education is one.

Warner is considered the single person most responsible for bringing Kearney State College into the University of Nebraska system. He also was a major player in the creation and passage of the constitutional amendment that created the Coordinating Commission for Postsecondary Education. Furthermore, he is known as a passionate supporter of the state's university.

Doug Bereuter leaves no doubt about that. Bereuter, now one of Nebraska's representatives in the U.S. Congress, was vice chairman of the Unicameral's Appropriations Committee during the first two years Warner was chairman.

"He has had a more favorable impact on the progress of the University of Nebraska than any other legislator. Period," Bereuter says.

But Warner's most long-term contribution may be his institutional memory, something that both stems from and contributes to the major legislative successes to which he can lay claim.

Ben Nelson calls it stability and being able to provide a historical perspective. Lee Rupp, former state senator, calls it a steady guiding hand. Retired Nebraska Senator Jim Exon puts it directly:

"He's Mr. Unicameral."

Scott Moore, now Nebraska Secretary of State, paraphrases Harry Truman: "The only thing new is history you haven't read yet." Then Moore adds, "But in Jerry Warner's case, he was there. ... He knows the intricacies of how things happened."

Moore says he has often gone to Warner to ask how some particular state policy or law transpired decades ago and has found him an amazing resource who can bring a historical and policy perspective to nearly every contemporary political issue.

"Senator Warner is the best argument against term limits," Governor Nelson says.

Not every politician who has been a powerful force in government for more than three decades continues to earn praise from colleagues, observers and constituents. But Warner is not every politician.

Abraham Lincoln said, "Nearly all men can stand adversity, but if you want to test a man's character, give him power."

From all accounts, Warner has met the test. Colleagues say he has earned their trust and that of his constituents—and the wider population of Nebraska—by being consistent, honest, self-effacing and kind. This book focuses on the major contributions Warner has made to the state of Nebraska and examines how he has managed to wield a great deal of power and at the same time maintain the respect of his colleagues, his constituents and the people of the state.

Warner himself says he's just doing what he was brought up to do: serve. As his father did, he works for the citizens of Nebraska.

Politics in the Blood

Warner admits his attitude toward government was something he learned from his parents, particularly his father. Charles Warner's life revolved around Nebraska politics and farming. So did his family's.

"The two things most frequently discussed at dinner were Hereford cattle and politics," Jerome Warner says.

Hereford cattle and a farm in northeastern Lancaster County are the first Warner family legacy; politics is the second. Three Warner brothers—one of whom was the senator's grandfather—came to the United States from Sweden in 1871 and homesteaded five miles north of where Warner lives now. Two worked for the railroad while the other farmed. Eventually, Warner's father, Charles, took over the farm.

Before he started farming, Charles Warner got an education that was somewhat unusual for a farmer of his day, attending first Luther College in Wahoo and then Lincoln Normal University before graduating from the University of Nebraska in 1899.

The next year, Charles Warner ran for the Nebraska Legislature, having been nominated as a Republican by the county convention. During his first two-year term in office, he initiated what has become a Warner family tradition: a reputation as a strong ally of the University of Nebraska. Chancellor E. Benjamin Andrews wrote in April 1901:

"I cannot let the occasion pass without thanking you, both officially and personally, for the care, time and patience which you were good enough to devote to university matters during the recent session. I hope you will be elected to the legislature as long as you are willing to serve, for I am sure that the financial interests of the state could not be in more suitable hands."

After serving in the 1901 legislative session, Charles Warner went off to Washington, D.C., where he enrolled in law classes at Columbia Law School. Lecturers for the courses included Supreme Court Justices John Marshall Harlan and David Brewer, who lectured on the Constitution and on corporate law.

Warner returned to Nebraska in 1902 and was elected to a second term in the Nebraska House of Representatives. Again, his legislative support for the university drew praise from Chancellor Andrews.

The letters from the Chancellor were included in campaign material supporting Warner's election in 1904 to a third term in the state's House of Representatives. The material also included reference to other Warner accomplishments and to his being nominated by acclamation and asserted, "It is purely on his record that this candidate makes his appearance for a third term."

Charles Warner was elected to that third term, but he was not nominated again in 1906. "He was fairly independent. I assume he fell out of favor with the movers and shakers in the party," his son says.

But a change in the way Nebraska's political parties did business let Charles Warner circumvent the good will of the party elites and get back into elective politics. Charles ran again for the Legislature again in 1914, after changed procedures provided that nominees be chosen by open primary elections. He lost the general election that time but was successful in 1918 and served from 1919 through 1937. That means Charles Warner survived the Nebraska Legislature's down-sizing from a two-house body of 133 people to a one-house body of 43. Not only was he elected to the smaller body, but he was chosen as the speaker of the new Unicameral Legislature's first session in 1937.

His son Jerome, born Nov. 23, 1927, was 11 years old in 1938 when Charles was the Republican nominee for governor. That campaign ended in defeat, as did a 1940 attempt at the state's executive office. But Charles Warner was elected lieutenant governor in 1948 and held the office until he died in 1955.

In the meantime, Charles and his wife Esther and their sons, Charles, Jr., born in 1922, and Jerome, farmed their land near Waverly. As one would expect of a Nebraska farm family in the early decades of the 20th century, Charles, Sr., was in charge of the day-to-day farm work and the 12-15 hired men the family employed during the summer when equipment was still powered by horses. But Charles' political and legislative obligations took him way from the farm on many an occasion. When his father was not there to run the place, Jerome remembers, no hired man or male relative took over: "Mom did it."

Esther Warner seemed to thrive on the responsibility of being a farm wife, both in the early decades of her marriage and later on, when her husband was a prominent state politician. She told a Lincoln paper in a 1956 interview that she found keeping the books for the farm and the registrations for the Hereford herd to be "fascinating." She also told the paper housework was not her first love and that she did it primarily out of necessity. "She'd rather watch the progress of the new irrigation pumps—installed this year on the farmland," the paper's story said.

Charles had to feel fortunate that his wife was willing to take a hand in the day-to-day operation of the farm. Her help made it possible for him to divide his time between the farm, his legislative career and other civic duties such as memberships on the school board, Waverly Farmers Elevator board, county fair board, state fair board and committees at several churches.

His younger son often accompanied him to the meetings and observed "how he handled himself in potentially controversial situations. I learned a lot, even though I couldn't identify it." For one thing, although people who had opposed Charles Warner on particular issues might hold grudges, Warner himself never did. "What was done was done," his son summarizes.

Charles Warner had the same attitude toward lost elections. He lost campaigns for six offices during his lifetime—for the legislature in 1914, for governor in 1938 and 1940, for the legislature in 1944, for lieutenant governor in 1948—and lost a bid to be a delegate to Nebraska's constitutional convention in 1919-20. Warner had really wanted to be part of the body that rewrote the state's constitution, and he was disappointed when he was not chosen to participate. That was the only loss he seemed to regret, Jerome says. "I never heard any remorse about the others. That was just how it was."

The younger Warner says that kind of attitude is something most farmers acquire naturally. "What the yield is, the yield is—and you start talking about next year."

Charles Warner the farmer was always willing to embrace new ideas. On the farm, the Warner family made the switch from horses to tractors earlier than many of their neighbors. And they tried out experimental equipment for International Harvester, including tractors with rubber tires instead of iron wheels. Warner was also ready to try new ideas in government. "He was very open to doing things different or better," Jerome says, including helping Nebraska switch from the traditional two-house, partisan legislature to the current unicameral system.

During his childhood, Warner recalls how his father was in and out of office and what that taught him about a politician's relationship to his constituents. "If he had won an election, people crossed the street to come talk to him. If he had lost, people crossed the street to avoid him. It's the office people came to see."

Warner says that early lesson about politics has stayed with him throughout his career. It is the power of the office that people appreciate and want to get close to, not necessarily the person holding the office. Knowing that, Warner says, has kept him from being overly impressed by politicians.

But, by watching the way his father, the politician, interacted with his constituents and watching the example his parents set, Warner learned to respect public office. He remembers an incident that occurred when he was 8 years old.

Incumbent president Franklin Delano Roosevelt came to Lincoln for a parade down O Street during his 1936 campaign against Alf Landon. Warner and his mother, a staunch Republican, joined the throngs along the parade route.

Naturally enough, "I had on Landon (for President) buttons," Warner remembers. "But when Roosevelt came along, my mother zipped my jacket shut (to cover the buttons) because, she said, 'It's the *president* coming by, not just Roosevelt.' She had lots of respect for the office," and her example had a lasting influence on her son.

Esther Warner had a feel for politics. Betty Schlaphoff, a long-time family friend, calls it "a natural sense of political fallout," an ability to see ahead of time the likely political consequences of a particular action. That may have been one thing that attracted the politically minded Charles Warner to her.

Born in Illinois in 1891 to Swedish immigrants, Esther Phyllis Anderson had come to Nebraska with her parents when she was 2 years old. After country school and Waverly High School, she attended Nebraska Wesleyan University in Lincoln for two years to earn a teaching certificate. She taught several years before marrying Charles Warner on Dec. 9, 1914.

Politics played a major role in the family's life, Warner says, but so did the church. "My parents were active in two or three churches," a tribute to their leadership in the community. The family belonged to the Bethlehem Covenant Church, where Warner is still a member, and his father chaired the congregation's building committee in the early 1900s. Charles Warner also chaired the building committee for the Methodist church at Prairie Home. The Warners attended the Waverly Methodist Church, and their mother taught Sunday School there when Charles, Jr., and Jerome were children.

The boys attended Waverly High School in the 1940s, and retired science teacher Betty Schlaphoff remembers they were both good students, both leaders. "He came up with some profound observations," she says of Jerome. Because of the interest he took in the wider world and his family's enthusiastic involvement in politics, "I could see he was headed toward the legislature."

In 1945, only five years out of high school, Charlie was stricken with spinal meningitis. Jerome, who was 18 at the time, remembers that he missed six weeks of high school so he could help Carl Hanson, the family's hired man, keep the farm running while the Warner parents were distracted by Charlie's illness.

Charlie recovered from meningitis in all respects but his hearing. However, being deaf did not quench his desire to serve or his interest in politics. As an adult, he served on the board of his local Natural Resources District and participated in political activities wherever he could. And, of course, he and his brother were partners in owning and running the family farm. Jerome says, "I probably could not have done what I did here (in the Legislature) if my brother hadn't farmed with me."

Before he went into farming and politics full-time, Warner earned a degree in agriculture from the University of Nebraska, even having a fling with Cornhusker football as a freshman in 1947. It didn't last long.

Warner suffered a separated shoulder in practice and remembers how the trainers taped his arm to his chest and sent him back out onto the field. The shoulder was dislocated again in the next play. Furthermore, the impact of Warner's collision with an opposing player yanked the tape loose—and the tape took some of Warner's skin with it. "I lost interest in football after that," Warner says with his trademark wry smile and understated irony.

The dislocated shoulder kept him from going on duty with the Nebraska Air National Guard when it was activated in March of 1951, during the Korean conflict. A viral infection of the heart that same spring kept him from graduating on schedule. Instead, he says, "I spent 70 days at the student health center." Because of concern that he shouldn't be moved until his recovery was far advanced, he stayed at the infirmary a few weeks after classes had ended for the semester. He finished his schooling in the fall, graduated in January of 1952 and went home to farm with his father and brother.

Charles Warner was still dividing his time between the farm and the Statehouse, where he was serving as Nebraska's lieutenant governor. In 1955, the last summer he was alive, the senior Warner was still talking politics with his son. "He'd be sitting in the front yard when I'd come home on the tractor, and he'd have a comment for me about policy or legislation."

Charles Warner told his son he expected him to be elected to the legislature, and he gave him some advice about what to expect. One piece of advice Jerome remembers—but that he says he wishes had not been necessary—was about lobbyists. His father said anyone in the legislature had to expect that someday some lobbyist would "get you someplace and try to feed you liquor to get you to do something." The solution to that problem, Charles said, was to take the drink along on a visit to the restroom, pour out a good half the liquor and add water. "They never know the difference," Charles Warner said, of the lobbyists. And the legislator will able to keep his wits about him.

Most of Charles' advice for his son had to do with issues and how to approach them. His father told him to make up his own mind and not just try to please people. Jerome has followed that advice, he says. He doesn't worry about how a particular vote he makes or stand he takes will affect the next election. Even those who vote with an eye to the next election sometimes lose, he says. It's not worth risking a sacrifice of principle. "If you start to vote against what you believe, you're going to end up doubly disappointed."

Charles Warner's involvement in banking also carried over to his son, albeit the impact was not permanent. The elder man and his brother-in-law had been among five stockholders in the Lancaster County Bank in Waverly during the 1920s. In 1929, the stockholders discovered their cashier had been keeping a double set of books for years, gradually embezzling from the depositors. When the cashier died and the stockholders discovered what he had done, they decided to try to cover the losses, borrowing the money and personally supporting the bank.

"We'd have been better off if the bank had gone under," the senator says, recalling his family's difficult financial times in the 1930s and 1940s as they tried to see the bank and its customers through what would otherwise have been bank failure.

Warner remembers his father's co-signing notes for people his bank loaned money to, a legal practice at that time. "He had confidence in them" during the Depression years, "and he never made a mistake. People were very appreciative. They didn't want welfare, and they honored their commitments." Watching his father work with his friends and neighbors, Warner says, helped him learn to judge people.

The fact that his family was in the bank business meant Warner would follow the custom of going to work for a correspondent bank to learn more about the business. He worked at the National Bank of Commerce in Lincoln for a year-and-a-half in the late 1950s. "I was kind of a flunky," he says, working as a teller for 3-4 weeks, then in the vault for a while, then recording summaries of financial statements for a few months.

"It was good training," Warner says now, but "my banking interests got sidetracked" by a series of events that still evoke regret and a touch of bitterness.

William Dick, who was running the Lancaster County Bank in those years, wrote to Warner, telling him he was ready to retire and get out of the banking business. Because of his family's emotional ties to the bank, Warner would have liked to acquire controlling interest when Dick retired. But "I procrastinated," Warner says, and made no arrangements. A month later, Bill Dick died.

By the time Warner went to First National Bank to ask for help acquiring the Waverly bank, the smaller bank had already been sold. Warner was convinced NBC had had a hand in keeping him from acquiring the bank, and, in his anger, he offered to quit the day he came to that realization. He did quit a few weeks later. Although he had enjoyed the "different world" he found at NBC, the circumstances under which he was shut out of the Waverly bank soured him on banking as a career. "It was very bitter for me," he recalls.

Throughout his brief experience with banking, though, Warner continued to farm—and to lay the groundwork for a political career. Knowing he wanted to run for public office, Warner began to join community and service organizations in the late 1950s. "I did it to become acquainted with people and so they could become acquainted with me."

He had been active in the Young Republicans since the early 1950s, but after his father died in 1955 he got involved in many more groups. He joined and became president of the Havelock Farmers Institute, which planned an annual community celebration. He joined a number of fraternal organizations: the Odd Fellows; Rebekahs; Eastern Star; Masonic Lodge No. 54, the lodge his father had belonged to in downtown Lincoln; the Shrine Patrol, a marching unit. He was a member of the board of directors of the Lincoln Jaycees.

He was also a member of the Lancaster County Extension Board and the Lancaster County Fair Board. By 1960, he says, "I was an officer in 15 or 16 organizations and president of 10 or 11." He enjoyed the work, the ceremony and the contact with people, but he also admits "I would be less than honest if I didn't acknowledge that it was another way to get your name known."

In fact, he volunteered to be the treasurer of the county fair board largely for that reason. "I enjoyed it. I like fairs, but it's also accurate to say that I figured 'Jerome Warner' on the awards checks that went into several hundred homes wasn't all that bad."

He has no concrete evidence to indicate that any of those activities made a difference, but his instincts tell him they gave him valuable name recognition. He adds, though, that he never directly used the connections he made in any of the organizations he served when he set out to campaign for office. It wouldn't have been appropriate, he says.

But the job that probably gave him the most solid experience in political matters during those years was one he did not seek out. He was not even present at the meeting where he was elected chairman of the Lancaster County School Reorganization Committee, a group charged with examining the possibility of consolidating some of the 35-40 school districts in the county.

"I was told later they wanted to put me on the committee because I had lots of land, so they thought I'd be unwilling to reorganize," Warner says. But his own personal situation was not as important to him as fulfilling the requirements of the law that instituted the state's reorganization committees. The law said the committees had five years in which to come up with a comprehensive plan. If the plan was not forthcoming at the end of five years, the group was to be dissolved and a new committee appointed.

Some committees in different parts of the state simply sat out their five years, intentionally delaying the consolidation process. But Warner says he would have been disobeying the law—and discrediting his own reputation—if he had allowed that to happen in Lancaster County. So he and his committee worked with the people of the county, holding countless hearings and meetings, listening to their concerns and fears. In the course of that process, "We developed a plan, and I went out to sell it."

Not that successful school reorganization ever came easy. Warner remembers that his father had been involved in a reorganization of the Waverly district in 1919, before he had children of his own. Warner knew that some of the neighbors who had opposed the plan Charles Warner supported were still angry about it in the 1930s. One man was particularly bitter: "If our cows ever got into his field, there was hell to pay," Warner remembers.

He was aware that fights over school districts have divided families and created hard feelings among neighbors. But he says, if people are given enough time and information, they usually will do the right thing. With that belief in mind, he led his committee on the long-term course to plan for school reorganization and to explain to people why the plan was needed.

The plan proposed four districts for the rural parts of the county, one in each geographic quadrant. Only the plan for the southeastern quadrant actually went to a vote—and it failed. By that time Warner had resigned from the committee because he had been elected to the Unicameral. But he believes the committee's work laid the background for later reorganization in what are now the Norris and Raymond Central districts and for the consolidation of other parts of Lancaster County with districts in other counties.

Of course, that committee was hardly Warner's only responsibility in those years. While he actively sought leadership positions in many groups, he says, some things also happened just by chance. For instance, he went to a county planning commission meeting one night with a lot of questions about zoning and the "attitude of a farmer" that the land in question was "*my* land." When Warner arrived at the evening meeting, the chair of the commission, Doug Brogden, introduced himself and gave Warner the news: Warner had been appointed to the planning commission that afternoon.

"I went with all those questions," Warner recalls, only to find out he'd been made a member of the body he was ready to take on in battle. "It's sort of the old saying: 'Yesterday I didn't know how to spell it. Now I are one,'" Warner says of the situation. He didn't raise any of his questions at the commission's meeting that day.

His service on the planning commission turned out to be good preparation for the Legislature, Warner says. He learned about a lot of public issues and also developed a feel for the impact a public body has on individual citizens. Although the planning commission was only an advisory body, "you were aware your votes affected individuals very directly." The people involved were neighbors and friends, and the members of the planning commission could see firsthand how their recommendations would influence people's land and livelihood.

The Legislature, on the other hand, deals with statewide issues and large numbers and often forgets how its decisions affect individuals, Warner says. His early experience on the planning commission has made it easier for him to remember the connection between government action and people's lives.

Ready to Run

By the time he was 30 years old, Warner had accumulated a lot of advice from his father and a lot of experience in public office and had forged a lot of connections with the people of Lancaster County. He was ready to make the run for the Legislature that he had always known would be inevitable.

In 1959 Otto Liebers, the incumbent senator from Warner's district and the chairman of the Appropriations Committee, told Warner he would not run for re-election in 1960. Warner filed for the empty seat. So did four other people.

One of those others was George Knight, president of the Citizens State Bank of University Place. "He was a pillar of the community," Warner says.

The 18th District of that day had not been reapportioned since 1935. It included Lincoln and Lancaster County land northeast of a line from the state fairgrounds to Cotner and O streets and another area east of 56th St. and south of Calvert. "A lot of it had been farmland in the 1930s," Warner says, but had since become part of Lincoln.

Warner and Knight were the two candidates to advance in the nonpartisan primary in 1960, and Warner found himself in his first legislative race.

"I spent right at $5,000," he says. "My own money." Most of that went to mail 15,000 pieces of campaign literature in each of two mailings. And Warner went door-to-door, asking people to vote for him.

They didn't. At least, the majority didn't. Knight was elected to the Legislature by a 54-46 percent margin, a turn of events about which Warner is philosophical. Knight was respected and well-known in the community. By comparison, "I was an unknown," Warner says, "pretty much trading on my father's name."

So Warner went back to his farming and his responsibilities in all those community organizations. But he didn't exactly lose interest in politics.

All the members of the Unicameral held only two year terms in those days, and in 1962, Knight decided not to run for reelection. Had Knight decided to pursue a second term, Warner would probably not have chosen to oppose him. But since the seat was open, Warner took the opportunity to run again. This time his opponent was Dick Duxbury, a man who was as unfamiliar to the voters as Warner was.

Once again, Warner went out to campaign door-to-door, and in the process he learned a lesson about the technique's effectiveness. He had suspected it would be important that people, especially newcomers to the district, see that he was interested enough in them to knock on their doors.

"In 1960 I intentionally skipped some precincts to see if I could tell the difference" in the vote, Warner says. "Largely, there was none." But the effect proved to be more obvious in the long run. Warner found when he went back to see people two years later that his earlier work had paid off. He got a larger share of the vote in the precincts where he had campaigned in 1960 than in those he had skipped. "I could see a significant difference," he says.

One thing about the 1962 campaign was no different from the 1960 race, though. Warner again spent as little as possible on the campaign: $3,200, mostly his money. "I accepted very little in donations," Warner says, and no more than $25 from any one person. Some friends did invite people to coffee to introduce him to the voters, but Warner says he didn't like to ask for much campaign assistance. "I still hate to ask," he says.

Today, when the public takes it for granted that candidates for everything from president to mayor will try to raise as much money as possible to fund their campaigns, Warner's attitude is unusual. He thinks raising campaign money for a legislative race seems inappropriate. In 1962 "I thought people who contributed would be under the assumption they could influence what I did." Thirty-four years and nine elections later, Warner still wonders if that may be the case.

Even accepting volunteer help makes him slightly uncomfortable. He says he feels funny when finds himself opposed on a legislative issue to the wishes of people who have given time—but not money—to his campaign. If they had contributed financially, he says, it would be even worse. "The potential for being influenced in how you vote certainly is there."

In those first campaigns and in every one since, Warner has been especially careful not to take contributions from individuals or groups associated with kindergarten-grade 12 education. "I was heavily involved in state aid to schools issues in the 1960s and '70s," Warner points out. "I didn't want to give the impression I was ever reacting to campaign contributions." He would accept endorsements from groups associated with school aid issues—but not money.

Back in 1962, what money Warner did spend in the campaign went for more mass mailings and for yard signs. He ordered a thousand signs, he says, and used about 500. "I still have some," he adds.

Complicating the 1962 campaign was Warner's continued service as chair of the Lancaster County School Reorganization Committee. In the weeks before the primary election, the committee came to the point of making a controversial recommendation that several school districts in southern Lancaster County be merged. Warner was invited to many events to explain the plan. "People said I was stupid to do it then," he says, right before the election. "But I figured I might as well learn now how to handle myself in a controversial area."

When he talked about the plan, Warner says, "I mentioned all the bad as well as the good—just like I do upstairs now (in the Legislature). There's virtually no issue that's all one side. There's truth on both sides. You need to evaluate which you think is best."

One last meeting on the school plan, just days before the election, was called by someone who opposed the reorganization, perhaps in the hope that Warner's leadership of a controversial plan would hurt the candidate and his chances of being elected to the Unicameral. Warner went to the meeting and made his usual two-sided presentation. The reaction was calm and thoughtful; anyone who may have hoped Warner's defense of the reorganization plan would make enemies for him had to be disappointed. "One person at the meeting told me later, 'I don't agree with anything you've done, but I appreciate the way you did it,'" Warner remembers.

That attitude prevailed through Election Day, and this time Warner was the victor with 59 percent of the vote. He would follow his father's footsteps up the steps of the Capitol and into the legislative chamber, a place in which he had always planned to serve—for as long as he could be re-elected. He has been re-elected 10 times.

His legislative philosophy was being shaped from the time he was a child, but it got some reinforcement soon after he was actually elected to the Legislature. On the first day of the 1963 session, Warner's first day in the Unicameral, friends John and Melba Scott brought him a copy of excerpts from a speech by Edmund Burke. "I carried it for years in my billfold," Warner says, until the paper fell apart. But the philosophy Burke expressed has stayed with the Nebraska senator and has framed his approach to public service.

Burke was a member of the British Parliament in the late 1700s. In his famous speech, he told his constituents he believed a legislator does a disservice to the people he represents if he yields his opinion to theirs. Warner shares the philosophy.

The representative is in the midst of the argument, Warner explains, but the constituent is at a distance and does not have the same information. In a representative democracy, the elected representatives are expected to make decisions, the senator says. "The voter concurs at the election—or does not."

"I've seen a legislator say he has seven letters for something and four opposed, so that's how he'll vote. I would never do that," Warner says.

"You can't always be at odds with the people, nor should you be," Warner says. "But direct democracy would be bad. Pure and simple majority rule gives no consideration to minority rights." Sometimes a legislator has to be more concerned about the people who would be adversely affected by a particular legislative action than he is about what the majority of his constituents might want.

He admits his philosophy may not be too popular in the 1990s, a time when many people seem to believe an elected official's vote should always reflect the wishes of the majority of his constituents. But Warner has never been one to shy away from controversy, as his early activities in the Legislature attest.

His request that he be assigned to the Education Committee went against the prevailing wisdom. Warner's friends in the Legislature, people he knew through his father's career, told him to avoid Education. "No matter what you did, you made everyone mad," Warner was told.

School reorganization was a statewide issue, an issue that stirred controversy on every level. A group called the Nebraska School Improvement

Association would bring 800-1,000 people to hearings on reorganizational matters, enough to make any legislative committee feel the heat. Senators who had chaired the committee in the previous decades tended to last only one or two sessions before leaving not only the committee but also the Legislature itself, Warner was told.

But the new senator from Waverly asked for Education because he was interested in the subject and thought he might make a difference there. The Public Works Committee was his other request. The committee was reaching the end of a decade in which public power was being reorganized and power review boards were being established. That, too, "was tremendously interesting," Warner says.

And public power—an arrangement unique to Nebraska—was and continues to be dear to Warner's heart. He has little patience with people who say government should operate competitively, like a business. Ultimately, the senator says, government has to fund both sides of the competitive equation, and that's inefficient and expensive. "I learned that concept from my years with public power," he says, a relationship that began well before the farmer became a legislator.

That kind of early experience, added to the atmosphere in which Warner grew up, may have prepared the new senator well for the opening of the 1963 legislative session. But his sense of well-being didn't last long.

A senator who had grown up in a political family, who had devoted hours of service to volunteer and local governmental organizations, who had always wanted to serve in the Legislature surely had a leg up on the average freshman senator. Warner had good reason to believe he was well-prepared to enter the Unicameral in 1963.

"I came in thinking I was fairly well acquainted with state issues. I heard about them all the time. But the first two or three days after the session started I hardly slept. I realized there was a whole lot I didn't know."

Senators would ask him to sign on to bills he didn't know anything about. Rather than bluff his way through, trying to impress people with his knowledge and background, Warner readily admitted his relative ignorance and worked hard to get himself educated. "If people would say, 'You already know about this,' I would say, 'No, I don't. Tell me about it.'"

People did tell him. And he learned. But, while Warner may have participated in a lot of legislation during that first session, he didn't try introducing much of it himself. A notable exception was a bill to provide state aid to schools.

"It was killed before I even explained it," Warner says. He smiles at the thought of that early defeat on an issue he was to become so closely identified with in succeeding years.

That first bill included a combination of ideas that Warner says he had never thought about until after he had been elected to the Legislature. And it flew in the face of his early beliefs about tax law.

Warner learned his tax law doctrine at his father's knee, and Charles Warner had consistently opposed broadening the tax base. In fact, Charles had convinced Jerome so thoroughly that, in the 1950s, the younger Warner joined the Farm Bureau in an effort to convert its members, generally in favor of a broad tax base, to his own point of view. "I was going to point out the error of their ways," Warner says. Instead, the potential converter became the converted.

To learn more about the issue, Warner attended several informational seminars on taxes led by the University of Nebraska's department of agricultural economics. The information he heard there and from the Farm Bureau influenced his thinking. "Gradually, over time, I decided I was wrong," Warner says.

In Warner's book, a politician who decides he's been wrong and then changes his mind on a matter is not waffling; he's learning.

Warner says he regularly tells his staff to point out to him everything that might be wrong or questionable about a position he's considering. "I can figure out what's good about it," he says, but he wants to be sure he has considered all sides of an issue.

"When I've changed my mind it's because the circumstances changed, because what I thought were the facts had been changed. ... Sometimes it's a change in how I feel about a policy, but not in terms of some principle as to right and wrong."

In the case of the tax structure, the latter situation probably prevailed. By the time he was elected to the Legislature, Warner was convinced that the old state property tax system was "no longer appropriate."

"I probably became like a convert for a religion. I became more adamant about change than had I grown up the other way."

But he still had not thought through the specific ways the tax structure could affect schools, he says. That changed soon after he was elected in

1962 when he had a routine introductory visit with Dick Herman, then a legislative reporter with the Lincoln Journal.

Herman asked Warner what he planned to do in the Legislature.

"I said I wanted to introduce a bill to provide state aid to schools, which really was a spin-off from all the years I'd spent with Lancaster County school reorganization."

Herman asked Warner whether he planned to introduce a bill with flat per pupil aid or one that provided for equalization.

"I said, 'What's the difference?'"

Herman explained that foundation aid was just a flat per-pupil distribution while equalization aid attempted to provide relatively more money for poor districts so that their students' education could be comparable to what was available to students in wealthier districts.

Without hesitation, Warner told Herman, "I'm going to do foundation and equalization aid."

"That was the extent of my homework," he says now, "but it was very obvious to me it was right."

Never one to delay action on something he believes is right, Warner had leaped into the aid-to-schools fray during his first session in the Legislature. A member of the Education Committee, he had introduced a bill that included both foundation and equalization aid.

The bill, though, drew the same kind of opposition similar measures had drawn in previous years. "In those days people were opposed to federal aid to education, and state aid was just as bad," Warner says.

"I didn't have the five votes to get it out of committee," Warner says. But another bill the committee had considered that year—and advanced to general file—actually would have taken money away from schools. That gave Warner an opening to make his point. He pointed out that, logically, if the committee members were going to give the entire Legislature an opportunity to take money from schools, they should also give the senators the opportunity to give money to schools.

"We had a little casual discussion, and all of a sudden it was five votes." His bill had advanced.

But during the bill's first encounter on the floor of the Legislature, the majority of the senators had voted to indefinitely postpone consideration—the equivalent of killing a bill. As a result, Warner did not have an opportunity to argue on the floor for what his bill would have accomplished.

In those first years, though, other issues also demanded attention. One of those was a bill to return the state to electing legislators on a partisan ballot, ending the nonpartisan nature of the body. Both major parties came in and tried to convince the senators to revert to a partisan institution, Warner says, but to no avail. The bill was overwhelmingly defeated.

Warner says the defeat was well deserved. His father had served both in the old, partisan body and in the nonpartisan Unicameral as had other senators of that day. "No individual who served in both systems ever said the old system was better," Warner asserts, "either the partisan part of it or the two-house part." Besides that, he adds, "a number of those elected were advocates of returning to the old system before they got here, but they changed their minds when they got here."

While the new senator may have been unsure of himself during the first days of his first term, it wasn't long before he had adjusted. He went home from that 1963 session knowing he wanted to come back for the 1965 session—the Unicameral met only every other year through the 1960s—as chairman of a committee, preferably Government and Military Affairs.

"It was one of the top three committees—with Revenue and Appropriations," Warner says, and many capable legislators sought to lead it. The position came open in 1965 when the former chairman decided to pursue a different leadership position.

In the meantime, Warner ran successfully for re-election to the Unicameral, this time for a four-year term. The 1964 election was the first in which senators ran for four-year instead of two-year terms.

But chairmen of legislative committees were still elected by the 12-member Committee on Committees rather than by the entire body as they are today. That committee, made up of three senators from each Congressional District, sometimes had trouble finding people to lead some of the committees. But they always had more than enough candidates for Revenue, Appropriations and Government and Military Affairs. Warner says the three had nearly always been the "most prestigious" in the Legislature.

Warner's bid for the leadership of the latter met with some opposition, he recalls, but was ultimately successful. So, two years after his arrival in the Unicameral, Warner took over the powerful committee that dealt with state, local, city and county government. He isn't really surprised that he was elected so soon to a leadership position. "I was accustomed," he says, "to being involved and doing something in whatever activity it was."

Warner says he assumes that people who run for office are competitive by nature and would want to be "out front." And yet, he says, the Legislature when he first arrived was like most any civic organization: a third of the people were "just there," a third had an interest in a few things and the other third were interested in everything. He was part of that third group, Warner says.

"I had also learned many times over that it took very little effort to make more effort than the average," Warner says.

In that era, the committee's single secretary was the only staff, and the chairman wrote all the committee statements. Furthermore, no senator had an office until the late 1960s. At that point the speaker moved into what had been the lieutenant governor's office, but the other senators still did not have their own office space, only desks in the legislative chamber and a few cardboard file boxes in which to keep materials. The senators were, to a large extent, on their own.

Despite the lack of staff support, Warner plunged into the Government Affairs Committee, taking up dealings that would lead to a major piece of legislation in 1965. A consultant hired by the Appropriations Committee had completed a three- or four-year study of the way state employees were hired and paid. "There had been no state classification system," Warner says, "so different agencies paid people differently for similar work."

The result of the consultant's study was a recommendation that the state establish a Department of Administrative Services and a state personnel department. Warner's committee wrote the legislation to accomplish both.

Since the beginning of his political career, Warner has frequently demonstrated concern for state employees. "Politicians come and go," he says, but the career people are the nuts and bolts.

"I've been supportive of state employees and (good) salaries, but that's nothing but a decent, logical business decision. If turnover is high, it's expensive. I believe in paying well to retain people."

That philosophy was clearly in evidence when Warner and the Government Committee wrote the legislation that would establish DAS and a personnel department. When the bills reached the full Legislature, Richard Marvel, chairman of the Appropriations Committee, and Warner attached 150 amendments on the floor. That was an unusually large number of changes to make at that stage of deliberation, but all were incorporated. The bill was passed, and the Department of Administrative Services was created.

Working with the experienced Marvel on the DAS legislation gave Warner intimate insights into the procedures and workings of state government, teaching him techniques he would put to good use in the ensuing years.

For one thing, Warner recalls, he learned that consultants may feed their clients what they think the clients want to hear. He also picked up some ideas about how to put votes together and keep them together. And he learned that it's not too difficult to get complex legislation passed when senators believe the sponsor to be knowledgeable about the subject.

"Dick was perceived to be knowledgeable—and he was," Warner says. It was the younger senator's first involvement with comprehensive legislation, and the experience was to stand him in good stead as he himself became knowledgeable about other complex issues.

The part of the bill dealing with personnel was not successful in 1965, though. "It was estimated that it would cost $4 million extra to equalize salaries," Warner remembers. "Today a one percent adjustment (for cost of living) is $18 million. But then the $4 million was an obstacle that was hard to overcome." He smiles wryly at the difference two decades of inflation has made to state government.

After just two terms of service in the Unicameral, Jerome Warner had already exerted his leadership and begun to influence legislation. He was quickly making a name for himself, attracting notice from the press and public. The attention would continue and intensify.

PART TWO
SETTLING IN

The Lure of Higher Office

T he attention Warner attracted during his stint as chairman of the Government Committee and leader of the battle to reconfigure state government may have been part of the reason the senator, with two legislative sessions under his belt, considered running for higher office in 1966.

It was not a novel idea. Many politicians enter office knowing they want to move up in the power structure from local to state to national level. And politicians who achieve early success and recognition—as Warner did—would be all the more likely to be encouraged to consider higher office.

Warner made a mark on highway legislation and tax restructuring when Norbert Tiemann was governor in the late 1960s, and Tiemann took notice of the "bright young senator. I always assumed he wanted my job," Tiemann says.

However, Warner's first serious flirtation with the possibility doesn't seem to have been his own idea. Early on in his legislative career, Warner says, both he and his supporters seemed to assume he might run for higher office. "It was just something I should do," he says.

In the spring of 1966, friends and supporters repeatedly urged him to make a run for the U.S. House of Representatives, but Warner wasn't sure the House was where he wanted to be. He told the Lincoln papers in February that he wanted to keep on working in the Legislature on taxes and education.[2] He was also concerned about two special legislative committees; he was chairman of a study committee on the valuation of agricultural land, and he was a member of a legislative study group on water resources. He had been interested in both those issues for a long

---

[2]Lincoln Journal, Feb. 10, 1966; Lincoln Star, Feb. 10, 1966

time. Besides that, he wasn't sure he wanted to leave the Waverly farm to move to Washington.

Ultimately, Warner decided not to file for the House seat. But that was not to be the end of the question of higher office.

A few weeks later, Warner's friends John and Melba Scott invited him for pizza at the original Valentino's at 35th and Holdrege. Still believing Warner should try to move on to higher office, the Scotts tried to talk Warner into putting his name on the primary ballot for Lieutenant Governor. The discussion over pizza was not rooted in deep ideological or strategic principles. "It was just sort of spur of the moment," Warner remembers.

Warner said no, he did not want to run for lieutenant governor. But the friends were not about to take no for an answer.

In those days, a person's name could be placed on the ballot if a petition bearing 25 valid signatures were submitted. Warner remembers. "By Friday they had 400 names, and I had 10 days to decide."

Warner's friends had gathered not just the minimum 25 signatures but 400 signatures in about seven hours on Friday, March 8, just beating the filing deadline for an incumbent.[3]

"The press assumed it was a gimmick," Warner says. Many reporters seemed to think Warner's candidacy was a done deal and that the petition drive was just a campaign stunt to earn him early publicity.

But that was not the case, Warner says. He appreciated the effort made on his behalf, but he really had not made up his mind whether to allow his name to be placed on the ballot. Again, Warner was concerned about pulling out of the legislative programs in which he was so involved.

By March 17, he had decided. He declined to accept the petition filing. The Lincoln Journal quoted Warner as saying he had great respect for the office of lieutenant governor but that he believed the two offices that offered the greatest opportunity to be effective for building Nebraska were governor and member of the Legislature.

"In many respects, the Legislature is more important because an executive officer of the state relies primarily on good basic legislation in the performance of his duties," the newspaper quoted Warner as saying. He added that he thought he could "best serve my state by remaining in the Legislature."

Two years later, when friends again urged him to run for the U.S.

[3]Lincoln Journal, March 13, 1966

House, Warner again declined. He says he didn't want to move to Washington and give up farming and the opportunity to be a "citizen legislator" in a body he believed was aptly suited to that purpose:

"I'm interested in policies and issues. There's no other place in government to bring change about as effectively as in the Legislature. My interest is in the mechanics of government at the policy level."

That put a temporary end to the question of running for higher office. And the next major crisis the Legislature faced gave Warner another opportunity to plunge into the public policy whirlpool and make a difference in the state's future. Undoubtedly, his success there just reinforced his conviction that the Nebraska Legislature was where he belonged.

First, though, he had to deal with the senator from Scottsbluff, a man whose legislative reputation was, to put it mildly, formidable.

Warner had intended to return to that chairmanship of the Government Committee after his first term there, but Senator Terry Carpenter also wanted the position. It was one of the first struggles between the senator from Scottsbluff, who had been in and out of the Unicameral since 1953, and the relative newcomer from Waverly.

"When I first came, he (Carpenter) was viewed with some reservations by the senior members of the body," Warner recalls, although "he became more acceptable" later.

"He didn't back down much," Warner says of Carpenter. Carpenter would fight tooth and nail for his positions and his bills, and defeat was something he took personally.

"In the '50s and '60s if he got beat on an issue, he was apt to go home for a week."

Both at the time and in retrospect, consensus has been that Carpenter was, indeed, a powerful state politician. But many Nebraskans have qualms about the way he gained and used his power.

"Part of his strength was to take on new members early and hard and belittle them." Warner recalls how Carpenter went after Cliff Foster, a freshman senator representing Seward and York Counties in the 1960s. In those days, freshmen were expected to keep silent through an informal initiation period, but Foster apparently had not gotten the word. "He was comfortable about pointing out where others were in error," Warner recalls with a wry smile. Carpenter was not about to let Foster get by with such hubris. The veteran senator proceeded verbally to cut the newcomer down to size by doing his best to question and humiliate Foster.

45

Carpenter liked to go after a person who was obviously not well-versed on a subject. Or sometimes he would "pick on a personality trait," Warner says. Or he would manage to pick a fight about the meaning of a word or words.

Warner recalls the general outline of a bill in the 1960s that had some relation to sexuality. Legislators were very careful about the language they used in public debate in those days, especially language related to sexual matters. Carpenter challenged the senator introducing the bill, asking for definitions of a long list of words related to "unusual" sexual activity. The other senator was too embarrassed to engage in that kind of verbal combat with Carpenter and finally just gave up and sat down, Warner recalls.

Watching Carpenter in action would often intimidate less hardy souls who didn't want to get the same treatment, Warner says. "They wouldn't want to cross him and be subjected to that." So Carpenter often got his way.

When Carpenter attacked people, he would do it "with some level of accuracy," Warner says, comparing the process to that used by current State Auditor John Breslow. "He wasn't completely off the mark, but he went to the extreme."

Carpenter made good newspaper copy, and the press nicknamed him Terrible Terry. "He took after all the sacred cows," Warner says, "which wasn't too bad a thing to do. In the long run, it was probably beneficial."

Carpenter's method of operation was unorthodox but did give him influence on legislation, Warner says. One such piece of legislation funded a building for Nebraska Educational Television. Carpenter received a lot of credit for NETV and, in fact, the building on Lincoln's North 33rd Street that houses the network is named after him.

Warner and others who were involved at the time say Carpenter got more credit than he deserved. It was actually George Gerdes of Alliance who was behind the creation of the network, despite the flamboyant Carpenter's well-publicized involvement. Carpenter was, indeed, responsible for the building itself, but he was less than consistent about supporting the network. "Terry tried to take it (NETV) apart several times after that. Once he was going to make a law college out of the ETV building."

Carpenter and Warner did not get along. "There was no combat on the floor; we just disagreed on the issues," Warner says. He learned that the way to handle Carpenter was not to try to lick him but to invite him to join in sponsoring a piece of legislation. "I went to Terry for help, gave him a bill to introduce." That assured Carpenter would support an idea rather than fight it.

Warner remembers making exactly that kind of move regarding the highway legislation of 1969. Carpenter had already caused trouble with one of the 16 bills in the package when Warner asked him to sponsor a related measure, the bill that would allow bonds to be issued for highway construction. Warner decided that was a safe bill to give Carpenter since the bond attorneys would dictate how the measure should be written.

Warner even remembers the number of the bill: LB1313. The designation was a deliberate choice—with a story behind it. At that time the Council of State Governments' office was situated at 1313 E. 60th Street in Chicago. Various groups at the time had accused the Council of being a subversive organization, associated somehow with the Communist Party and trying to establish regional governments that would destroy the states. Some of those same groups were opposed to the idea of allowing bonds to be issued for roads construction, "so we thought it would be kind of fun if the bond bill would be numbered 1313," Warner says.

That required a little manipulation of the numbering process. The bills included in the highway package ran from about LB1290 to LB1306. Carpenter had already signed the bill to allow bond issues, but Warner held it and did not formally file it until it would be in line for the designation 1313. "It wasn't a very big deal, but at the time we thought it was entertaining."

In that case, Warner got Carpenter's cooperation on a major piece of legislation, and he admits that he was never the victim of one of Carpenter's bitter personal attacks on the floor. But in 1967 Warner wasn't sure he wanted to take on Carpenter in a contest for the chairmanship of the Government Committee. Warner was sure Carpenter didn't have the votes to beat him in a head-to-head contest for the chairmanship of the Government Committee, but Warner didn't think a confrontation would be useful for the committee or the legislature. While he was considering what to do, he discovered another option, leadership of the Executive Board.

"Initially, I didn't like the idea" of running for Executive Board, Warner says. "But I knew I'd run for Speaker in 1969 ... so I went for Executive

Board." The committee included only five people then, as opposed to nine today. In those days the board included the Speaker, the chairman of the Committee on Committees and the chairman and vice chairman of the Executive Board plus one member elected at large.

Never one simply to accept things as they had always been, Warner assessed the Executive Board and decided some changes needed to be made if it were to be truly effective. He immediately established written guidelines for conduct of the committee. He anticipated the kinds of things the Executive Board would be asked to do and developed policies that would enable the group to function consistently rather than simply dealing with individual requests as they arose.

"It worked out pretty well," Warner says. "I didn't have a lot of problems while the Legislature was in session. I had more afterwards."

The problems arose when Senator Fred Carstens of Beatrice asked for an appropriation of $5,000 to hire a consultant to do a study on the state's crime problem. He even had the consultant in mind, someone he knew from outside Nebraska. The Executive Board interviewed the man and declined to hire him.

"That made Fred very unhappy," Warner says. "Next session he introduced all this legislation to completely restructure the Exec Board," arguing that the small group meant too much power was concentrated in too few hands. The restructuring increased the committee's membership from five to nine, where it stands today. Today's membership includes the chairman, vice chairman and Speaker, all elected from the floor of the Legislature, and two members from each of the state's three Congressional Districts, selected by the caucus from that district. It does, Warner admits, diffuse power and give broader representation.

If he had chosen to battle Carpenter for leadership of the Government Committee, Warner would not have had a chance to help streamline the Executive Board's functioning. Of course, he would also have avoided the confrontation with Carstens. On the other hand, that particular incident allowed Warner to contribute to another significant change to the structure of the Unicameral.

All that, however, pales in comparison to that of the biggest issue of 1967, an issue that always has and probably always will raise hackles and blood pressure. The issue was taxes. And Warner was in the thick of it.

Rebuilding Nebraska's Tax Structure

W hen Nebraska celebrated its centennial in 1967, the foundation of the state's tax structure was basically the same as it had been for 100 years. The property tax produced the vast majority of state revenue with the remainder coming from fees and fines. Nebraska had no income tax and no sales tax. The arrangement made sense in the agrarian economy that was Nebraska at its founding, but the state's economy had changed a lot by the late 1960s. The tax structure had not changed with it.

As early as the 1940s, legislators and state officials had been discussing the need to change the tax structure, and Warner remembers official attempts to revise it during his first session in the Unicameral. A 1963 bill, based on the so-called McClellan Report, a study sponsored by state, proposed that the state abandon its nearly total reliance on property tax and institute an income tax. The report said nothing about a sales tax.

The 1963 bill went nowhere.

In 1965, proponents of a state income tax tried again. Warner remembers strong opposition from the Omaha business community. Some of the business leaders sent a plane to Lincoln to transport senators to Omaha for meetings about the tax plan. "I was only in my second term, but I got to go along for some reason," Warner says.

At the meeting, a group of 10-12 business people, CEOs of some of Omaha's major companies, made no bones about how much they disliked the effect the proposed income tax would have on their businesses. They showed little concern for the way the new tax would affect the state.

"I was so shocked at that meeting," Warner says. "It was one of the more elementary discussions that I had sat in on tax structure. These guys didn't take time to look at the state's tax structure. They thought they were going to be adversely affected. ... They had no interest or knowledge of the broader picture. ... That's always kind of stayed with me." Warner is still known to be wary when big business comes asking the Legislature for favors.

Despite the opposition the business community mounted against the income tax, the Legislature passed the measure. Governor Frank Morrison declined to sign the bill, so it became law without his signature, a clear indication of the tepid support the income tax engendered. In fact, support was so weak and opposition so strong, that opponents mounted a successful petition drive to place a referendum repealing the law onto the ballot for the next fall.

At the same time, the Farm Bureau and other organizations started a petition drive to place on the ballot a measure to prohibit state property taxes. Farmers were particularly fed up with property tax and what they saw as an unfair burden on landowners; the Farm Bureau's petition drive was also successful.

Both measures appeared on the ballot in November 1966. Both passed. The result was that the state was left with few visible means of support. It had lost its ability to levy property taxes and had been forbidden to institute an income tax. The double whammy cut off more than two-thirds of the state's revenue and threw it into a fiscal crisis.

Norbert Tiemann, elected governor in 1966, led the drive to design a new tax structure that would save the state from insolvency. It was also designed to provide state aid to schools, improve financing for higher education, create an agency for economic development and make highway improvements.

As governor, Tiemann drafted a revenue proposal that established a progressive state income tax and a 2.5 percent state sales tax. The Legislature's Revenue Committee, however, had its own ideas about what should be done and crafted its own bill from scratch. Part of the committee's package was a provision setting an individual's state income tax as a percentage of his or her federal liability.

"Tiemann accepted a lot of the responsibility for what the Legislature did. He concurred with it," Warner remembers. "He lost the election in 1970 in part because of 'Tiemann taxes.'"

It was an unfair accusation, Warner says, and many Nebraskans involved in the crisis agree. The tax structure changes were forced on Tiemann because of the people's vote to deprive state government of most of its income. Thanks to the vote on the initiative petition, there was no going back to dependence on property taxes and no going forward to include the income tax approved by the Legislature. The state had no choice but to devise some other structure for raising revenue. Besides, Warner says, the combination of sales and income taxes was a more appropriate answer to the problem than any single-tax source—including the property tax.

"The whole session was oriented toward writing a good tax law," he adds. The Legislature mightily resisted any attempts to manipulate the tax law to give an advantage to any particular group, Warner remembers, despite pressure from many special interests, broad and narrow.

Warner's primary interest and involvement in the tax package lay in the proposed state aid to schools. He had introduced similar legislation unsuccessfully in 1963—the bill he says was killed even before he could explain it—and in 1965. Even Governor Frank Morrison's support in 1965 couldn't save the measure.

In 1967 he introduced a bill to establish the School Foundation and Equalization Fund. The bill would do two things: provide aid to schools on the basis of average daily pupil attendance during the previous year—the foundation part—and create a formula to regulate distribution of aid in relation to the wealth of the district—the equalization part. It was a combination of ideas Warner had been trying to promote ever since he'd been elected to the Legislature.

By 1967 the situation was different, and Warner's plan to provide state aid to schools became part of the overall tax restructuring effort.

The bill was designed to provide enough state aid to schools to cover, on average, 40 percent of their costs. Estimated cost for the measure was $67 million. (That would be more than $400 million today, Warner says.)

The 1967 bill got out of general file with no problems, just another part of the huge tax reform bill working its way through the Legislature. At some point an amendment passed that limited to $25 million the amount to be appropriated the first year, with increases to be added in subsequent years.

The matter became more complicated when the Legislature repealed the personal property tax on intangibles, the poll tax and some of the tax on household goods, all taxes that helped support schools. Those repeals took $10 million in revenue away from schools, and that's when the arguments began that the state aid bill did not really provide any property tax relief, Warner says. "Of the $25 million in the state aid bill, $10 million went to replace the lost revenues. That left us $15 million for property tax relief."

Several other factors also had an impact on the bill, whittling away the amount left to contribute to relieving property taxes. "What it boiled down to was out of that whole $25 million that was, quote, property tax relief, there was probably $5 million that did not get utilized in some other fashion. That hardly made a dent in relieving property taxes for schools.

"So people would argue, 'Well, we got all these new taxes, and my school tax didn't go down.'" People forgot, Warner says, about the taxes that had been repealed.

He did succeed, in the following years, in getting the dollar figure for state aid to education up to $35 million and then to $55 million. But he fell far short of his original aim, to start the process toward full state funding of education. Besides that, the emphasis shifted, in the decade following the 1967 reforms, from the equal educational opportunity Warner hoped state funding would provide to property tax relief.

Dick Herman, who covered the 1967 legislative session for the Lincoln Journal, says Warner's plan to equalize educational opportunities throughout the state was "corrupted" by politics as senators were pressured by constituents to concentrate on reducing property taxes. Over the years, state aid to education bills have been weighted toward tax relief and haven't done much for equalization. "The state failed to take Jerry's view," Herman says regretfully.

Regardless of whether people really understood what they were getting—or liked it—Warner's plan for state aid to schools passed, part of the package of tax reform bills that the governor and the Legislature had devised to meet the state's fiscal crisis. Indeed, that probably is why any kind of state aid to schools bill passed that year.

The legislative session in which senators fought their way through the thicket of tax reform to devise a system of state sales and income taxes and leave the property tax business to local subdivisions had been, arguably, the most significant session since the Legislature became a Unicameral in 1935. Warner calls it "a significant portion of Nebraska history." He remembers it as an exciting time to be involved in state politics.

Not often is a legislative institution galvanized from its usual incremental movement into the kind of massive reform enacted in the 1967 session. When such change does take place, it is usually the result of a set of circumstances that simply come together at the same time. In 1967, it was a combination of a tax crisis, an activist governor and a forward-looking Legislature.

It was not a quick and easy procedure, however. The package of bills finally passed the Legislature on a 39-7 vote on July 17, 1967. It included the sales tax provision that was to be used successfully against Tiemann in his 1970 re-election campaign.

Warner was part of a group in the Unicameral that wanted to keep the sales tax as low as possible and raise the income tax to make up the difference. "I thought sales tax was regressive," he says.

But it soon became obvious that a two percent sales tax would not bring in sufficient revenue to provide an appropriate cash flow for a state just coming out of an enormous tax restructuring. So the Legislature set the initial rate at 2.5 percent but included a provision to drop the rate to two percent as of Jan. 1, 1969.

But Tiemann called a special session of the Legislature in 1968 to repeal the two percent provision and stay at two-and-a-half. Between the successful action to keep the sales tax rate at 2.5 percent and the earlier adoption of the new income tax rate set by the Board of Equalization, the state took in more income than it needed.

By the time the 1970 election campaign was in full swing, the state's coffers had a balance of $39 million, and the surplus became a major election issue. Nebraskans were outraged. Taxes are never popular, and a system that allowed the state to collect more than it actually needed to meet its budget caused a statewide furor.

Looking at the dollars involved, Warner can't resist drawing a contrast with today's situation. "Now we run a reserve of five percent" of the total budget. That amounts to about $85 million annually just in reserves. However, in 1970 the $39 million looked like a lot of money. To most people it looked like far more than the state needed in reserve. Jim Exon campaigned heavily on the issue, and it was widely regarded as one of the principal reasons he defeated Tiemann for governor.

Warner thinks the defeat was unfortunate. "He'd turned out to be a really great governor," he says of Tiemann, calling the governor a visionary. Tiemann created what is now the Policy Research Office, an agency designed to develop long-term planning for the state in an era when anything that looked like centralized control was suspect. "Not many governors are willing to talk about where the state should be in the next 10 years," Warner says. Most are usually content to support the status quo.

"Nebraskans tend to kick governors out who take strong positions. ... Tiemann certainly was aggressive. We seem to like governors who don't do much."

Tiemann paid the political price for being a leader. Even though Warner believes it was the Legislature that was actually responsible for the tax restructuring plan, Tiemann's support for the change helped get the package passed. The Governor was willing to stick his neck out and take the lead even when he didn't have to, something the senator admires. He calls Tiemann "by far the best governor I've worked with."

The total tax package may have been fatal to Tiemann's campaign for a second term. But it was only the first of a series of major legislative successes for Warner and established him as a leader in aid to education.

The Road to
Highway Reform

Nebraska got its new tax structure in 1967 thanks to a fiscal crisis. But not everything that was part of that package was created in response to the crisis. Warner's education bill, for instance, was a reflection of his growing reputation as a long-term thinker and planner. Not content simply to react to problems as they arose, Warner was always urging his colleagues to plan ahead, to work toward a vision of what the future could be.

No example better illustrates that fact than the next major issue Warner took on. It was to be one of the major building blocks of his reputation as a leader: roads.

"The heart and soul of highway legislation in Nebraska was authored by Jerome Warner," says Jack Pittman, now finance administrator at the State Highway Department. Pittman was employed in the department's finance office in the late 1960s and worked with Warner to develop the 1969 package of highway legislation.

It wasn't that Warner necessarily had had a deep and abiding interest in highways. Like every other senator, he had been concerned about the roads in his own district, but he had not made the topic a priority in his legislative life. Once he got involved, though, he was not content simply to address the surface issues. Instead, he insisted the Legislature plan for the state's roads as far into the future as possible.

A study of highway needs had begun in 1965 under the leadership of Senator Jules Burbach of Crofton, spurred by the fact that $.5 million worth of federal highway money was available to states. The state senators were eager to get their hands on that federal money, and each had his own ideas about where and how it should be spent—preferably in his or her home district. "Everybody wanted on that study committee in '65," Warner says.

However, by 1967 it became apparent that the study had recommended more changes than the state would be able to handle and that many of the recommendations were going to be controversial. The proposals included changes in how counties and cities operated, increases in gasoline taxes and registration fees—a lot of mandates.

In those days the Legislature's interim study committees were not standing committees but were appointed by the Executive Board at the close of the legislative session. As chairman of the Executive Board, Warner sent out a form to all senators, asking them to rank the interim study committees on which they would be willing to serve.

"Where two years before, at the end of the '65 session, everybody wanted on it (the highway study committee), by the end of the '67 session, nobody wanted on it," Warner says. That included all but one of the members of the original study committee.

Since no senators wanted to serve on the committee, the Executive Board decided to make itself the study committee. As chairman of the Exec Board, Warner became chairman of the study committee.

The 1965 study committee had held close to 20 public hearings throughout the state even before the consultants did their work. When Warner and the Executive Board took over, they held another round of hearings to solicit comments specifically about the consultant's report. "That's when it started to get controversial," he says.

But the senator, with five years of legislative experience under his belt, did not go into the controversy unprepared. "I listened to all 40-some hours of tapes" of the previous committee's hearings, taking notes on what people had said.

"I've always had a good memory," Warner says. When he prepares for a hearing or debate on a bill, he tries to refresh his mind with everything he can remember about the bill. "If I really concentrate, I can do it well," he says of his memory. "Of course, sometimes I remember dead wrong."

In the case of the roads hearings of the 1960s, he remembered correctly enough of the time that the process worked well. Many who had testified and asked questions at the first round of hearings came back to talk again when Warner and the Executive Board went out to make their own rounds. "They'd make their remarks, and then I would look at my 'crib' notes, and I'd say, 'Well, two years ago you said'—whatever it was they said. Which immediately flattered them."

Lee Rupp says Warner has a gift for handling public hearings like the ones involving roads in the 1960s. Rupp, now a lobbyist for the University of Nebraska, served in the Legislature from 1983-88. He remembers the patience Warner exhibited at hearings during the session and in the interim.

"He is a bottomless pit of patience," Rupp says. Warner will be sure his committee hears out all citizens who come to testify. "They will patiently listen to 3-5 hours of things—probably two or three minutes of which would encompass stuff they've not heard before."

The preparation and the patience served Warner well during hearings on the roads bill and, the senator remembers, "those public hearings went exceedingly well."

But then came the hard work of putting together a plan that the public could support and the Legislature could pass. Warner's biggest help with the highway plan, one of the most important influences in his career, came from a person who was to be one of the most important influences in his life, his future wife, Betty Person.

Person was the Legislature's sole researcher in the late 1960s, a no-nonsense former newspaper reporter who took seriously her job to serve all the senators' many diverse needs for information. In the case of the roads study, she wrote the actual legislation.

Warner and Person based their plan on the consultant's recommendations but modified it to include suggestions from the hearings or simply what they thought would work better.

One thing that fell into the latter category was the formula for distributing highway dollars to counties and cities. "We had a formula we just knew wasn't acceptable. I remember the consultants who did that one said they knew it was a bad formula, but they thought for another $15,000 they could come up with another formula. And I know my reaction was I think we can come up with a better formula ourselves that won't cost anything, and that's exactly what we did."

Warner and Person came up with a weighted formula, which is still in effect. "It was no secret we had done that, but I assumed we'd be very vulnerable because this was not 'done by the consultants.'" In that era, Warner says, a great deal of deference was paid to consultants' recommendations. "But what these consultants wanted to do, we didn't want to do."

Instead, Warner and Person applied their own expertise to the problem and came up with their own plan. Warner's skill at guiding the plan through the Legislature illustrated again his growing leadership and influence.

But before he could introduce his study committee's proposed highway plan, he had to run again for reelection. Once elected, he had to decide whether to seek a leadership position in the Unicameral—and which one. This time, he ran for speaker.

In 1969 the position carried far less authority than it does today. The speaker was more of a figurehead, without many of the powers that have since been granted to the position. But it was still considered the highest honor the body could bestow upon a member and, as one of relatively few leadership positions in a nonpartisan body, it did bestow a share of influence.

In 1969 the speaker's post was considered the culmination of a senator's political career. While the law did not demand it, most speakers served only one two-year term and then retired from the Legislature. Warner did not intend to follow that tradition.

"It was no secret I was not going to retire," Warner says. For one thing, he was not up for re-election until 1972, so he would almost surely be back to serve out the remaining two years of his term.

As a result, some senators did not relish the possibility of Warner's becoming speaker. In fact, Terry Carpenter had proposed at the last minute that candidates for the job should stand before the Legislature and explain why they wanted the leadership post. But Carpenter didn't tell Warner that's what he would have to do, probably intending to surprise and fluster a rival for whom he felt little affection.

One of Warner's friends in the Legislature warned Warner the night before the vote was to be taken that he would be expected to speak. "At least that gave me a little time to think why did I want to do this," Warner says. He talked about what he would do to keep the session short and the number of bills low. "And that came out OK."

Warner was 41 when he was elected to the post that usually went to older senators who had served in the Legislature longer. Moreover, he is the only man to follow his father as speaker of the Nebraska Legislature.

A Lincoln Journal editorial was enthusiastic about Warner's election as speaker. "Since he was first elected six years ago, Jerome Warner has made the Legislature his life. He has worked tirelessly at his official duties and at studying issues, night and day, in session and out. During that period, he has developed a mastery of the intricate details of some of the most vexing legislative subjects."[4]

Despite his promise to keep the session short and the number of bills low, that year's session was the longest in history and saw a record number of bills introduced. "So much for campaign promises," Warner says.

One reason for all the bills and the lengthy session, of course, was the highway plan, Warner's own special project. Shepherding it through the legislative process was not without peril.

That year, 1969, was the last of the Unicameral's biennial sessions and the last year in which there was no limit on the number of days the body could meet. There was, however, a limit on the number days in January during which bills could be introduced; the deadline fell at noon on the 20th legislative day.

Betty Person, the Legislature's only full-time researcher, had completed work on the 16 highway bills and taken them to the bill drafters in December, Warner says. He had checked on them periodically after the Unicameral convened in early January, but each time he checked, he was told the bills were not finished. On the 20th legislative day, the last day on which bills could be introduced, Warner finally received the pile of highway bills from Emory, one of the Legislature's bill drafters. As the senator looked through the drafted bills, he found plenty of surprises: wordings that were different from what he had asked for in the bills and items that were brand new to him. He was horrified at the potential for political mischief in the incorrectly drafted bills. And he knew he had very little time to try to correct the errors.

Warner had a page take the bills to Person with a note saying, "These things look bad." Person came to the legislative chamber about 11:30 a.m. and told Warner the bills contained wordings that would have killed the legislation and would have "had people stirred up to no end."

When Warner checked the dates on the backs of the forms, he found that the bills actually had been drafted Jan. 3, 5 and 7. The fact that they weren't delivered to him until the last minute led him to believe somebody did not want him to be able to change the mistakes he found.

[4]Lincoln Journal, Jan. 8, 1966

Something drastic needed to be done if the highway plan were to survive long enough even to be considered. "I stood up about quarter till 12 and moved that the rule for introduction of bills in the first 20 days would be interpreted to mean that any bill requested by 4 o'clock that afternoon would be considered as having been introduced," Warner says. The motion passed, partly, he says, because other people had bills in mind that they still wanted to introduce and partly because it was the speaker who requested the extension.

Warner and Person took the bills back to the bill drafting office and asked that they be redrafted. The drafting office said it was too late to request redrafting; the deadline had passed. But Warner said, "No, it's not too late. The floor just adopted my motion to consider any requests made by four this afternoon, and I'm now making a request for 16 new bills. ... Except this time you're going to bring them to me in rough draft."

Swept into the pot along with the roads legislation that afternoon in early February was another bill that would not have made it to consideration under the traditional deadline, a proposed constitutional amendment that would bring the Legislature into session every year instead of every other year.

It was not a bill Warner supported. "No public policy needs to be changed every nine months," he says of the switch. He believes public policy should evolve slowly and not be open to fiddling and adjustment every few months.

A number of factors contributed to Nebraska's move to annual sessions. A national movement to improve and professionalize state legislatures was having an effect in most every state by the late 1960s and early 1970s. The movement recommended adding staff to provide the legislators with more information and support. As Warner notes, it's easier to retain staff when the Legislature meets every year. The reformers also stressed that quality people would be more likely to run for and stay in the legislature if they could count on fitting an annual session into their private lives and work. Warner acknowledges that is also true.

However, the amendment also set a limit on the number of days the Legislature can meet each year. "There was talk about how the Legislature was in session for so long—and we were," Warner says. It was Sept. 24 when the Legislature adjourned in 1969. But the total number of days in session during a two-year period was about the same then as it is now. Furthermore, every bill introduced was disposed of—either passed or killed. Today, many bills are simply not dealt with before the Legislature is forced, by law, to adjourn.

Until the 1990s measures gave the speaker authority to set priorities on legislation to be considered, the body's rules included no efficient way to be sure that the most important matters were considered. Allowing each of the 49 senators to select one priority bill out of the more than 800 introduced each session was an attempt to solve the problem, but the results had been mixed.

The Legislature will take care of the matters it must take care of—budget, revenue, crises involving existing laws. But other matters that may be vitally important in the long run may never reach consideration, thanks to the time limits set by law. Warner is not comfortable with that outcome.

But when the proposal for annual sessions was put to a vote, the people approved it, probably believing that "the less the Legislature meets, the less harm they do." However, senators respond by trying to do more in less time. As a result, both senators and the public have less time to learn about the issues behind the legislation.

"But reality goes against perception, and perception will always win," Warner says.

For good or ill, the amendment to change the Legislature's schedule to annual sessions slipped into the legislative machinery in 1969 thanks to the highway package. But, although he had avoided a total washout along the road to highway legislation when he sent back the last-minute bills, Warner knew he would have to proceed with caution as he steered the legislation to success.

The roads plan was nothing if not comprehensive. In keeping with Warner's commitment to long-term thinking, the plan included a classification system for every road in the state, from major highways to county gravel. It included increases in the gas tax and motor vehicle registration fees. It established a highway allocation fund and, for the first time, allowed the state to go into debt to construct roads.

In a story in the March 2, 1969, Sunday Journal and Star, Warner commented on the package of roads legislation, admitting it was involved and complex. He assured citizens the state did not intend to dictate to local government what each jurisdiction should do about individual roads. But the classification bill would establish a structure for the states, counties and cities to work together to eliminate duplication and conflict and benefit all of them.

Many lobbyists were in favor of the plan, and so were cities, which stood to receive more money for roads based on the consultant's recommendations. But cities historically had little support in the Legislature, Warner says, and that situation held going into the 1969 session. So he made good use of the contacts he had developed across the state during the hearings, asking supporters to call their senators and encourage them to vote for the plan.

Action on the floor also required some maneuvering, Warner recalls. Terry Carpenter and Jules Burbach had managed to amend the measure dealing with the gas tax so that the increase would have been higher than the Legislature was likely to approve.

"It would have killed the bill," Warner says. "So that night Betty and I sat in her office, and we wrote speeches for six senators on the floor, to get it reconsidered.... We had the order in which they were to speak; we had them spaced in different areas on the floor so people seemed to be coming up from different locations."

Warner gave the speeches to senators who supported his version of the bill. He gave the list to Lieutenant Governor John Everroad and asked Everroad to recognize the people on the list in order, mixing in any other senators who wanted to speak to the bill.

The plan worked. Each senator spoke, according to schedule, and the motion to reconsider was approved. Carpenter did not appreciate what had happened, and "as he usually did when he got mad, he went home for a week." Jules Burbach, another opponent of the plan, did not protest the reconsideration. As a result, Warner did not have much more trouble with the bills. Eventually, the entire package was approved, "with every bit of the controversial stuff in it," Warner says.

The process demonstrated Warner's understanding of how the Legislature works: One person alone cannot accomplish much of anything. Instead, a measure needs a reasonably large number of people who support it and a few who know enough about it to convince others to get on the bandwagon.

But the person who orchestrates a presentation the way he did on the subject of the gas tax shouldn't talk about it, Warner says. In the case of that 1969 debate, no one knew about the plan except the six senators who made Warner's case and the lieutenant governor who presided.

"If you're successful at doing something up there (on the floor), the last thing you want to do is talk about it," Warner says. "In some respects it makes the others sound used, and that's not true. We structured the arguments. But the Legislature has a very efficient internal balancing system. And if the majority feel like they've been maneuvered or used or someone takes more credit than they ought to, it will always get balanced out in time."

Gary Hannibal says he has heard Warner make similar observations more than once. "He said to me in private conversations that some of the best things he ever did he couldn't tell anybody for 10 years."

Hannibal, an Omaha senator and member of the Appropriations Committee from 1985-90, considers Warner his mentor. The senior senator knows a lot about human nature and realizes the best way to get things done is not to be obvious about his own influence.

And those who have worked with Warner through the years are unanimous in their respect for his intelligence and capability.

Jack Pittman says Warner was able to get the highway bills passed in 1969 largely because of his familiarity with the system and because "he's so damn smart.

"I thought I knew my job well," Pittman says. "But he's six days ahead of me. He knows the legislative labyrinth."

Sandy Scofield, who served with Warner on the Appropriations Committee in the 1980s, agrees. She thinks Warner's intelligence is one of his greatest strengths. "But he comes across as so modest, it's hard to realize you're dealing with someone with maybe genius capabilities," Scofield says. "I marvel at his ability to take in information and remember it."

Ron Roskens, the former university president, who became a close friend of Warner's through the years, agrees that the senator is "a brilliant man. His capacity with respect to funds is unbelievable...the man never uses a book or set of documents as a resource. He uses the back of an envelope from his pocket" and a steel trap mind that never seems to forget a number that is of any importance.

In addition to that kind of intelligence and ability to catch on quickly, Warner's family background was a major factor in his quick rise to leadership. Warner learned leadership from his father. With that kind of background and six years of legislative experience under his belt, Warner was well-prepared to lead the fight to revolutionize Nebraska's roads.

His success in that campaign only increased his status in the Legislature and the state.

Perhaps most importantly, though, the battle for the highway system brought Warner something personally important. It brought him together with Betty Person, who was to become his wife. "We got to know one another quite well," Warner says of their hours of work together on the highway plan.

Betty

"We were very discreet," Warner says, partly because of his belief that the relationship between senators and their staff members should maintain a level of formality.

Furthermore, Person was the only researcher in the Legislature in those days. She worked for the entire body. Had the two been open about their growing personal relationship, people might have suspected that Warner had some influence on research Person was doing for other senators or knew confidential material involving that research.

"She would never have done anything like that, though," Warner says.

The two did attend social functions together in those days, "but people were so used to seeing us work together on roads and taxes" that they weren't startled to see Warner and Person together socially.

"It's also true that I guard my personal life fairly carefully," the senator adds.

The man who describes himself as reserved and the reporter-researcher described by many as warm and outgoing were married April 24, 1970.

While the highway bills may have been the catalyst that made the couple serious about each other, they had known each other for a number of years before that time. In fact, Warner had known of Betty Person before he actually met her. He had read her stories when she was Betty Craig, a reporter for the Lincoln Star in the 1950s.

"If her byline was on it, you would read it cause you always felt sure that it was accurate," the senator says.

Craig, a Lincoln native, had always wanted to be a reporter, Warner says. "She asked for and got her first typewriter at age 4 so she could write." She actually got her start in journalism when she answered an ad for a United Press International reporter in 1944, during her first year at the University of Nebraska.

During a phone interview, Maggie Davis, head of UPI's Lincoln bureau, asked Craig, "Have you had experience?"

"No."

"Can you type?"

"Yes, but not very fast."

"Can you operate a teletype machine?"

"What's that?"

"But you do want to be a reporter?"

"Yes."

So Craig went for an interview the next morning. Before leaving home, she told her mother that if she had to reach the UPI office by walking up three flights of stairs with pea green walls and a bulb hanging from the ceiling, she was going to go back home.

When she reached the building, she climbed up three flights of stairs, the walls were pea green and there was a light hanging from the ceiling on a cord.

But Craig didn't go back home; she interviewed with Davis and was hired.

Craig's first assignment was to cover an athletic event at the university. Craig didn't know anything about sports, but Greg McBride, sports writer for the Omaha World-Herald, was a longtime friend of Craig's family, and he helped her get the story together.

"After that, it got better," Warner says. Craig soon moved from sports to the statehouse, where she covered a special session of the Legislature in 1944, a beat more to her taste.

Craig learned a great deal from Maggie Davis's insistence on accuracy, discipline and professionalism. When Craig would write a story, Davis would ask her questions about the content. If Craig could not answer all the questions to Davis' satisfaction, "Maggie would send her back," Warner says, even though UPI and Associated Press reporters were constantly competing to beat each other on stories by minutes or even seconds. "So she learned that that's how you did things," the senator says.

UPI paid its men and women reporters the same salary, equal treatment that was somewhat rare in that era. Craig's starting pay was $15 a week, more than many women made after long careers as newspaper reporters. It wasn't until some years later that Craig was to experience firsthand the discrimination against women that was common in society of that day.

After several years learning her craft with UPI, Craig became news director for KOLN Radio in Lincoln, a job she held until 1952. She had an interview show each morning. After World War II, all kinds of foreign dignitaries toured American university campuses. Many who came to the University of Nebraska-Lincoln talked to Betty Craig on KOLN. The only one who ever turned down Craig's request for an interview was Winston Churchill's son.

In addition to international visitors, Craig interviewed prominent Americans on her daily show, including Senator Joseph McCarthy of Wisconsin, who later earned notoriety for his Congressional hearings on un-American activities. In his interview with Craig, McCarthy was open and direct about what he was trying to accomplish as a member of the U.S. Senate.

McCarthy had spoken in Nebraska on several occasions, and Craig had covered his speeches. But one of McCarthy's appearances, in Omaha, was before an organization that allowed only male members. The organizers refused to allow Craig into the room, even in her capacity as a reporter.

When McCarthy learned that Craig was being excluded from the event, he threatened to cancel his speech. "Betty tried to talk him out of it. She didn't want to make that fuss," Warner says. But McCarthy insisted she be allowed in the room, and she did cover the speech.

Craig left KOLN in 1952 to join Fred Seaton's staff when he was named to fill out a Senate term after Kenneth D. Wherry died in office. In Washington, D.C., Craig worked both for Seaton and for the Republican National Committee during Dwight Eisenhower's campaign for president.

After Eisenhower was elected, he appointed Seaton Secretary of the Interior, and Craig was out of a job. Seaton hadn't been in office long enough to develop the clout to help her find another position in government, so Craig turned to McCarthy. She had renewed her professional relationship with him when she moved to Washington, and he helped her get a job at the Library of Congress. In that position, Craig wrote a history of the U.S. Capitol, the first official work of its kind.

Warner says he and Betty had tried to find a copy of the book in recent years but had finally given up. But, as he sorted through boxes at his home in the spring of 1995, he was delighted to discover a copy of the book among other papers and memorabilia.

Craig was married and had a son, Jamie, while she was living in Washington. She was expecting her second child when her marriage ended and she decided to return to Nebraska in 1956 as Betty Person. Her daughter, Liz, was born in Lincoln.

Person went to work for the Lincoln Star as its statehouse reporter. Thorough and fair, she earned the trust of the people she covered. In fact, she was so respected that she ended up with her own office in the heart of the Capitol.

"When Vic Anderson was governor, he offered her office space between the governor's office and the chief of staff's office," Warner says. "As a result, she knew what was going on most of the time in the governor's office."

During the 1950s, a reporter could easily make daily contact with every state agency and all branches of government, because they were all situated in the Capitol. Person became well-acquainted with the workings of state government.

As she covered the Legislature, she observed that the senators needed more help researching issues that came before them. So she approached the Executive Board, asking that they consider hiring a researcher. The board hired her in November 1964 as the Legislature's only research staffer.

That meant Person worked on the 1965 bills that established the Department of Administrative Services and the personnel department, the 1967 bills that established the state sales and income taxes and state aid to schools and the 1965-69 highway studies and bills. In the process of researching the highway bills, Person had her own tangle with Warner's nemesis, Terry Carpenter.

As the Legislature's researcher, Person started preparing for the highway legislation by applying many of the recommendations the consultant had come up with to counties and cities and statewide to calculate the effects. One thing she did was calculate how many dollars of highway money each city was getting per mile of road. The allocations had traditionally been made on a purely political basis, whatever the Legislature could work out in negotiations and deliberations. The most recent allocations had been made in 1955.

It turned out that Terrytown, the section of Scottsbluff named for Senator Carpenter, was getting far more dollars per mile than any other municipality in the state. "Terry had nothing to do with the fact that Terrytown was getting more money," Warner says. It was just a result of the way the allocation had been set up.

But when the numbers were published, Carpenter thought they might make him look bad. He told Person he was unhappy that she had allowed the information about Terrytown to be made public. "Your job is to protect the legislators," Carpenter told her.

"Like hell it is! My job is to protect the taxpayers," Person snapped back.

Despite confrontations like that, Warner says, Person and Carpenter usually got along just fine. "Terry would say what he thought, and Betty would say what she thought, and that was how it was."

But once Betty Person became Betty Warner, Carpenter's attitude seems to have changed. In 1971, Person had been approached about doing the reapportionment that was required after the 1970 census. She had had a lot of experience with the process and had agreed to do it again. "But then Carpenter came in and fussed," Warner says, "primarily because she was married to me. So Betty quit. She didn't need that."

Warner has no doubt, though, that his wife would have been ethical and even-handed to a fault had she gone ahead with the reapportionment. "If she'd had to stick me to be fair, she'd have done it," he says. The two had worked together long enough before they were married that Warner had plenty of opportunity to appreciate his wife's integrity.

"It was a wonder we ever got together," Warner says. The relationship got off to something of a rocky start thanks to the 1965 bills produced by the Government and Military Affairs Committee when Warner was chairman.

"A whole slug of amendments" came out of committee hearings on the proposed bills, Warner says. He took all the amendments to Person and asked her to correlate all the information and "put it together so it made some sense and we could act on it." He asked to have the finished product in a week or two.

"The day the Government Committee was to meet, she had been there all night the night before, putting that stuff together," Warner says. "Jamie and Liz were sleeping on a couch" in the office while their mother worked.

Person took the completed amendments to Warner just before the committee was to meet at 2 p.m. the next afternoon. "I had decided, probably the day before, that we wouldn't take up the bill that year. But I didn't tell Betty. Didn't think about it." It was the cost of creating a personnel department that concerned Warner and made him decide to postpone action on the proposal.

When Person came to the committee meeting with the material she had worked all night to prepare, Warner thanked her and then nonchalantly mentioned that the committee probably wouldn't take up the matter in the current session after all. "Needless to say, she was a bit put out with me," Warner says, "and appropriately so."

But if Person was disgusted with Warner after that 1965 incident, the emotion didn't last. As the researcher and the senator worked together in the ensuing years, they began to develop a personal relationship that also included her two children.

Jamie, now 41 and living in Phoenix with his wife and three children, remembers when his mother was dating the senator. The Persons lived a few blocks from a Lincoln bowling alley, and Jamie, then a teen-ager, would often stop by to bowl a line in the early evening.

One night Warner came along to bowl with him. On one of his attempts the senator slipped and fell—but still managed to bowl a strike. "I gave him a trophy for Christmas that year," Jamie says. "He was one of the few people who could fall down and still bowl a strike."

Jamie was 15 and Liz 14 when Warner married their mother in April 1970 and subsequently adopted the children. The new house Warner was building, across the section to the east of the home place, was finished in October, and the family moved in then.

The senator had always been "a strong family person," says Betty Schlaphoff of Waverly. But marriage at age 43 and to a woman with two teenage children changed his life a lot.

Jamie and Liz went to school in Waverly, but Jamie remembers that he was never particularly active in school activities. "I spent most of my time on the farm," he says.

"He taught me about farming right away," Jamie says. "He was pretty patient" and a good teacher, he recalls.

During one of his early attempts at field work, Jamie started out driving across the contours in the field. His dad stopped him and, in the dust on the tractor, drew out the pattern that the young farmer should follow around the field.

Although he didn't demand perfection, Warner was always concerned that the farm work be done right. For example, when crops were planted in spring, Warner wanted the rows to be straight, planted the way his father had taught him. Rather than scold his hired hands or his son for work that didn't quite measure up to his standards, Warner would often do a lot of the farming himself. "He ran himself ragged," his son says.

Farmers experience frequent problems with equipment and conditions, problems that can lead to all kinds of frustrations. But Jamie Warner says his dad refused to allow himself to waste time in anger when something broke down or didn't go right. Jamie remembers only one exception.

"We were getting irrigation motors ready and using a front-end loader to pick them up," he says. Somehow, "Dad crunched the radiator on one of the motors. He was really mad. He threw the radiator cap and busted it."

"He never let me throw anything," Jamie says, remembering his surprise at his father's reaction. But Warner's anger didn't last long. "He walked in the barn, and he was back in two minutes, starting to figure out how to fix it," Jamie says.

Warner seldom lost his temper with things or people, Jamie says. "He only yelled at me twice." One of those times, not surprisingly, happened in the field.

"He yelled at me once when I was moving hay bales. He told me how to do it, but I didn't want to do it that way. I got mad, and he got mad." The two didn't speak for a while that afternoon, but their anger didn't last.

Things didn't go as well for Warner and Liz during the early years of their relationship, the daughter says now. "It was a rocky road in the beginning," she says, although it was obvious "he cared a lot about all of us. ... I'd never had a dad before, and I didn't know how to relate to it. And, also, I was an extremely rebellious teenager."

Liz attended UNL for a while after high school, but her heart wasn't in her school work. She started working on the farm with her dad and going to the university part-time when she was 21. At that point, her relationship with Warner changed dramatically.

Warner was bothered not at all by the fact that Liz wanted to do work that was not traditionally done by women. "He had all this open acceptance of me," she remembers. "He taught me everything he could about running the machinery and making decisions about the farm. He trusted me to do the right thing."

Not all the men on the farm were as supportive of Liz's non-traditional role, she says. "I remember thinking I was so sorry Dad and I couldn't just do it all ourselves."

"He was a great teacher," Liz remembers, always calm and patient. "My mom was very much a worrier," Liz says, "but Dad had a different way of approaching things."

She knew her father worried sometimes about her operating the power equipment on the farm, but instead of warning her to be careful, he'd say, "Don't go out and break that thing now," or "Don't go too fast and mess things up." It sent Liz a message that he was treating her as an adult, but she also knew he was concerned about her safety. "He just had such a good way of getting his message across without saying that."

The experience of working together transformed the relationship between father and daughter. By the time she spent a summer in England in 1978, Liz would write fondly about her father in the journal she was keeping. Included was this passage: "An atmosphere of stability prevails when he is with me. I like to watch him work — so careful, diligent, knowledgeable and patient. His calmness is remarkable, and I find that comforting. ... He's been a wonderful teacher, friend and father to me. How fortunate I am!"

Liz recalls how Warner would "sing these dumb little jingles" while they worked and "laugh and joke at things about himself."

And she remembers the polka music. "One time he was driving the tractor up to the house, and I was behind him, and I could see him bouncing up and down. I wondered if he even had his hands on the wheel and what was going on. Then he stopped and opened the door to the cab, and I could hear the polka music."

"He's such a sweetheart," Liz says of the senator, "so shy but so kind."

Now, at 40, Liz manages the University of Idaho's field campus at McCall and doesn't see her father as often as she'd like. But she has fond memories of her years working with him on the farm. "We had some good times back then," she says.

Jamie recalls an incident when he was in college at UNL that illustrates his father's interest in his adopted children. A business administration major, Jamie and a few other students had gone to talk with some state senators about the business college's need for more faculty. Later, at a meeting with a lot of business majors, the dean asked

Jamie to talk about their visit to the Legislature and the status of potential legislation.

"I hadn't expected that," Jamie says, and was not prepared to make much of a speech. "I was trying to fumble my way through, and then I looked up and Dad was standing in the back of the room." The dean asked the senator if he'd like to speak, and Warner did, explaining where the college stood on its request for more faculty.

"I really appreciated that," Jamie says. "He'd go out of his way for Liz and me."

"He's a kind, considerate person," Jamie adds. "His parents really raised him well." As a result of that upbringing, "he always expected a lot of himself but not so much from others, so he was never real disappointed when people didn't measure up. He'd just accept it and go on."

Life After Being Speaker

After Warner and Person's victories in the highway legislation in 1969 and their marriage in 1970, Warner returned to the Legislature for the first of its annual sessions in 1971. "There wasn't even the slightest thought on my part or anybody else's part of doing anything more than a two-year term" as speaker, Warner says. He was looking forward to serving as a member of the body with no formal leadership responsibilities.

He recalls joking at the time that "I was looking forward to coming back 'cause I didn't have to be nice to anybody anymore. That sounds bad," he admits now. "It probably wasn't a very smart thing to say," he adds, even though it was said in jest.

As he had planned, Warner wasn't elected chairman of any standing committee that year, but he was appointed to chair the Rules Committee, a select committee. He was chosen for that post, he says, because he had become very familiar with the Legislature's rules during his term as speaker.

Lieutenant Governor John Everroad, the Legislature's presiding officer, had been absent quite a lot from the 1969 session, Warner says, leaving it to the speaker to preside. "I knew the rules frontwards and backwards," the senator recalls, a trait that is vitally important for a speaker, he adds. "It's essential to know the rules and be quick" to prevent the senators' being distracted from the substance of legislation by arguments over the rules.

So the Rules Committee chairmanship was a logical position for Warner to occupy as the first speaker to return to another term of service in the Unicameral. Even without a powerful committee position, Warner was a leader who got noticed. An editorial in the Lincoln Star in October

1972 called Warner a "lawmaker of demonstrated leadership and tenacity in pursuit of sound legislative goals."

It was earlier that same year, when Warner held no major leadership post, that an incident happened that the senator still regrets. It involved Senator Sam Klavar of Omaha.

Klavar had been involved in a scandal in 1955 and was censured by the Legislature at the end of the session. A legislative investigating committee concluded that Klavar was guilty of taking a $1,500 bribe from a trade association in return for agreeing not to introduce a bill the association disliked. Warner's father was serving as lieutenant governor then and told his family a lot about the Klavar scandal.

The whole thing came at the end of the session, and the senators assumed the censure would mark the end of Klavar's political career. Instead, Klavar used the censure to his advantage, convincing his constituents that he had been mistreated by the Legislature while trying to represent their best interests. The censure was soon forgotten, and Klavar continued to be re-elected until he retired in 1972.

At the end of the 1972 session, the customary resolution was introduced to thank the senator for his service to the body. Warner was one of the few who remembered and still cared about Klavar's involvement in the scandal nearly two decades earlier. He left the legislative chamber rather than be swept along in the traditional resolution of thanks and approval. Now he wishes he had stayed and voted "no."

His silent protest backfired. When Warner returned to the chamber, Orval Keyes, the senator who sat in front of him, said, "Warner, I pushed your (voting) button 'yes' for you since you weren't here."

Warner was furious. He remembers the incident as one of the few times he blew up at a fellow senator. "I said, 'Never touch my button. Never!'"

The upshot was that Warner was listed in the legislative proceedings as voting to commend Klavar for his long and distinguished service. "Fortunately, resolutions don't mean much," Warner says, "but it sure disgusted me."

Warner's distaste for a senator who he believed had misused his office is a reflection on his own ethical standards. Along with his love for politics—and Hereford cattle—Warner's ethics were learned at home.

"It's relatively simple," he says. "As I grew up, if I had to ask myself 'Would my mother approve?' I knew she wouldn't—and I shouldn't."

Further, Warner has tried to pattern his character after his father's. "He idolized his dad," says Dick Herman, the retired reporter. "He tries to emulate his habits of responsibility, prudence, vision and respect for the institution."

The senator tells about something his father had written on a scrap of paper, a scrap the son has had framed. While he can't recite the exact words, Warner says the essence of what his father wrote was "You never build yourself up by tearing someone else down."

Lessons learned from examples like that, Warner says, are what make a person who he is.

As a senator, Warner says, the way he has addressed issues has been a mixture of what he grew up with and what he's learned. He say he never tried to design a system to build his credibility in the Legislature. He was told as a child, he says, "that you do what you say you will do."

In the cattle business, for instance, the Warner family sold hundreds of head of livestock, and "nothing was ever in writing." They simply lived up to the commitment they had made.

The habit stayed with him, Warner says, and it drew attention. For instance, when he met with the Lincoln firemen during the 1962 campaign, he says, he did his best to tell the firemen what he thought he would do about the various issues they raised.

When he returned to talk to the group again during the next campaign, two years later, "they made such a thing out of the fact that I had ended up doing exactly what I said I would do.

"It never dawned on me that I shouldn't do that," Warner says.

He has followed much the same pattern in every election campaign. "There are always things I want to get done," he says, "and I talk about them in the campaign. I don't know how much influence that has on voters, but it does have an influence me. I've said I'm going to do it, so then I do."

Once he's in the midst of trying to follow through on those campaign pledges, though, Warner tends not to go back to his constituents to ask them how they feel about a specific issue.

That's one of the reasons Warner seldom answers constituent mail until after the legislative session ends. "It's distasteful for me to write people the customary letter: 'Thank you for your suggestions on LB Whatever, and I'll keep that in mind as I vote on this issue.' That's a response, not an answer," the senator says.

If, at the end of the session, he finds he voted differently from the way the constituent had urged him to do, he writes a long letter, explaining why he voted as he did. "I've had people say they still disagree but understood or appreciated the rationale," he says.

That doesn't always reconcile the differences he has with a constituent, Warner says, but he adds that he believes most people will accept a genuine explanation. "The one thing they won't accept is if you try to con them," he says.

"Honesty with everybody and surely with your constituents is the easiest thing to do. First of all, you don't have to remember what you said," he adds with a chuckle.

While almost no one would fault Warner's penchant for honesty, not everyone agrees that he should postpone answering constituent mail until a session ends. Shirley Marsh says she thinks it is a mistake not to answer a constituent's letters. Marsh represented a Lincoln district in the Unicameral from 1972-88 and served on the Appropriations Committee with Warner during most of those years.

After the 1980 census and the ensuing redrawing of legislative district lines, Marsh says she heard from people who were now her constituents but who had previously been in Warner's district. "People would complain that he didn't respond," Marsh says. In the American system, she says, constituents expect their elected officials at all levels to listen and respond to their concerns.

Marsh, a Warner fan, excuses Warner's habit as at least partly a result of trying to farm and serve in the Unicameral at the same time. That situation placed extreme limits on his time, she points out, even during the years when he was not serving as chairman of a committee.

Warner, however, made the decision on the basis of principle, perhaps a reflection of his belief that he should serve his constituents more as a trustee—someone who weighs all the facts in making a decision — than a delegate—someone who votes simply on the basis of his constituents' wishes. Waiting until after the session to respond to their letters made it possible for him to preserve that distinction.

During the brief time between his term as speaker and his election to a new leadership position, Warner was able to bring to fruition a piece of legislation he had been working on since he got to the Legislature. The concept came to be known as greenbelt legislation.

Warner became interested in the issue in 1959, when he was on the city/county planning commission for Lincoln and Lancaster County. During his first session in the Unicameral, he had introduced a bill to reclassify all real property because of contradictions in the way the system was working.

But the issue really came home to him when he heard the story of one of his own constituents, Mrs. George Snyder. As is often true in legislative matters, this one grew from a situation that affected relatively few people at the time it surfaced.

Mrs. Snyder, a widow, owned a quarter of land at the east edge of Lincoln where Southeast Community College now stands. It was her sole source of support, but taxes were taking most of her income from the land, Warner recalls.

Land near urban areas—like Mrs. Snyder's—was being valued and taxed at a rate higher than agricultural land because it was in the path of potential development, making it worth more on the real estate market.

But the assessor had no way of knowing where Lincoln's next growth spurt would come. When Mrs. Snyder asked the county to change the land's zoning from agricultural to development, the county refused, even though the land was being assessed at a higher value than normal for ag land.

Mrs. Snyder was caught between two branches of government with conflicting aims. On one hand, her property was being valued at a relatively high rate because of its potential for development. On the other hand, Mrs. Snyder was being told she could not use the land for development.

"It made absolutely no sense to me," Warner says. "It seemed totally unfair."

Warner decided the legislature needed to act to correct the unfair situation. He talked to the bill drafter and told him what he wanted, based on his own research. "What they brought me was a constitutional amendment to classify all property," a lot more bill than Warner was expecting. It would have allowed the greenbelt legislation to be passed, but it also would have allowed classification of real property with no limitations. He introduced it without realizing the ramifications that were included.

As soon as the bill was introduced, Warner heard plenty of protests about what a bad thing the bill was. And he agreed. "I'm unalterably opposed to classifying real property for tax purposes. I think it all should be at 100 percent" of market value. Instead, the bill he had casually introduced would have valued property differently depending on its classification.

Minnesota had had such a provision and had ended up with about 30 property classifications, all of which could be and were changed frequently as a result of political maneuvering. "You could manipulate who paid taxes and who didn't," Warner says.

Warner didn't have to worry long about supporting a measure that went against his own principles. "The bill went down the drain," he says.

He came back the following session with a constitutional amendment to try to eliminate the trap Mrs. Snyder and others like her had fallen into. This time the proposal made it through the Unicameral but failed at the polls that fall.

Warner let the issue ride for a few years, then proposed a measure that the Legislature adopted and an amendment the voters approved in 1972, allowing ag land to be assessed as ag land rather than as development land until the land is likely actually to be developed. The law took the "guessing game" away from county assessors and allowed for higher valuations as dictated by the market, Warner says.

Despite its successful passage, the measure "has been a problem child for me," he adds. "We've had problems with it because people want to use it as a gimmick to reduce their taxes rather than as an orderly development tool for a municipality and to allow people of average or less means to hold onto their property until it is ready to be developed." He still hears criticism about greenbelt legislation, he says, although "I still think the concept is right."

And he points to the matter as an example of how long-term persistence is sometimes necessary if a legislator wants to be successful. "If I'd been here for anything less than 10 years, it's not likely anybody else would have picked it up," he says of the issue he pursued until 1972.

Former Senator Loran Schmit says the greenbelt measure was, indeed, significant legislation, "but the most significant thing is that he could pass it without anyone raising the question of whether it benefited him personally." It may, eventually, do that, but no one questioned Warner's motives in supporting the legislation. Because of his reputation for integrity, people assumed he was interested in greenbelts for policy reasons, not personal reasons, Schmit says. He agrees.

Warner's ability to lead the Legislature toward what he believed to be an ideal tax system even while he did not hold a leadership position is another tribute to his growing reputation in the Unicameral. Whether or not he enjoyed being "just a senator," Warner's recess from leadership was short-lived. In 1973, almost by accident, he became the chairman of the Education Committee. Once again he would find himself embroiled in the controversy that state aid to schools always seemed to engender.

Warner hadn't intended to make a bid to lead the Education Committee. The opportunity arose, however, when an Omaha World-Herald reporter called Warner and told him that only one senator, Orval Keyes, had indicated an interest in chairing Education.

The reporter asked Warner what he thought about that. "I had some reservations about Orval as chair of Education," Warner says. "I said I thought I'd just become a candidate for the chair of Education." And he was elected.

Actually, he says now, chairing the Education Committee at that point was convenient since he was still involved with state aid to schools legislation, particularly with the contested distribution formula. It was best, he says, that the Education chairman introduced bills and held the interim hearings on the topic "if you wanted to keep it intact."

A bill involving the distribution formula that Warner introduced in the 1973 session was passed two years later, he remembers. To that date, it was the most expensive state aid to schools bill passed, providing 65 percent of school funding from state sources.

Although he was no longer chairman of the Education Committee in 1975, Warner still carried the ball on the state aid bill that year. He was its chief supporter and the one who best understood what it would accomplish. The bill passed on final reading with more than 30 votes, and the Legislature recessed for a few days that spring.

Warner was home, trying to get some farm work done, when he got a call over the noon hour from the governor's office. A staffer invited him to come to the Capitol that afternoon and talk with Governor Jim Exon about the state aid bill. Warner assumed the governor wanted to discuss the bill one-on-one in the privacy of his office.

When Warner got to the Capitol, he ran into Dick Herman, the legislative reporter for the Lincoln Journal, who told him Exon had called a press conference for that afternoon. Oddly, the press conference was scheduled for the same time as Warner's meeting with Exon. Warner began to be suspicious. He was expecting an informal meeting with the governor. The situation he was apparently going to face was very different.

The governor's hearing room was filled with reporters waiting to hear from Exon, tax commissioner Bill Peters and other officials. Warner came to the quick conclusion that Exon and his staff wanted to feed the press reasons why the aid to schools bill was a bad piece of legislation. The governor and his people had already been making public statements questioning Warner's projections about the cost of the bill and implying that it would be far more expensive than projected.

The issues were the same as they had always been—and still are—regarding state aid to education. Any cut in property taxes for schools would have to be made up by increases in sales and income taxes. People doubted that property taxes would actually go down and stay down, and many also feared losing local control of schools. Those were the fears Peters and Exon were trying to stir in the minds of Nebraskans by attacking Warner's bill.

"They were probably trying to make me look bad," Warner says, and to justify Exon's impending veto of the bill. But the senator was not about to give up without a fight.

When it was Warner's turn to speak, he began by questioning Peters' numbers and conclusions, figures that made the cost of the measure look considerably larger than Warner believed to be true.

Warner asked Peters why the public should trust the figures the administration was touting. The senator pointed out that the tax commissioner's regular revenue projection always was a broad range of possible numbers. How could Peters be so precise about state aid figures when he never seemed able to be the least bit precise about any other numbers?

"The argument started there," Warner says, and got hotter. The senator gave no ground.

"I felt really good when I walked out of there." But, he concedes, "It was probably like the challenger fighting the champion. If you win on points, at best it's still a draw." The press reported the argument as a draw, Warner says. The governor vetoed the bill.

The measure came back to the Legislature for an override, facing a lot of publicity—just as Exon had planned—about how much state taxes would go up to pay for the new state aid to education. State taxes certainly would have gone up, Warner admits, but local property taxes would have gone down commensurately. That was the whole point behind the bill.

Warner needed 30 votes to override the veto; he got only 25. In the process, Warner came close to losing control of himself on the floor, he recalls. He knew he wasn't going to get the 30 votes he needed, but his goal was to get at least 25 in favor of the override, at least a majority of the body to make a respectable showing.

"Somebody was playing with his button, voting 'yes,' 'no,' 'yes,' 'no.' We'd go from 25 to 24 to 25. ... That got to me for some reason," Warner says. He tried to make a motion to thank those who had voted for the bill, "but I know I wasn't emotionally very well under control." He recalls the experience as one of the few times he has had trouble staying calm.

But that 1973 aid bill stands out for another reason, too. It was the last time Warner sponsored a measure involving state aid to schools. He had sponsored such a bill every session since he'd been in the Legislature and saw the major 1967 legislation and several follow-up bills enacted.

"It became obvious to me by 1974 that the issue of state aid to schools was controversial itself but that I was becoming part of the controversy as well," Warner says. "It was time to assist somebody else who was willing to do the battle and not necessarily be the one who was carrying it."

So he began supporting measures sponsored by Jerry Koch of Ralston and Frank Lewis of Bellevue and, more recently, Ron Withem of Papillion.

"And that's important upstairs in the Legislature," the senator says. Helping someone else on an issue instead of continuing to take the lead himself lets a senator preserve the balance Warner believes is necessary in the body. "If there's a perception that someone is dominating over a period of time, eventually it wears thin, and it's time to step aside."

So he decided to do exactly that regarding aid to schools. By that time, however, the senator had already made a major impact on aid to schools and on roads and highways. "And taxes," Warner says. "But that's because roads and education can't function without taxes."

In order to be successful on major, expensive legislation, the senator had learned how to make his views heard, how to work with his fellow senators, how to line up votes to advance legislation to final approval. He developed his own method for doing that.

"I don't go around and lobby people to get a bill out," he says. Part of the reason is philosophical: "It's hard for me to ask anybody to do anything, generally. I feel like I'm imposing." Part of the reason is practical: "Inevitably, you run into those who say, 'Yes, I'll help you. And, oh, by the way, I've got a bill in your committee.' I don't like to be put in that position," Warner says. "If I don't ask, I'm not asked."

But that doesn't mean he doesn't talk to people about issues and bills in which he is interested. He says he visits with people and offers to answer questions.

Lobbyists can also be a big help, Warner says, "and then I don't have to get involved." The senator says he often works closely with lobbyists working for a group that is on the same side of an issue that he is. "I also will use them to help tell me where I've got problems."

And then Warner will set out to try to solve those problems, to provide more information, to soothe ruffled feelings, to answer questions. "But I'm not going to go support something I don't want to support. It's not that I'm all that pure, but I just don't like getting into this 'I'll scratch your back if you'll scratch mine' because there's no place to end."

Ron Roskens, president of the University of Nebraska from 1977-89, says that unwillingness to trade votes is one of Warner's strengths as a senator. "He has refused adamantly to make deals," Roskens says. "He's a role model." Even people who often disagree with his stands—like Senator Don Wesely, who is generally more liberal than Warner—admire Warner's honesty and willingness to take a strong position.

Vote trading, for Warner, is out. But persistence over the long haul has been successful for him. When he loses a legislative battle over something he believes is important, chances are good he'll just come back and try again the following year. "If we got along without it for 125 years, 126 won't make any difference," Warner says.

Fond Memories of Legislative Life

Not all Warner's memories of his early years in the Legislature concern hard work and legislative intrigue. Those years were also full of friendships and camaraderie—and an occasional dramatic event.

In 1976, for instance, during the nation's bicentennial, Warner dressed in costume and began doing programs as Ben Franklin, one of the leaders of the American Revolution.

The role seems logical for a person as involved in government as Warner has been—and who looks like Franklin to boot.

"When people tell me I look like Ben Franklin, I tell them the resemblance is in appearance only. His life was a little more risqué than mine," Warner says.

But the surface resemblance is hard to deny. Scott Moore, now Nebraska Secretary of State and a member of the Unicameral from 1986-94, says he remembers thinking, long before he arrived in the Legislature, that Warner could be Ben Franklin reincarnate.

The resemblance arose in the early 1970s when Warner let his hair grow out of the crew cut he had worn through the 1950s and 1960s. "It was mostly by accident," he says now. "I was irrigating one summer, and I didn't have time to get my hair cut. Betty liked it that way, and my daughter did, too. If they liked it, it was OK with me."

The longer hair around the sides couldn't camouflage a growing bald spot on top, though, Warner says. At one point in the mid 1970s, his barber recommended a hair piece. "He put it on and sent me home with it. Liz and Betty were sitting at the dining room table as I came in, and they both burst out laughing when they saw me. That was the end of that," Warner says.

The hair piece would have destroyed the Franklin look anyway and maybe would have prevented Warner from playing the Boston statesman on several occasions.

One of those performances took place one evening in the old East Chamber of the Unicameral, the room that had been home to the state's House of Representatives under the bicameral system from 1867-1937. In that formal room, dressed in costume, Warner spoke to his fellow senators about what Franklin would have thought of the Unicameral. It was a piece Warner wrote himself.

Although he portrayed Franklin that evening, the speech was based primarily on *The Federalist Papers*, written by James Madison and Alexander Hamilton in 1787 and 1788 in support of the newly drafted U.S. Constitution. Warner remembers studying The Federalist to try to determine how the framers of the Constitution—including Franklin—would have regarded the Unicameral. He doesn't remember the specifics, but he believes the framers probably would have had their doubts about a one-house legislature. It would not have measured up to their standards for checks and balances among governmental branches.

Although he doesn't remember precisely what he told his fellow legislators, he recalls that he had a good time making the presentation. "I'm no actor," the senator says, "although you do a lot of acting in public office, I suppose." He enjoyed the opportunity to do it openly on that occasion.

He has fond memories of other aspects of life in the Unicameral in the 1960s and 1970s, too, especially in the days of biennial sessions. Today senators are invited to dozens of social activities—many sponsored by organizations hoping to lobby them. That was not true three decades ago, Warner says. Instead, senators had time to spend socializing together.

"Almost everyone stayed at the Cornhusker or the old Lindell Hotel," Warner says, except some members of the Omaha and Lincoln delegations. He himself would stay in town much of the time, going home to the farm to catch up on work as necessary.

The senators spent many an evening in Lincoln in the card room at one hotel or the other, discussing public issues as they played poker or blackjack and drank pop or coffee, Warner remembers.

The number of senators gathered in the card room varied from just a handful to about a dozen. The informal discussion "gave you the opportunity to understand where people were coming from on different issues" and helped develop a consensus.

Warner believes the process of establishing sales and income taxes in the late 1960s was eased considerably because of the background work that went on in the card rooms. The same was true with major state-aid-to-schools bills. Informal give and take helped people learn to know more about the various sides of the issues.

"It wasn't that deals were made," Warner emphasizes. "It wasn't what people think of as a, quote, smoke-filled room."

The card-players limited themselves to betting nickels and dimes and set a $3 maximum on losses. "That was a deliberate thing so nobody could lose a lot of money. ... If it became a gambling room, that could certainly have had adverse effects on legislation."

"You could play up there all night and have a terrible night and maybe lose two or three dollars at most" before the room closed at midnight, Warner says.

Some of the best card players were Ross Rasmussen and Jules Burbach, Warner remembers. He won't say whether he considers himself a good card player but does admit, "You'd learn and get better as you sat there."

But what he remembers most about the card sessions was the valuable discussion that went on. "I used to say if I had to pick between 9 a.m. and 4 p.m. or 8 p.m. and midnight, I would pick 8 to midnight to get more things done," Warner says. The discussions in the card room went a long way toward resolving issues that would be dealt with formally during the session.

The gatherings in the card rooms gradually died out in the late 1960s and early 1970s. More senators commuted from home rather than stay in Lincoln during the session or rented apartments so their spouses could stay with them. The old Cornhusker Hotel was torn down. And the senators had fewer free evenings because they were invited to more and more social events.

The trend accelerated when the Legislature went to annual sessions in 1971, Warner says, and when the ranks of lobbyists increased. Those lobbyists wanted to schedule events—often dinners—at which the senators could hear from the groups the lobbyists represented. "The theory was the way to a legislator's heart was through his stomach," the senator says.

And so the informal camaraderie of the card rooms disappeared. Today, Warner says, if he wants to see another senator, he has to call the senator's office to make an appointment. It was different in the days when legislators had only their desks on the floor of the legislature and "nowhere else to go," he says. And no telephones on their desks, either.

In fact, the closest telephones were in the cloakroom on the south side of the chamber, Warner says, and the south side became the "prestige" side for a senator to sit on. The senior members sat there to be close to the phones.

As long as he's been in the Legislature, senators have chosen their seats on the basis of seniority, Warner explains. No senator is allowed to bump another—no matter which has seniority—but the members who have seniority get first choice on open seats.

"As a freshman, the only place I could get was on the north side," Warner says. In 1965, though, 20 new senators joined the body. That alone called for a major seat reshuffling.

But it was also in that year that the legislators decided to spread out more and fill up more of the rows of the chamber. Through the 1963 session the senators sat 10 across and filled only the first four-and-a-half rows of seats. Lobbyists were allowed to sit in the remaining rows, behind the senators.

The lobbyists' presence on the actual floor of the Legislature had been criticized ever since Nebraska became a one-house body in 1937, and Warner agrees the arrangement didn't look good. On the other hand, he says, "Everyone knew who was talking to whom" and if another senator or a member of the press wanted to go listen in on a conversation, he did.

"It was very public," Warner says.

But the perception of inappropriate behavior got the better of what may have been reality, and the senators ejected the lobbyists from the chamber's seats in 1965.

Warner had sat in the back row during the 1963 session, and in 1965 he actually moved one row farther back—although that row was no longer the back row. He declined to make the move to the south side of the chamber.

"I intentionally stayed on the north side. That was my way of rebelling" against the common tendency among elected officials to inflate their own importance.

Grabbing power in the Legislature is not possible, Warner says. "I'm assumed to have power, I guess," he says. "I read that from time to time over the years. But power in that body is not grabbed, it's given. And the people who sustain themselves over a period of time don't abuse it."

John Kelly, a member of Frank Morrison's staff when Morrison was governor in the 1960s, would send sayings and aphorisms to Warner from time to time, the senator says. One he likes best is "Deal with things the way they are, not as you wish they were." The motto comes in handy in his day-to-day dealings with the Legislature, Warner says.

The advent of annual legislative sessions may have ushered out the era of the card room gatherings, but it also helped usher in a new era in legislative life. Legislators were expected to be more professional, to devote more time to the job. The workload increased, and Legislative staff began to expand rapidly.

To that point, staff had consisted largely of one clerk for each standing committee and one researcher: Betty Person. By 1973, each senator also had his own staff person.

Annual sessions created a need for full-time, year-around workers, Warner says. And, while many who have studied legislatures say state government improves as legislatures professionalize by adding staff, Warner is not so sure.

"I strongly believe in the citizen legislator," he says, but the annual sessions have made it harder to maintain that concept. Nebraska pays its state senators $12,000 a year, which means most of them must hold nearly full-time jobs outside the Legislature, too. Annual sessions have made that more difficult, Warner contends.

"You have to fit your personal schedule to the government. It doesn't work the other way around," he says.

Under those circumstances, staff is increasingly important, Warner says. Most senators cannot begin to do by themselves all the work associated with their legislative duties.

"But you lose, at the same time, when you accept someone else's research," Warner says. "You don't know how many decisions they made as to what they're going to bring you and what they're not."

One unofficial staff member whose information Warner trusted implicitly was his wife, Betty. Those who watched the two at work remember how they complemented each other.

When she came to the Legislature, Betty worked for Jack Rodgers as the body's only full-time researcher. Rodgers remembers her as "bright, friendly and outgoing. ... Her influence was important on all of us," Rodgers says.

Loran Schmit, a state senator from 1968-1992, says when Warner married Betty, "he doubled his expertise. ... She had an astronomical memory."

Corliss Young, a member of Warner's staff, says, "He measured everything by how she reacted. She was more outgoing and fiery than he was."

Ron Roskens describes Warner and his wife as "about as remarkable a team as I've ever known." Although Warner valued her ideas, Betty didn't try to dictate what his position should be on the issues. "It was an ideal partnership."

But professional legislative staff have also become increasingly necessary as communications have improved and constituents expect a faster response from their state senators. "There was very little constituency work done when I came here," Warner says, "primarily because you didn't have staff."

When he started in the Legislature, Warner heard from his constituents by telephone and letter and, occasionally, telegram. The pace was slower. "It was whatever time you wanted to spend."

And, too, he admits, today's issues are far more complex than the ones he dealt with 30 years ago.

"On the whole," the senator says, "staff is beneficial," particularly for senators who are involved with complex legislation. "I could never handle the Revenue Committee today the way I handled Government and Military Affairs in 1965. Timewise, it would be absolutely impossible" without the help of staff.

In fact, Warner was one of the leaders in the move to increase legislative staff. He is quoted in a March 22, 1965, Lincoln Journal article as promoting the idea of adequate research staff and asking the public to respond to the idea.

Despite his occasional misgivings about the professionalization of the Unicameral and senators' increased reliance on staff, Warner is known as someone who treats staff members well.

Eleanor Stratton was Warner's secretary during his term as speaker in 1969-70 and was committee clerk for Appropriations from 1985-89. She was a Unicameral staffer for more than 20 years and worked for a variety of different senators. Warner was one of her favorites.

"I felt if I had made a huge mistake, he would have stood behind me," Stratton says. "He was easy to work for."

Sandy Myers Sostad, of the Legislative Fiscal Office, and Stratton both say Warner treats staff members with kindness and consideration—and no condescension.

Sostad remembers a time during Warner's tenure as Appropriations chairman when the staff members in the Legislative Fiscal Office received invitations to a dinner in Warner's honor. "He was really upset," Sostad said. He did not want the staff to feel pressured to attend an event to honor him.

On the other hand, "He was happy to come to my wedding," Sostad says. "He's really down to earth."

And Kathy Tenopir, who specializes in higher education issues for the LFO, says, "He has a great sense of humor. We've had a lot of laughs."

Corliss Young, Warner's research analyst, went to work for him right out of law school in 1980. She thought she'd stay two years rather than 15, but she says, "This is the perfect job for me, and working for him makes it more perfect."

Warner says he has been fortunate to have had excellent staff members. "I want people around me who are brighter than I am," he says of the staff he has worked with.

Warner is careful to keep his personal senatorial staff's duties separate from the committee staff's duties. Young works for him; the other people in his office work for the Revenue Committee. "Basically, committee staff does only committee-related activity," Warner says. He followed the same guideline when he was chairman of Appropriations.

He makes another distinction, too. "If other senators ask committee staff to do things for them, it's confidential," Warner says. For instance, George Kilpatrick, Revenue Committee counsel, "can do work for other Revenue Committee members. I don't expect to be told." Not all committee chairmen follow that dictum.

Warner comes honestly by his respect for legislative staff. After all, he married the first—and at that time the only—legislative researcher in 1970. But he also remembers with some fondness the days when secretarial staff was provided only to the speaker and committee chairmen. Life was simpler then—and so was legislative business.

"The only thing that has not changed is human nature. We deal with the same frailties—people who are vindictive, people who try to get power by force."

If he could design the Unicameral's staff system from scratch today, Warner would put more emphasis on a pool of staff for each committee that would remain intact even as committee chairmen came and went. If a term limits measure is ever approved in Nebraska—by both the voters and the courts—Warner says, the continuity provided by staff will be even more important. "It will be the only institutional memory you have."

So says the only state senator who has served during biennial and annual sessions, the only one who has served two-year and four-year terms and the only one who knows from personal experience what life in the Nebraska Unicameral was like in the 1960s.

PART THREE
PERFECTING LEADERSHIP

Becoming a
Powerful Chairman

He had known since the 1960s, Warner says, that he wanted to lead Appropriations, especially after becoming chairman of the Executive Board and then speaker. But he also decided he would not try to unseat Richard Marvel, a respected senator who had been holding the Legislature's purse strings since 1961. Marvel was chairman of the Legislature's Budget Committee until it became the Appropriations Committee in 1971; he was chairman of Appropriations through the 1976 session.

Warner had been involved with the Budget/Appropriations Committee from early on, particularly when he was chair of the Executive Board and then as speaker. In fact he was the Executive Board chairman who hired Marlin Rein to be the state's legislative fiscal analyst while Marvel was chairman of the Budget Committee and officially in charge of the fiscal office.

Warner met with Rein, Marvel and several others when Rein was interviewing for the position. After the meeting, Warner asked Senator George Gerdes of Alliance what he should do next. Gerdes said, "If you think he's good, hire him 'cause it's likely Dick won't want to make up his mind."

Warner says, "Dick had lots of trouble making up his mind a lot of times." Marvel seemed to enjoy raising questions about policy issues and examining all sides of a question, but he was slow to make a decision. "He didn't like that part," Warner says.

So Warner went ahead and offered Rein the job. He accepted.

Perhaps because of the relationship, forged when Rein was hired, Warner worked with Rein a lot in the ensuing years, even before he chaired the Appropriations Committee. Warner's interest in state aid to schools involved him in revenue and appropriations matters, and Rein was helpful in figuring out the impact of the state aid bills.

Warner got a good introduction to the power of the Appropriations Committee leadership during a 1969 budget crisis. During that busy legislative session, the last of the Unicameral's biennial sessions and the one in which the 16 highway bills were passed, the appropriations bill was not reported out of committee until August, Warner says, even though the fiscal year had started July 1.

When the bill reached general file, senators started offering amendment after amendment. In those days, a committee amendment needed 25 votes to pass, but amendments offered by individuals required only a simple majority of those on the floor.

Many senators were absent from the floor a lot during those days, and amendments often passed with eight "yes" votes and six "no" votes and the rest of the senators not voting. As a result of all the amending, the final appropriations bill included a budget far larger than what the state's resources could fund.

The Legislature moved to recess for two weeks so that the Appropriations Committee could meet to work out a solution. But Chairman Richard Marvel went home, and the committee did not meet. Nothing was happening.

During the second week of the recess, Warner went to the Capitol and worked with the three members of the Appropriations Committee staff to develop amendments to decrease the budget by about $8 million, a significant amount in 1969.

When the Unicameral reconvened, Speaker Warner took his regular spot on the legislative floor; the lieutenant governor presided. Warner introduced his amendments, and all were adopted.

The victory led to what the senator still says was "one of my favorite headlines: 'Warner cuts $8 million from budget.'" What better publicity could an elected official ask for?

In the wake of the 1969 crisis, Warner proposed that all amendments to the appropriations bill should require 25 votes rather than just a majority of senators present. "It became very apparent that all kinds of mischief could be done the way the old rule was," he says.

Warner's 1969 maneuverings to solve the appropriations crisis may have been behind Marvel's saying in later years that he had always thought Warner would challenge him for the chairmanship of Appropriations during his tenure in the 1970s. Warner says he never intended to do that, but he adds that chairing Appropriations after Marvel stepped aside was certainly his goal.

Warner saw Appropriations as a committee with a lot of influence, a place a senator could make a difference.

"I've never thought of myself as, quote, seeking power in the sense that some people do, but I did think if I was going to spend time here, I want to have some impact on what happens. I want to be involved in what happens."

If a senator wants to exert influence in the Nebraska Unicameral, chairing a committee is the thing to do. If it's the Appropriations Committee he chairs, he exerts influence in spades.

Appropriations is widely regarded both within and outside the Legislature as the most powerful committee, and the person who leads it is regarded as one of the two or three most powerful in the Legislature. The Appropriations chairman is nearly as powerful as the speaker because all legislative policy is guided by the money available.

Besides that, Appropriations touches most other issues, so the chairman has a chance to have broader influence than any other committee chairman.

Warner sought the opportunity to have that kind of influence in 1977.

Ordinarily, a senator who seeks to be elected chairman of a committee has had experience on the committee in question. That wasn't true in Warner's case. Although he had been active in Appropriations Committee business, Warner never had been a member of the committee whose chairmanship he sought. His competition for the job, on the other hand, had more experience.

Doug Bereuter, who now represents Nebraska's First Congressional District in the U.S. House, was on Appropriations and wanted to be chairman. So did Glenn Goodrich of Omaha, another committee member.

Warner and Bereuter had become friends when Bereuter worked in the Tiemann administration. So when the Appropriations post came open, the two got together and decided only one of them should run for the position. They decided each of them would take an informal poll of senators to see who was likely to vote for whom.

When they compared notes, they found some of the same names on both lists. But Warner's support looked stronger than Bereuter's.

The upshot was that Bereuter decided to drop out of the running. Goodrich did make a run at the chairmanship, but "it wasn't much of a battle." Warner was elected.

Warner quickly began to look for ways to improve the Appropriations Committee.

"I knew I was in trouble by the third day."

At the first few days of hearings, two or three small agencies came in to testify. After their testimony, Warner followed the same procedure he had followed as chairman of other standing committees: He asked for discussion and a vote on the agency's requests.

Nearly everyone on the committee voted "yes" on nearly everything. "And they had no basis not to," Warner says. "Nobody had come in and asked for something that was bad or wrong. But you quickly knew it was all going to add up to too much."

After a few days, Warner told the committee they would no longer be voting after each agency's presentation. Instead, they would hear what all the agencies had to say before making a decision.

In the meantime, Warner and Bereuter, who was vice chairman of the committee, spent each evening developing a budget for the agencies that would testify the next day.

Sometimes they handed out the proposed budgets. Sometimes they just steered the discussion toward what they believed was the proper decision.

The senator recalls that he and Bereuter got some criticism for the way they were handling things. Some people suggested they were setting the committee up, doing government business in secret. Far from trying to do business in secret, Warner remembers, the two senators were simply trying to get their committee through the year without completely abandoning budgetary integrity.

Actually, the new procedures meant the committee members were more involved than they had been under Marvel's chairmanship. Bereuter, who had served two years with Marvel, says Marvel and his staff had done most of the work on the budget themselves. Most of what went on in committee meetings was simply jockeying for special projects.

By contrast, the new chairman and vice-chairman offered real options for the committee.

Those procedures that Warner and Bereuter developed are essentially in place today. So are some others that Warner instituted early on. For example, the committee adopts a total budget figure early in the session, based on what is projected to be available for spending.

As a result, the committee is obliged to establish priorities for budgeted expenditures.

Under Warner's leadership, Appropriations always abided by the revenue projections given them by the Revenue Committee—with two exceptions. First, if a major new program were to be instituted, Warner would always ask for additional dollars to fund it. He opposed proposals to phase in new programs over a period of time.

"That's dumb," he says. "All it does is take money away from the rest of your ongoing programs."

The other circumstance occurred only once or twice when the Legislature was cutting programs right and left to try to trim the budget to match revenue projections. Once they had made all the cuts they believed reasonable, the only alternative was to ask for an increase in taxes to meet the budget demands.

One of those occasions arose in the early 1980s. The committee had made many cuts and still was $30-40 million short. They would have to ask for a half-cent increase in the sales tax to make up the difference.

Either that or make some dramatic cuts; the University of Nebraska became a likely target. Higher education is one of the few discretionary areas in the state budget.

At that point, a conservative senator on the committee took a stand against the cuts. Jim Goll of Tekamah, who had supported the effort to keep finding places to make cuts, pointed out what an adverse impact the major cuts would have on the university. Goll said the committee had gone far enough, Warner remembers.

It was one of those times when all the committee members recognized they had reached the bottom of the barrel. "We went for the new revenue," Warner says.

Appropriations Committee members often sense each other's positions on an issue. They can feel which way the committee is likely to move. Of all legislative committees, Appropriations is widely regarded as the most cohesive.

One reason is that the nine members of Appropriations serve on no other standing committees. Another is that the appropriations process is long and time-consuming. Senator DiAnna Schimek of Lincoln, who served on Appropriations in the 1980s, describes it as "falling into a black hole."

In addition, the state's budget is complex, and only those who work with it regularly are likely to understand it. Finally, the committee writes only one bill each session, and that bill is reported out under the committee's name. Members sink or swim together.

As chairman, Warner built on the committee's cohesiveness to advance policies he believed were in the state's long-term interest. He took advantage of his opportunity as chairman to influence the committee.

Part of that opportunity arises because when people become part of a group—like a legislative committee—and begin to understand the issues the committee deals with, they are likely to move toward an ideological center. Scott Moore, who served on Appropriations under Warner, puts it this way: "You understand there are real needs out there. ... You see real people with real problems and try to help."

Senator Don Wesely of Lincoln notes Warner's role in bringing people to the center: "I saw him take the most conservative members and turn them into liberal spenders. The 'Thone Clones' (very conservative senators) were put on Jerry's committee in the early 1980s. We figured he could handle them, and he did. By the end of the session he had them singing out of his choir book. ...

"Under Warner, people became more liberal on Appropriations. But if they were liberal to begin with, they almost had to become more conservative. Warner always brought people back to the middle."

Two incidents from the 1950s, before he was elected to the Unicameral, influenced Warner's beliefs about group dynamics.

The first involved a Waverly school bond issue that failed in 1956. Unwilling to give up, supporters of the bond issue organized a citizens committee to examine the matter once more. The school board selected committee members, being careful to include people they knew were opposed to the project so that the committee would be balanced.

One opponent refused to serve on the committee. "He had the most beautiful reason," Warner says. "He did not care to serve because he was afraid he might change his mind."

The other incident is actually a story Warner heard from Art Ward, a member of the university's College of Agriculture faculty in the 1950s. Ward told about a group of Nebraskans who didn't like what their school board was doing. So they rounded up other candidates who, they believed, better represented their own views and helped them get elected. "In a couple years, they were voting just like the people that got kicked out," Ward told Warner.

They were good people who found that the decisions that had been made were really the decisions that needed to be made.

"Those people didn't change. All they did was acquire knowledge or information."

Warner says the same phenomena apply to legislative workings. As Appropriations chairman, he would be sure the committee members had a lot of information about the matters before them. Once committee members understood the depth and breadth of the issues, they might still argue over how something should be done but they usually stopped arguing over *whether* anything should be done.

The committee chairman, in other words, didn't have to manipulate committee members to his point of view. When members are given the opportunity to see the same things, they come to similar decisions.

Of course, the chairman has a lot to with presenting members with opportunities to see the same things. "I was pretty good at putting things together," Warner says. "That was partly 'cause I could read people pretty well."

It was also because of the way Warner operated as chairman. For one thing, he allowed people plenty of time to be comfortable with the issues. "You've got to give them time to change their minds," the senator says.

One of his practices sometimes raised criticism outside the committee. "I took a lot of show-of-hands or voice votes. It was a reverse show of hands. If you objected, you could raise your hand. And that was the end of that issue."

Warner did not want roll call votes early on, because members would tend to make commitments before they knew all the ramifications. So Warner avoided roll call votes all the way through the process. That procedure probably had a lot to do with the committee's ability to come to consensus.

The process allowed people to feel their opinions were being considered, too. If even one committee member objected to removing an item from the budget on initial consideration, Warner left it in. Eventually, committee members would get to a point where they knew an item should not be included and would be ready to drop it. At that point, a committee member often would ask for a vote so he or she could be shown voting "yes" on something the committee would eventually drop. The "yes" vote would be something the senator could claim credit for with his or her constituents.

Vard Johnson, chairman of the Legislature's Revenue Committee during the 1980s, told a World-Herald reporter in 1986 that "Jerry Warner is a master at causing members (of the Appropriations Committee) to feel they are part of the whole. He has elevated institutional dynamics to an art form."

Lee Rupp puts it more bluntly. "He cultivated that committee like a row of radishes," the former state senator says. Rupp served in the Legislature from 1983-88 and is now the University of Nebraska's only registered lobbyist.

Rupp and others who have worked with Warner remark about how the senator tends to carry a bunch of envelopes around in his coat pockets. When he was leading Appropriations, one of those envelopes would have Warner's version of the state budget written on it. "It was always amazing how that was how things turned out," Rupp says. The senator usually managed to take the committee where he thought it should go.

Don Wesely, considered one of the more liberal members of the Unicameral, tells a story involving a very conservative senator who was assigned to the Appropriations Committee under Warner. Part of what Appropriations recommended that year was an increase in state employee salaries that Wesely thought were too generous.

As the Legislature debated the proposal, Wesely, the liberal, found himself arguing for less spending while the conservative senator in question argued for more. Wesely remembers how astonished he was by the role reversal and how impressed he was by what Warner had obviously accomplished to get the professed conservative to that point.

"I congratulated Warner on teaching his course on government spending," Wesely says. "He played the committee like an instrument. They started with screeching and scratching, but by the end he could play whatever he wanted."

Corliss Young, a member of Warner's staff since 1980, tells a story that illustrates how Warner's procedures worked. She was sitting in on Appropriations Committee hearings on an issue in which she was involved during the late 1980s. Although she doesn't remember the specific

topic, she says the issue was one on which she knew Warner's preference.

And she remembers Warner at work. She knew the discussion that
day had not gone in the direction Warner preferred, although he didn't
say so.

The senator makes it a habit to go last in committee discussions and in
asking questions at hearings, Young says. On this particular day, when
it was his turn to comment, instead of allowing the matter to come to a
vote, "he discretely changed the discussion to another topic," and the
issue in question was set aside for that day.

The next time the committee met, members' comments indicated they
had moved a little farther toward Warner's point of view. "But I could
tell there were still not enough members on his side," Young says. "He
avoided coming to a vote again."

By the time the matter came up for discussion a third time, people's
inclinations seemed to have changed even more. When the vote was
taken, the result was the one Warner was working toward all along, Young
says.

"To me this illustrates how Senator Warner works and why the method
he uses gathers so much respect. He can wait until the people involved
get enough information to arrive at an informed decision, at a consensus."

The incident illustrates one of Warner's basic philosophies: Give the
people (or a committee or the Legislature) enough information to make
an informed decision and whatever they decide will be OK, even if he
personally disagrees with the decision.

Warner believes a couple of basic factors hold the key to getting a
committee to work together: "They need to have confidence in a person's
judgment, and they have to feel they have an opportunity to differ or to
work out those differences." The procedures he followed as chairman of
Appropriations tried to provide both of those.

Warner's impact at Appropriations was due to more than just procedures, though. He also worked outside the committee's formal
proceedings to build committee cohesiveness. He says he didn't spend a
lot of time with committee members outside the regular meetings, but
he tended to be close to several in each session. Usually, he says, it was
simply a matter of compatible personalities; some people just tend to get
along well together.

At times, however, he chose his listeners carefully. "If I had something in particular that I was trying to get done, I probably would have talked to one person primarily. ... I usually knew things people were particularly interested in. You may have to visit with everybody to some extent, but there were some you counted on more than others."

Gary Hannibal was one. Hannibal, of Omaha, was elected to the Legislature in 1982 and served his first two years on the Revenue and Miscellaneous Subjects committees. He joined Appropriations in 1985 and served there until retiring from the Legislature after the 1990 term.

"I consider Jerry my mentor," Hannibal says of Warner.

"He used to call me his translator because Jerry doesn't always speak as clearly as you'd like except when he gets into something really heartfelt. Then everybody understands exactly what he's saying.

"When he's rattling off numbers and all kinds of technical things and millions of dollars of things, he kind of mumbles. And I was the one who was designated on the floor to explain what he said."

He agrees with the assessment that Warner forged a cohesive committee but says he did it in such a way that he enhanced not only his own influence but also the respect others had for him.

"He has forever been a consensus builder. And in order to build a consensus that works out the way you want it to, you have to know exactly where you want to be at the end," Hannibal says. Warner knew where he wanted to be and would subtly steer people in that direction.

That often meant Warner would find out from the other Appropriations Committee members what they really wanted to see included in the final product. Most people would suggest several things, and Warner would latch on to at least one of those and say, "That sounds pretty good." Then he would work to build consensus among the committee to include the items important to individual members.

The whole process reminded Hannibal of a story his father-in-law had told him. During his first year on the Appropriations Committee, Hannibal passed the story along to Warner when the committee was working on the University of Nebraska budget.

Under Warner's guidance, the NU budget was deliberated toward the end of the committee's hearing schedule, "supposedly because it was a big item," Hannibal say. "In retrospect, I realize it was to wear us down on all the other stuff" and make it easier for the university's budget request to survive intact. Warner's interest in the university's welfare has never been any secret.

The committee had an entire book of figures and information to examine and hardly knew where to start. It was late, and committee members were tired.

Warner made a few suggestions as to what the committee might do with the request, Hannibal recalls. "He said, 'I do happen to have a little sheet here I put together just in case you were interested.'" The committee looked at the plan, discussed it a little and said, "Sounds good. Let's go."

After the discussion of the university's budget was over, Hannibal told Warner the story he'd been told by his father-in-law, who had spent 35 years as a menswear merchandising manager for Brandeis department store. Hannibal's father-in-law said a customer who would come into the store looking for a shirt would often be overwhelmed by the number and variety of shirts available.

A good salesman would ask the customer what color shirt he wanted. If he said blue, the salesman would bring two or three blue shirts for the customer to consider.

"So all of a sudden the salesman has focused this customer from 200 down to two," Hannibal told Warner. "That's called merchandising. That's called selling. And that's exactly what you do to us in this committee."

A week or two later, as the committee was considering another budget item, Warner turned to Hannibal and said, "I've got a shirt for you." The line got a good laugh.

Warner would sometimes tell Hannibal how a plan that Hannibal or another committee member had suggested—after Warner had presented a few facts—was exactly what the chairman had hoped someone would suggest. But he wouldn't say it himself to start with. Instead, he would focus the committee's attention on a few alternatives so they could arrive at a consensus.

"His timing was incredible," Hannibal says. "He would let you (the committee) muddle around until you were tired and desperately looking for an answer, and then he'd throw you this shirt."

Tom Bergquist of the Legislative Fiscal Office remembers one year when the budget was due to be presented to the total Legislature in two weeks, and the appropriations process was at stalemate.

So Warner distributed copies of the hand-written budget plan he had come up with. "He wasn't heavy-handed," Bergquist says, but "he always had a sheet—or a shirt—ready to go."

In a situation like that, the committee would usually think Warner's plan sounded great, Bergquist says, and would be happy to go along. If Warner had started out by telling the committee what he thought should be done and how they should vote, he'd have gotten nowhere.

Steve Fowler agrees. Fowler, a Lincoln senator who served on Appropriations with Warner, says Warner's patience and willingness to concede on small points help him maintain his influence.[5]

Lowell Johnson, a member of the Appropriations Committee from 1980-92, describes Warner's interminable patience as a factor in his success. The chairman would give every committee member his complete attention as they made their opinions known.

Warner always seemed willing to keep working to perfect a budget even after most committee members were ready to give up. In that case, the committee members often would agree on a general policy and then direct Warner to work out the details. He never betrayed the trust of his committee members in such situations.

Or in situations that had more to do with kindness and courtesy than with public policy. Shirley Marsh testifies to that.

Marsh served in the Legislature from 1973-90, the entire time as a member of the Appropriations Committee. Because she has asthma, Marsh had requested that smoking be prohibited during committee hearings. The committee, then under Richard Marvel's leadership, had agreed on a 5-4 vote.

When Marvel left the committee and Warner took over as chairman, Marsh was concerned about the no-smoking policy. She knew Warner was a smoker—he still is—and she had already begun to count votes to see whether she could expect the smoking ban to continue.

As it turned out, she did not have to worry. Warner told the committee, "I'm aware of the tradition of non-smoking in these hearings. And if I can keep from smoking, so can everyone else." Warner was careful never to smoke in Marsh's presence, during hearings or elsewhere.

Warner showed respect for her in other ways, too. Marsh was the only woman in the Legislature from 1972-78 and one of only a handful for

[5]Lincoln Journal-Star, January 1983

many years after. "He always acted like he respected me as an individual," Marsh says. "I didn't receive that kind of respect from my colleagues across the board."

On-the-spot Wit;
Long-term Wisdom

Marsh is not the only person to have commented that Senator Warner treated her with respect. He is known as a man who, as a matter of course, treats everyone with respect. Perhaps that is one reason he has, in turn, continued to be so respected.

But that doesn't mean Warner is overly formal or stiff. In fact, he is well-known for his dry humor and ironic remarks—often made at his own expense but also gently applied to legislative life and to his fellow legislators.

Warner's wit and humor contributed a great deal to his relationship with the Appropriations Committee. Hannibal, who served on Appropriations from 1985-90, recalls an evening committee hearing that hundreds of people were expected to attend and at which many would testify on a bill about state employee salaries.

"We were tired," Hannibal says of the committee members, and were speculating how long the hearing might last.

Warner said, "I'd say we'll be done at about 8:59."

The committee convened at 7 p.m. and listened to five or six people present testimony. That was followed by questions and answers, by discussion and by presentations from a few other speakers.

Finally, Warner asked if anyone had other comments or questions. When no one replied, the chairman declared the meeting adjourned. "We looked at the clock. It was 8:59 right on the button."

The committee kidded Warner about the accuracy of his prediction.

"How often have you done that?" he was asked.

"Once."

"When are you going to do that again?"

"Never."

In a Journal-Star column in March 1981, Tom Fogarty pointed out some other funny exchanges between Warner and the committee. Warner always insisted that every committee member have a chance to be heard, but sometimes none of the members had much to say. In one instance, Warner had suggested a course of action no one on the committee seemed to care much about one way or the other. So the chairman declared the matter closed.

"Not hearing an objection, I'll assume that what happens is what we'll do."

Warner could do a little arm-twisting, though. Scott Moore recalls a time when he was a new member of the Appropriations Committee.

"I was not the best Appropriations Committee member," Moore says. He quickly established a reputation as something of a rebel, not always willing to go along with Warner and the rest of the committee — at least, not without a fuss.

Moore remembers two times when Warner was provoked enough with his younger colleague to cuss at him. Once was in 1988 or '89 when Moore had met with a group of people to plan a strategic action involving an issue before the committee. Warner knew the meeting had taken place and asked Moore what he was planning to do.

"I told him what we were going to do, and he looked me straight in the eye and said, 'Well, if you want to——it up that bad, just go ahead,' and he walked away," Moore says, laughing at the memory.

"The only other time he used that same word with me—I remember clearly both times, and I never heard him use that word any other time—was in 1991. It was something to do with roads," Moore says. By that time, Moore was Appropriations chairman, and Warner was Revenue chairman.

The issue involved roads money, and Moore had filed an amendment that went against Warner's wishes. When he told Warner what he had done and the information on which he had based his move, Warner told him, "Whoever told you that didn't know what the——he was talking about."

Moore also remembers Warner speaking clearly and directly to help him out of a political misstep. It happened when the Republican senators in the Unicameral were "having a problem communicating" with then-Governor Kay Orr, Moore says. The senators met and decided to send two of their number to meet with the governor and "open some dialogue."

The governor had heard about the senators' meeting and was concerned about what they might be planning. She asked Moore to meet with her at 8:30 one morning to fill her in on what was going on. Later that morning Moore told some of the senators involved in the original meeting about his visit with Orr. And by noon the contents of that second discussion had gotten back to Orr. She was not happy.

A few days later, Warner took Moore aside and gave his inexperienced colleague some advice. "Knowledge is power around here," he said, but a person who is told something by the governor would be wise to keep it to himself. The governor, Warner told Moore, was not at all happy with him.

"He gave me this fatherly advice that I remember very well," Moore says. He took the lesson to heart.

While Moore may have tried, in his early days on the committee, to assert his independence from Warner's leadership, he is proud, now, that Warner approves of his record in politics. After Moore took office as Nebraska's Secretary of State in 1995, he sat with Warner at an informal dinner. "I didn't know about you the first time you came in," Warner said several times, "but I think you've done a good job." Moore believes those words are the ultimate compliment.

Long before Moore became part of the Appropriations Committee, Warner had put his stamp on the group by helping it adapt to the changing needs of a changing state. In addition to revising the committee's procedures so that the entire budget would be considered before any decisions were made on specific requests, the committee reviewed individual agency budgets, trying to find ways to move some of the costs from the general fund to user fees.

The committee developed a general formula to ascertain what portion of the agency's activities was a benefit to the public in general and what portion was protecting somebody's turf. That was particularly true of some of the licensing boards whose purpose was, ostensibly, to protect the general public. The committee tried to apply a consistent policy to agencies across the board.

A December 1990 editorial in the Lincoln Star assesses what Warner accomplished as chairman of the Appropriations Committee. The editorial praises his leadership in establishing the procedure for biennial budgeting and the process that requires the Appropriations Committee to look at all state spending, both new and old. That means the committee is forced to consider the effects on the future of spending decisions the Legislature makes today.

Some of the Appropriations Committee's policy and procedure actually was ahead of the national curve, Warner says.

For instance, the Legislature enacted sunset legislation during the 1980s. Under sunset laws, an expiration or sunset date was set on laws and regulations at the time they were passed. The law or regulation would have to be reviewed by the Legislature if it were to continue after its sunset date.

In Colorado, the state Nebraska took as its model, the sunset legislation applied especially to regulatory agencies. Up to that point, the state's legislature had not been watching such agencies much at all.

That was not the case in Nebraska. Agencies in this state were being reviewed every year by the Appropriations Committee. The committee would regularly question agency representatives about the way their money was allotted, something many of those representatives resented.

"We had some fairly healthy discussions at times," the senator says—"healthy meaning angry."

That kind of watchdog policy paid off for the state. Once sunset legislation had been enacted and the Legislature had examined the state's 20 regulatory agencies, "the only thing that was abolished was a licensing board. ... and it had last met in the early 1960s," nearly two decades earlier. The Appropriations Committee's regular reviews had prevented dead wood from accumulating in this state.

So much for the impact of sunset laws in Nebraska. The Appropriations Committee had beaten them to the punch.

But Warner didn't want the Appropriations Committee to beat the rest of the Legislature to a pulp, something that could easily happen. The committee and its chairman are arguably the most effective and powerful of their kind in the Nebraska Legislature.

"If you have a competent chair and a good process, there's lots of deference to Appropriations on the floor," says Doug Bereuter, now a member of Congress.

At times that deference has turned to resentment as non-committee members have begun to feel they were being run over by the budget-wielding Appropriations Committee. To defuse such resentment Warner moved to find a more effective way to share power with other legislators.

For example, when Warner became chairman of Appropriations the committee's final spending recommendation to the Legislature would equal the total amount available in the following year's budget. That meant no latitude was left for senators who wanted to change the Appropriations bill on the floor. It meant individual senators could not sponsor any spending measures dear to their hearts or those of their constituents. It meant a lot of senators were feeling a lot of frustration with the Appropriations Committee.

Warner convinced the committee that one percent of the total budget allocation should be left undesignated and available for senators to spend via amendment on the floor. Because the state's budget was growing at five percent a year in those days, the amount to be designated outside the committee was 20 percent of the new money available—approximately $16 million in the late 1970s—enough to satisfy senators' needs to make their own marks on state appropriations.

Of course, when the state's economy slowed during the mid-1980s, the amount represented by one percent of the total decreased from $16 million to only $1 or $2 million. The practice Warner established remains today, but the amount available for designation on the floor is far less than it used to be. "Times are different," the senator says, and growth is far slower.

Another example is the rule that gives the entire Legislature the opportunity to debate the year's spending limit before the Appropriations Committee begins to develop a budget. That helps prevent some battles that previously arose whenever senators would try, at the end of the session, to increase or decrease an appropriations bill that the committee had carefully crafted to a different total.

Despite both those procedural changes, however, unrest with the Appropriations Committee boiled over during the 1984 session. The insurrection was led by then-Senator John DeCamp of Neligh. Warner tried to placate the unhappy DeCamp by playing down the Appropriations Committee's power.

"Any committee has an edge on the subject matter it deals with," Warner says.[6] Other senators could have even more impact on the appropriations process if they had more time.

[6]Lincoln Journal-Star, Feb. 5, 1984

"Knowledge is strength; there's no question about it. It's not anybody's fault, and there's nothing you can do about it."

But DeCamp didn't quite buy that philosophy. He said Appropriations' control over the budget was quite different from any other committee's control in its own subject area: "It's the difference between being in charge of the chickens or the cows or the corn and being in charge of the entire farm."[7]

DeCamp has not been the only senator to complain about the power of the Appropriations Committee and its chairman. Some senators new to the committee sometimes thought Warner was "heavy-handed," but they usually changed their minds over time.

Senators outside the committee would sometimes grouse about Warner's dominance over the committee and the committee's dominance over the appropriations process. However, Ron Withem, current speaker, says he has heard similar complaints about the two more recent Appropriations chairmen.

It was no secret to Warner, either; he was aware that Appropriations is often resented by other senators. In a 1984 Journal-Star story he observed that part of the problem is circumstances: Committee members serve only on Appropriations. Other senators do not have the time to understand the budget as well as the Appropriations Committee does. As a result, they often feel left out of the process.

Furthermore, the committee unanimously introduces one bill on behalf of the entire group. Nearly always, the committee members support the bill as introduced, standing steadfast against substantive amendments from the floor.

In both perception and reality, the chairman of the committee has an enormous impact on what the appropriations bill looks like and what kind of progress it makes on the floor. One year Warner was unalterably opposed to the bill as the committee approved it. He told the Unicameral he would not support the bill, and the whole budget was changed on the floor. The whole appropriations bill stopped. "We had all kinds of negotiations off the floor for three days to a week," Warner says, "and then I got my way."

Neither Warner nor any other Appropriations chairman could get by with that kind of thing on a regular basis. Nor would he pull a stunt like

[7]Ibid.

that simply to demonstrate his own political power. If the chairman is to bring down the entire appropriations process, it had better be on the basis of principle, not political whim.

It may have been principle or it may have been politics—or some mixture of the two—but under Warner's leadership the Appropriations Committee made it very clear that responsibility for the state's budget lay with the Legislature. The Legislature was not about to take taxpayer heat over something the governor had set them up for.

Exon was governor when Warner took over at Appropriations, and the governor had a habit of submitting a budget he knew was less than what the state agencies needed to function. So the directors of the agencies would alert their interest groups, and they would begin to inundate the Appropriations Committee with letters, pleading that they needed more money to continue to function.

"The Legislature would always put the money back in, so the Legislature's budget would turn out to be higher than the governor's. That annoyed me," Warner says.

"The second year I was chair, I said we wouldn't accept a letter request budget. And agencies asking more than the governor requested for them had to send their requests through the governor's budget office," Warner says. No way was he going to allow the governor to set up the Appropriations Committee or the Legislature at large to bear the blame for burgeoning state budgets.

Nor was he willing to give up the Legislature's power of the purse to any governor. "The governor could veto, of course. I always thought we should include some harmless things (in the budget) the governor could veto without doing any damage, so he could get his headlines." Warner was willing to concede the headlines; he was not willing to concede the control.

The Appropriations Committee's battle with Exon over "letter request budgets" was indicative of Warner's relationship with Exon in general. "I disagreed with him and got annoyed with him more than any other governor," Warner admits. Exon was popular, the senator thinks, because he often would criticize the Legislature for its actions rather than taking any kind of personal leadership to make change happen. Exon was also the most partisan governor Warner had served with or known. And partisanship never has sat well with the senator.

Regardless of his relationship with the governor—or perhaps at least partly because of it—Warner built his influence in the Legislature as he built his leadership of the Appropriations Committee. From his position as "powerful chairman" of the "powerful Appropriations Committee," he was able to make a difference not only to the state's budget process but also to other major legislative initiatives. One of those was already a favorite interest: roads.

Roads Revisited

The second round of major highway legislation took shape in 1980, just three years after Warner became chairman of Appropriations. Once again, he was able to leave an indelible stamp on Nebraska's highways, this time by establishing a financing system that was well ahead of its time.

And, as had been true during the first round of highway legislation, both Warners were involved in the second round. This time, though, Betty played a different role.

For the first eight years of their marriage, Betty had not worked outside the home. But when Charlie Thone was elected governor in 1978, he asked her whether she would be interested in heading an agency in his administration. Thone knew Betty Warner had had a lot of experience in state government.

Betty declined the offer to lead an agency, although she told Thone there were two areas of government she was interested in. One was roads and the other was taxes, two topics she had learned to know extensively during her work as a legislative researcher during the late 1960s.

A few months later, Bill Peterson, assistant to the director of the Nebraska Department of Roads, asked Betty if she would be interested in doing some research and writing for the department. Her first response was no, but Peterson wasn't willing to take that as a final answer. A few months later, he repeated the offer, and this time Betty agreed to do work part time on special projects, particularly writing projects.

"For the next 12-14 years she had a great deal to do with the direction of state policy for roads," Warner says.

The situation might have looked a bit fishy: the senator heading a committee that had a major impact on highway legislation; his wife working for the Department of Roads. But Warner says it was never a problem.

"I had absolute trust in what Betty did—as did other people," Warner says. "If she didn't know that some course of action was totally above-board and right, she wouldn't do it. ... You could totally trust her judgment."

Far from viewing the Warners with suspicion, most people seemed to admire the way they worked together and complemented each other's interests and abilities.

Kay Orr was one of those admirers. "They were the epitome of service," says Orr, who was state treasurer during the late 1970s and early 1980s and governor from 1986-90. Orr supports Warner's contention that Betty would not have misused her relationship with him when she worked at the Department of Roads. "She was so very mindful of the delicate role she played as an employee of the Department of Roads married to a state senator," Orr says.

Because Warner was sure Betty would give him only accurate and appropriate information about what was going on with the state's highways, "it made it much easier for me to advocate some road policies I may have been reluctant to advocate otherwise," he says.

And Nebraska's roads, like the nation's roads in general, surely needed help in 1980.

The nation was in the midst of what came to be known as the energy crisis. Arab oil-producing nations had banded together to form OPEC, and oil prices skyrocketed. In response, the United States put an embargo on purchase of oil from OPEC nations. The results were gasoline shortages and high gas prices.

In Nebraska that meant the state's income from gasoline taxes fluctuated dramatically. People bought less gasoline, sometimes because they couldn't get it and other times because they were unwilling to pay unusually high prices. The Department of Roads was no longer able to project what kind of income it could expect from gasoline taxes. As a result, the department didn't know how, when or whether it would be able to meet its commitments to build and maintain roads.

"Enter the champion of highways, Jerry Warner," says Jack Pittman of the Department of Roads. Warner's goal was to come up with a stable source of funding for the highway program.

The measure was called the Variable Motor Fuel Excise Tax. Before the variable tax hit the scene, Nebraska's gasoline tax rate was fixed by the Legislature. The Department of Roads would try to project how much revenue it could expect each year and then develop its budget around the projection. "It had nothing to do with planning," Pittman says.

Furthermore, "Each time it (the tax rate) needed to be changed, it was a major legislative battle," Pittman says.

An increase of even a penny became an emotional issue. The upshot was that the needed legislation often died on the battlefield, leaving the roads program struggling.

This time, Warner came up with a mechanism to avoid those battles. He reversed the entire process and made the reversal permanent.

Warner said the state needed to talk first about what roads needed to be built, repaired and maintained and then find a way to make the funding available. Under the new procedure, the department would make its case to the governor, who would submit his budget proposal to the Appropriations Committee. Once the budget had been approved by the committee and the entire Legislature, the gasoline tax would be adjusted automatically to fund it.

"It was a brand new concept," Pittman says. "Most states would kill for this kind of concept today."

"This was Warner," Pittman adds. "It was his brain child."

Dick Herman, the retired reporter and editor, says Warner brought rationality and consistency to the state's highway funding when he sold the variable gasoline tax to the Legislature. The plan is also one of the reasons Nebraska's gasoline taxes are among the highest in the nation, Herman admits.

On the other hand, the plan allows the state to provide farm-to-market roads to its 1.6 million people spread across a huge geographic area.

Clearly, Warner has a vision that goes beyond parochial districts. However, it's not the kind of vision that is necessarily easy for a politician to sell. Don Walton, the Lincoln Star reporter who covered the Statehouse in the 1960s, says the highway plan, at every stage, was a tough battle. "The political pressures were enormous."

Nor did those pressures disappear once legislation was passed. Warner has taken criticism—usually good-natured but sometimes not—for establishing a trust fund for highways that cannot be touched for any other purpose.

"The system has withstood a number of onslaughts, including some I led," says former senator Vard Johnson of Omaha.

Ironically, Warner is known for opposing legislative schemes to ear-mark funds for particular uses. He also is known for asserting that highway money is dedicated, not ear-marked. He admits there's probably no real difference between the two.

"It's my own definition," he says. "It's kind of a standard joke. Many would tell you there is no difference."

But he goes on to draw the distinction: A dedicated fund is one in which the source of income is clearly related to its use, i.e. gasoline and roads; an ear-marked fund does not exhibit that kind of relationship.

Thanks to the various parts of the Warner-led highway plan for Nebraska, much of the politics has been taken out of the process of building and maintaining roads and finding the means to fund them. Warner's leadership in shaping such a plan demonstrates his conviction that he represents the entire state, not just one of 49 districts.

"I'm a state senator, not a local senator," Warner says. "I'm not here to pluck what I can from the state to return to my local governments. ... I don't like pork barrel politics."

Warner frequently reminds his colleagues of their obligations to the entire state. Moreover, he practices what he preaches, even if it costs him.

In fact, Warner has sometimes supported legislation that actually hurt him personally. At one point Warner backed a change in the regulation fee on trucks, including farm vehicles, that hit his own pocketbook.

His pocketbook was hit again when the interstate system took some of the Warner farm land in northeast Lancaster County. In spite of that, the senator was a big proponent of the interstate system. "He shot himself in the foot," Pittman says, "but he took on causes for the general good of the state."

That philosophy has sometimes made Warner's political life difficult. The variable gasoline tax caused him some discomfort when he was campaigning for re-election in 1980. The two-cent increase in the tax took effect in October, the month before the general election.

An unhappy taxpayer confronted Warner at a meeting just a few weeks before the election, accusing him of sponsoring the bill that raised the gasoline tax.

Warner admitted he had sponsored the bill. But he pointed out that no politician would introduce a tax increase to take effect five weeks before the day he stood for re-election unless he thought it was really necessary. "I thought it was really necessary."

People laughed, and that was the last he heard of the matter. It may have been that the tax was really not so controversial after all. Or the absence of backlash may have had something to do with the senator himself.

Warner, unwilling to take credit for his own successes, admits his credibility with the voters was probably a factor in reducing people's animosity toward the tax.

The legislation didn't affect his re-election much, either. He won that year with 72 percent of the vote.

The round of legislation that established the variable gasoline tax rate was not to be the last battle in Warner's fight to improve Nebraska's highway system. Another skirmish arose almost by accident in the late 1980s. This time it had to do with cleaning up a scam that was cheating the state out of its legal share of gasoline taxes.

That fall Warner was doing his usual stint at the Nebraska State Fair, something he continues to this day. A member of the fair board since the mid-1970s, the senator helps staff an information booth in the Devaney Sports Center.

The job also gives Warner the opportunity to visit with people about their state government. Many people tell Warner they appreciate the work he is doing in the Legislature while others are "rather blunt as to why don't I get out of there and I should have done that a long time ago."

In 1982, a retired farmer from Otoe County stopped to visit with Warner as he had done in previous years at the fair. "Would you like to buy some cheap gas?" the man asked. Apparently the man was trying to do the senator a favor and save him some money. All Warner needed to do, the man said, was to buy at least 2,000 gallons of gasoline at a time and pay cash.

The proposal struck Warner as suspicious. He asked the man how he could get the gasoline and was given a name and phone number.

Warner passed the information along to the State Patrol, which, it turned out, was already investigating the scam whereby dealers were trying to avoid paying state gasoline taxes.

An item in the March 23, 1983, Lincoln Star explained the scam. A distributor would purchase gasoline in a state with relatively low fuel taxes and fill out the form that said he would also sell the gasoline in that state. Instead, the distributor would sell the gas in another state and simply not report the change in destination.

The distributor would gain 6.9 cents per gallon between Missouri and Nebraska, 5.9 cents per gallon between Kansas and Nebraska and 5.9 cents per gallon between Colorado and Nebraska. George Watters, director of the Nebraska Petroleum Marketers Association, told the paper he estimated the state had lost millions of dollars in uncollected taxes over the previous decade.

Even more important, Warner says, the honest operators who make up the vast majority of dealers couldn't compete with the ones perpetrating fraud. The motor fuel industry supported the investigation and clean-up, he said.

Warner, referred to in the paper as a "patron senator of state and local roads," set out to help state law enforcement plug the leaky spigot. In the 1989 session of the Legislature, the senators established a task force made up of all the agencies with responsibilities related to motor fuel—fire marshal, roads department, revenue department, attorney general, etc. Jack Pittman and State Patrol Major Don Niemann were co-chairs of the task force.

The task force did a major rehab of the laws surrounding motor fuel taxes, and the new system has made a significant dollar difference to the highway trust fund.

When he first looked into the matter, Warner estimated the state would gain $7-9 million if it could collect all the taxes to which it was entitled. "I'm not sure we achieved that, but I would guess it's at least between $5 and $7 million a year."

Later in the decade, roads cropped up again in Warner's legislative life. This time the topic had nothing to do with a scam and nothing directly to do with funding. This time the issue was long-range planning.

Warner decided in the late 1980s that the Highway Department would do well to abandon its practice of working from biennium to biennium and move, instead, to a 20-year highway plan. Essentially, Warner was asking the department to look 10 times farther ahead than they had been doing.

Warner included a measure in the 1988 appropriations bill asking the department for a statement of its 20-year needs and an inventory of all the state's roads and their condition. The measure included specific long-range goals the department was to reach: reconstruction of parts of Interstate 80, completion of a system of four-lane highways, improvements to sharp curves and narrow bridges.

The bill required that the department report every December to the Appropriations and Transportation committees what progress had been made, what items were next on the agenda and how much money would be required to fund them. Once that figure had been determined, the variable gasoline tax, established in 1980, would take effect. The Legislature adopted the entire measure.

"That was probably one of the most effective things that ever happened for our agency," Pittman says.

During the consideration of one of the 1980s roads-related bills, Hannibal learned a lesson in highways from Betty Warner.

The two became acquainted when Hannibal served on Appropriations and would stop to visit in Warner's office after hearings and sessions. Betty was often there and would join in the conversations, but Hannibal didn't know much about her background.

One day as the Appropriations Committee was considering a bill that would change allocation of highway trust funds, members had received a flow chart to illustrate the current and proposed systems. "It looked like spaghetti," Hannibal says, with boxes connected by lines that crisscrossed each other back and forth.

Someone had used a marker to draw new lines over the old, trying to indicate how the flow of funds would be changed. "It almost looked to me like a five-year-old kid had taken a crayon and scribbled all over this thing," Hannibal says. "I just had to laugh. I didn't understand it."

That day, after the committee hearing, Hannibal accompanied Warner to his office, where Betty was waiting. "I said, 'Hi, Betty! Here, explain this to me, will you?'" Hannibal thought he was making a joke about the impossible intricate flow chart.

"She looked at me and very soberly she said, 'All right.'"

"I looked at her, and my mouth dropped open. I said, 'You understand this?'"

"Jerry said, 'Understand it? She wrote it.'"

Between them, the Warners knew Nebraska highways coming and going, Hannibal says.

Bill Swanson, who served with Warner in the Legislature during the

1960s, says the fact that Warner lives on a farm makes him conscious of how important roads are to the people of the state.

People in their 40s and younger take hard-surfaced roads for granted, says Ron Withem, speaker of the Unicameral. Older folks remember when many people in rural states like Nebraska had to drive 10 miles or more to reach a hard-surfaced road.

"There are people today who may think we've gone overboard, that we've kind of sanctified the road-building industry and are spending money for a higher quality of roads than are really needed," Withem says, "But whatever your view is on that issue, you can't underestimate the impact to the state of a stable transportation system."

The Big Cuts

By the early 1980s Warner had chalked up nearly 20 years of experience in the Legislature, making his mark on education and roads and the appropriations process. State government services were growing, and Warner was an important force behind that growth.

During Warner's first decade in the Legislature the state's economy was growing, and state government services were expanding.

"It was great fun to be here." Senators felt they were making significant changes and improvements for the state.

But things were about to change.

The expansive mood was beginning to wane by the time Warner was elected chairman of Appropriation. "In part you had a governor who was critical, always, of change," Warner says. "Exon built his reputation on opposition."

Also, people began to rebel somewhat against what the Legislature had done during the 1960s, particularly major reapportionment and huge changes in the tax structure. The rebellion wasn't a result of the Legislature tricking people into anything. As has always been the case in the American democracy, most citizens are simply not sure what it is they want government to do. For many Nebraskans, legislative action had not produced what they thought they would get.

The citizen unrest and dissatisfaction wasn't all bad, though, Warner says. If government is to remain representative, elected officials must reassess and adjust to situations and demands they had not anticipated.

The situation became truly serious during the early 1980s when the state was hit by a triple whammy: high inflation and an oil crisis on the national level and a farm crisis on the state and regional level. The combination brought an abrupt halt to government growth and intensified citizen dissatisfaction.

Nebraska's reaction to the farm crisis was more a political reaction than a substantive policy reaction. There simply wasn't much state government could do, although the state did try to address the problem in a limited way.

However, state government was affected by the chaotic condition of the national and state economy. Revenue simply was not coming in, and prices were going up.

Furthermore, changes in federal tax structure undertaken during Ronald Reagan's first term had a definite impact on the state. Nebraska's income tax rate was set as a percentage of a person's federal rate; when federal tax rates were cut, the state's income automatically declined. Moreover, federal outlays to the states also declined.

Warner took the lead in warning the state about what lay ahead. An editorial in the May 1981 Lincoln Journal said Warner had, during the session, "sought manfully to prepare both the Legislature and the state for the coming Reagan austerity." Another Journal editorial in August of that year said Warner, whom it referred to as the "far-sighted senator from Waverly," was continuing to warn that the state better be prepared to receive less federal money.

During the 1982 session, Warner and the Appropriations Committee moved to try to remedy the state's tax dilemma. The committee recommended increasing Nebraska's individual income tax rate to 16 percent of federal liability from the 15 percent then in effect. That increase would have allowed the committee to recommend a budget $15 million higher than the one Governor Charlie Thone had sent to the Legislature.

The incident was, according to a Lincoln Journal story in February 1982, another skirmish in the ongoing philosophical battle between Thone and Warner. The governor believed the state should simply swallow its revenue shortfalls and cut the budget; the senator believed the state also should consider adjusting its income tax rate in the face of federal tax cuts so that state revenue would remain close to the level it had been before the Reagan cuts. That would have allowed the state to continue to provide most of the services the people had come to expect, a move in line with Warner's philosophy that government is, indeed, useful to its citizens.

Thone won that round. The rate was not adjusted, the extra income was not raised and the budget was balanced by means of spending cuts.

At the end of the 1982 legislative session, another battle arose from the philosophical differences between the governor and the senator. Thone had vetoed state employee salary increases, effectively cutting them from the 3.75 percent included in the Legislature's budget to 2.5 percent. As the Legislature considered an override, some state senators suggested forcing the issue by threatening to withhold votes on another measure Thone dearly wanted to see passed.

The bill in question would have given the governor authority to move non-general fund money into the general fund to pay the state's bills that spring and summer. It was a measure Thone desperately needed if he were to be able to keep state government functioning.

Warner firmly opposed Thone's veto of the Legislature's salary increase bill. He told his colleagues Thone's version of salary increases would make no difference to the tax rate increases, which would be going into effect anyway. He said the smaller salary increase was symbolic and not financially necessary. It would hurt the employees without helping the state budget.

Warner still remembers his irritation with Thone's stand on employee salaries. He says he thinks Thone may have hoped to gain political points by beating employees down. That is precisely the opposite of Warner's view: "I believe in paying good people good salaries. ... Turnover is expensive."

Furthermore, state employees are essential to effective government. "Politicians come and go," Warner says. "People like me come and go. Essentially, state government depends on these career people that make it function."

Nonetheless, two attempts to override failed, leaving Thone with the victory. Then the senators returned to the matter of the funds transfer. Some senators, longing to get even, urged the Unicameral to defeat the measure and leave the governor hanging.

However, Warner encouraged the Legislature not to be vindictive. He told his fellow senators he himself had most reason to feel betrayed by the salary veto. He pointed out that the Appropriations Committee had cooperated with the governor, working and reworking its budget proposals in the face of steadily declining state revenues. Warner said he believed it was important that the budget include at least a small salary increase for state employees and that his committee's final product was a balanced budget that included a 3.75 percent pay raise.

Because Thone had insisted on cutting that amount for nothing more than symbolic reasons, Warner told his colleagues the possibility of retribution was enticing. He was tempted to urge the Legislature to defeat the fund transfer bill and leave Thone to face the financial music. But his concern for the welfare of the state made Warner resist the temptation. He urged the Legislature to approve the fund transfer measure, which required an emergency clause and 33 votes to pass. The senators did exactly that on a 34-7 vote.

At least two senators said later they voted for the bill only out of respect for Warner. A Lincoln Star story refers to the senator as "the hero of the evening ... a respected legislator and head of the Appropriations Committee, who eloquently urged his colleagues to be responsible and not vindictive."

"Charlie got mad at me on that one and chewed me out," Warner says. "I just shrugged. We just didn't agree."

In retrospect, though, Warner thinks Thone turned out to be a pretty good governor, despite the senator's sense that Thone didn't really enjoy the job. Warner thinks perhaps it was Thone's noticeable discomfort in the governor's office that contributed to his defeat after one term.

The following fall, the Unicameral was back in Lincoln for a special session, a common occurrence during the late 1970s through the mid-1980s A story in the Nov. 14, 1982, Omaha World-Herald describes how Warner led the action in that year's special session, urging spending cuts and tax hikes to allow the state to meet its obligations. Thone was a lame duck governor, having lost the election earlier that month to Bob Kerrey, and the World-Herald story reported that many people were referring to Warner as "acting governor." The senator, of course, denied that he was playing that role.

Regardless, Warner and the Appropriations Committee were far from being out of the budget-cutting woods. Revenues decreased, and budgets grew tighter as the committee developed an annual budget for the state.

By the mid-1980s the situation was approaching crisis. One year the committee was purported to have cut $25-30 million from the budget. "But we didn't really do that," Warner says. The cut came out of the general fund, but some expenditures were simply shifted to other parts of the budget, and some state tax dollars were simply replaced by fees. That was a shift, not a cut.

Other times the committee transferred money out of the state's cash reserve funds rather than increase taxes. Sometimes the transfer was intended to be temporary, but paying money back to the reserve funds was often difficult. It was something that made sense in the short run, Warner says, but ultimately, "all you're doing is pushing that snow bank out in front of you, and it's just going to keep getting deeper and deeper."

Despite efforts to shift costs and find revenues from fees instead of taxes, the Legislature finally was being forced to cut agency requests and squelch growth in order to balance the budget. It was not fun, Warner remembers.

For one thing, the number of budget items that could be cut was limited; more than half of the total was for entitlement programs or for items that would automatically come back from the agencies as deficit requests.

"Discretionary money essentially was only in higher education. So much of the state budget you couldn't cut."

The senator had tried to take some of the heat off education several times while he was chairman of Appropriations. He had proposed that his committee be allowed to suspend any statute in the Budget Act for two years if an emergency arose. The committee would not have been allowed to repeal a program, just to adjust it to get through hard fiscal times.

One year Warner's bill actually made it as far as select file, the second stage of legislative floor action. But that was as far as it went. A lot of senators thought the proposal would give the Appropriations Committee too much power over state programs.

"I didn't think so at the time," Warner says. If a similar measure were introduced today, though, Warner—now an outsider to Appropriations—admits he'd be as concerned as his critics were more than 15 years ago.

One year during the early 1980s, the state was facing a $23 or $24 million predicted shortfall in revenue. The papers were saying the Legislature needed to make only a 3 percent cut in the total budget of $735 million to make up the shortfall. However, $490 million of that total budget could not be touched, so what the Legislature actually had to do was make all its cuts in the discretionary part of the budget—the remaining $245 million. That amounted to a 10 percent cut.

"A 10 percent cut does not go unnoticed," Warner says.

A cut of that size meant the affected agencies had to eliminate jobs or entire programs. Ironically, it was the Revenue Department that usually got cut most frequently and heavily. "Over a period of time, we had fewer and fewer auditors ... fewer and fewer people to review things," Warner says. "So the error rate grew."

A result of less oversight meant the income from sales and income and fuel taxes dropped, a situation that made the deficit problem even worse. Later, when the Legislature restored money for Revenue Department auditors, the income started to increase. "Those cuts were very dumb cuts," the senator says, saving relatively few dollars in the short term but making it harder to collect legitimate revenues in the long term.

But that wasn't the only short-sighted cut the legislature made. The State Department of Agriculture had submitted as part of its budget a request to replace an $80,000 truck. The Appropriations Committee had slashed and snipped at the budget, trying to get it to match projected revenues. The members were within $500,000 of the goal, and the $80,000 truck was a tempting target. They decided to delay the purchase for a year.

"Any decent farmer like myself should have known better," Warner says. The old truck broke down the next year, leaving the state with a big repair bill and a couple of employees who were unable to use their time as fully as they should have.

"We didn't spend the $80,000. ... But we wasted a whole lot of money," the senator says.

But the days of slash and burn budget cutting were not over yet.

By 1985 it must have seemed to many in the Legislature—and the Appropriations Committee in particular—that their job had been reduced from planning and negotiating to meet the state's needs to just saying "no" to nearly every request that came along. State revenues continued to drop, and budgets continued to be trimmed and cut. It was a painful and frustrating process for lawmakers.

Perhaps the darkest moments came at the end of the 1985 session. Those involved remember the occasion as the Memorial Day Massacre.

It was another case of a change in the revenue forecast. The Appropriations bill had been hammered out in committee and presented to the entire Legislature when the revenue projection changed drastically and downward. Suddenly the Appropriations Committee's budget was more than $20 million above the projected revenue. In a state whose constitution requires a balanced budget, the discrepancy presented an enormous problem.

Besides that, the budget was growing steadily as the end of the session approached and senators offered amendments to add more spending items.

The Appropriations Committee met during a noon recess to decide what to do. Hannibal suggested Warner move that the Legislature postpone any decision on the budget until after the four-day Memorial Day weekend and that, over that weekend, the committee would meet to put together a package of budget reductions.

The committee followed Hannibal's advice and spent the holiday weekend lopping dollars off the budget. In the process, the committee eliminated funding for a number of pet projects its fellow senators had added only days before, via amendments from the floor. Warner expected trouble and moved quickly to avoid it.

He knew that, when the budget was taken up again on the floor of the Legislature, any senator could move to divide the question. That would have meant that the Appropriations Committee needed 25 votes to sustain each of its proposed cuts. "I knew that was virtually impossible to do," Warner says.

So he encouraged the senators to vote for the committee's amendment intact and then go back and examine it piece by piece. Any of the cuts could then be restored—with 25 votes.

It was a strategic move. It put all the advantage on the Appropriations Committee's side.

The committee's rewritten bill survived pretty much as submitted, and the result was a much reduced state budget, actually below what it had been the previous year.

"We actually cut the budget for the first time in modern history," Hannibal says.

Usually, when a Legislature says it is cutting the budget, it is only slowing the rate of growth or maybe putting a freeze on some expenditure. But in 1985 the Legislature made real cuts and came up with a real total that was less than that of the previous year. The senators could feel satisfied that they had accomplished what needed to be done, but few of them were happy about doing it.

Furthermore, the Memorial Day Massacre wasn't the end of it. The Legislature was called back into session later in 1985 to cut the budget some more, and Warner and the Appropriations Committee were, as usual, at the center of the procedure.

The special session was made necessary because, just three weeks after the Legislature went home on June 6, state revenue prospects had eroded further—and drastically.

Governor Bob Kerrey said the state faced a revenue shortfall of $28.3 million. He asked the Legislature to cut the budget $18.7 million and make up the remainder by means of funding shifts and extra revenues from fees or special taxes.

Warner disagreed. He said the shortfall was actually $49.4 million, and he proposed $19.7 million in budget cuts and $29.7 million in additional revenues, including a cigarette tax and a 1985 surtax on income. He told the Lincoln Journal-Star that the difference between the governor's figures and the Legislature's arose from a difference in opinion as to how much should be set aside for a budget reserve and for deficit appropriations.

Many people see the budget reserve as just extra money the state doesn't really need. Warner has always seen it as the beginning balance for the following fiscal year. Cutting that balance would simply push the state's 1985 fiscal problems into 1986.

Warner proposed an income tax surcharge that raised a furor because the possibility of increasing the income tax had not been included in Kerrey's call for the special session. Ordinarily, only matters specifically included in a governor's call for a special session may be considered during that session. So the Legislature and the governor faced off over a variety of issues, some clearly defined, some not.

Kerrey told the Journal-Star, "Senator Warner and I need to talk on Monday. We've been at loggerheads the last few weeks."

It comes as no surprise to veteran observers of Nebraska state government that the governor would find it necessary to consult with Warner about a matter of such vital urgency to the state. Henry Cordes, Omaha World-Herald reporter, says Warner has been a force Nebraska's governors have had to reckon with for the last three decades. "It's better to have him on your side," Cordes remarks, because Warner will almost surely have an influence on any major piece of legislation the Unicameral considers.

In fact, Kerrey's chief of staff, Don Nelson, told the World-Herald during one of Kerrey and Warner's face-offs that Warner "is the Great Oz, and you had better pay attention to the man behind the curtain."

But, despite their occasional public clashes, the governor and the senator had a remarkably close and amicable relationship. In fact, the morning after he was elected governor in 1982, Kerrey called Warner to ask for a meeting with him and Betty to discuss the state's future and the governor's role in it. Kerrey and Warner met frequently during Kerrey's term in office, and Warner says they got along well, especially considering they were from opposite political parties and disagreed on many things.

So in the case of the tax problem, Kerrey and Warner did what they usually did in such circumstances: They talked. About 10 days later, Kerrey surprised nearly everyone by expanding his special session call to include the income tax issue and then proposing his own bill to increase the income tax—just as Warner had proposed. That prompted arguments among the senators about the legality of Kerrey's actions and temporarily diverted attention from the purpose of the tax increase bills themselves.

When the Legislature finally worked through its procedural differences and returned to the matter of solving the revenue shortfall, it followed Warner's advice to the letter. The senators adopted the increased income tax that Warner had proposed and trimmed all state agency budgets by three percent—with one exception. The state's higher education system received only a two percent cut, just as Warner had proposed.

Warner's leadership as the state faced its fiscal problems earned him praise within the Legislature, in the press and among citizens at large. In recognition of the long-term influence he had had on the state, the Omaha World-Herald named him 1985 Midlands Man of the Year.

The four-page article in the paper's Jan. 5, 1986, Magazine of the Midlands cites Warner's "contribution as the steady hand on the tiller of state spending." Acknowledging the power of the Appropriations Committee and its chairman, the article reports, "Few other entities, including the governor's office, have more impact."

The article points out that the Legislature followed Warner's advice for the state's financial situation during its November special session and says that action was "an indication of Warner's influence on state government and helps explain why Kerrey ranks Warner 'right at the top' among the state's most powerful senators."

Kerrey told the magazine: "He (Warner) is an awfully good senator. I have always had an easy time working with him. We've had our differences, but he is easy to work with, and you know where he stands."

The article quotes Vard Johnson, then chairman of the Revenue Committee, and Bill Nichol, then speaker, praising Warner's hard work, institutional memory and ability to work with his committee. It gives Warner credit for being one of the Legislature's best-informed members on matters of both spending and taxes as the state wended its way through difficult financial times.

But Warner, never content with crisis management, also took steps to help the state plan against getting caught in a similar bind in the future. He introduced a bill in 1985 to move the state from annual to biennial budgets. The nearsighted thinking had led to some expensive mistakes, Warner says. "The public paid a high tuition price" until the Legislature learned its lesson. Twelve months is far too brief a time to plan for budget, revenue or even policy, the senator says.

Considering his experience with the appropriations process, the bill was part of a natural progression for Warner. When he became chairman of Appropriations, the committee was making decisions based on separate agency requests without even looking at the entire budget. After Warner instituted new procedures to make committee members consider all requests before making decisions, they were at least looking at 12 months of spending at a time. But even that proved not to be enough.

The state's fiscal problems continued, and budgets had to be adjusted before even a year had gone by. Biennial budgeting would provide more stability, forcing the state to look four years ahead as it did its planning.

Scott Moore, who succeeded Warner as the head of Appropriations, says Warner's role in shaping the state's fiscal planning has been amazing. Moore says he attended national meetings of state legislators in the early 1990s at which instruction was given about how to improve state budgeting processes. Very often, the recommendations were things Nebraska had already done under Warner's leadership, Moore says.

The same is true with revenue. Warner basically shaped the state revenue system in Nebraska. Ditto for the state's aid to education system and policies. In each of those broad areas, Warner accomplished several monumental feats.

The Legislature passed the bill to establish biennial budgeting in 1986; the procedure went into effect in 1987. Had the state made the switch 10 years earlier, many of the problems of the early 1980s could have been avoided.

Senator Warner's official legislative portrait, 1993.

Lt. Governor Charles and Esther Warner at a governor's inaugural ball in the early 1950s.

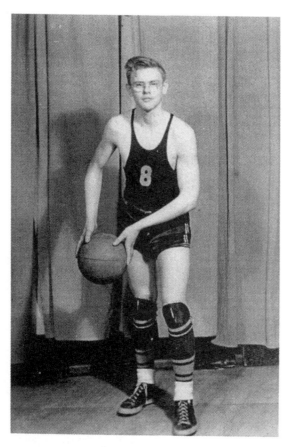

Jerome Warner as a member of
the Waverly High School basketball team in 1944.

Jerome Warner, 14, with the Nebraska State Fair champion Hereford heifer.

Warner, a University of Nebraska student, at the 1947 Nebraska State Fair.

The Warner family when they received the Conservation Pioneer Award, September, 1989; from left, Jamie, Liz, Charles, Jr., and Jerome.

Signing the 1969 highway bond bill; from left, Jerome Warner, an unidentified man, Bud Johnson, Governor Norbert Tiemann.

Jerry and Betty Warner, about 1990.

PART FOUR
COMMITTING TO LEGISLATIVE
LEADERSHIP

Moving on up?

Despite—or maybe because of—those trying financial times in the first half of the 1980s, Warner took another serious look at mid-decade at the possibility of running for higher office. It seems a logical consideration for a politician who had earned praise and respect for helping the state meet its fiscal crisis. Many a political career has advanced to a higher level of government on the strength of such recognition.

Warner's leadership of the Appropriations Committee and the Legislature had added to the public's awareness of and respect for him. Exercising that leadership had allowed him to realize for himself just how much he could accomplish for the state through its political system, how much influence he was able to wield. Perhaps the recognition he received as the Omaha World-Herald's 1986 Man of the Year also played a role in his decision.

For whatever reason, Warner probably came closer in 1986 to running for statewide office than ever before or since. Bob Kerrey announced he did not intend to seek another term as governor, leaving the seat wide open to candidates of both parties. Warner nearly took the plunge.

"That was the year a lot of people were pushing him to run," his son Jamie says. "I tried, too. It was really his last best shot."

Warner admits he considered a run for governor that year. "That was the closest I ever came."

He saw the governor's post as an opportunity to push for changes to help the people of Nebraska. He believes a governor who is willing to push particular issues can often see them through.

"Politically it would probably kill you, but you'd get things done."

Warner never took the opportunity to put that proposition to the test. He recalls sitting in a meeting with five or six people in 1986 to discuss a possible run for the governor's office. He also recalls how irritated he was by comments from one of those people as to how influential Washington Republicans would look on a Warner candidacy. The assessment was: not favorably.

What the "Washington influence" thought of him was of no concern to Warner. But he was annoyed at the idea that out-of-state people should have any say in what Nebraska needed or wanted.

He also thought he came too late to the 1986 governor's race. He told a World-Herald reporter January 12 of that year that the Legislature's two special sessions the previous fall had put him way behind on his farm work. In fact, he hadn't finished harvesting until December. So it was January before he was able seriously to consider the governor's race.

The same World-Herald story quotes Senator R. Wiley Remmers of Auburn as saying, "I'm quite sure Sen. Warner would get a lot of support." Warner himself told the reporter many people had encouraged him to pursue the office.

Warner could have drawn support from bipartisan sources because of his stature in the nonpartisan Legislature.

But that very nonpartisanship—and Warner's enthusiastic embrace of it—may have worked against him. Charlie Thone, active in Nebraska's Republican party politics for more than four decades, says he believes some in the party's power structure were opposed to Warner's running for any office outside the Legislature.

"There were a group of influential people who thought that the Unicameral was the place for Jerry Warner," Thone says, "and that if he would try for a higher office, there might not be the necessary support."

That lack of support from the Republican hierarchy may have been a result of Warner's loyalty and commitment to the nonpartisanship of the Legislature, Thone says. "It may have been that he burned some Republican bridges along the way by his fierce allegiance to the nonpartisan Unicameral. In fact, I know that was the situation with some party leaders—but not all of them."

Warner says he was not aware at the time that some Republican regulars didn't want to see him run for higher office, but he says he's not surprised. While he has always been reasonably active in the party, he was never part of the hierarchy. He's always been too independent to fit in very well.

Jack Rodgers, the Legislature's retired director of research, says Warner is not doctrinaire. That has made him appealing to people on all sides of the ideological spectrum. "He's a Republican, of course, but he's not as set in his views as some. He's more willing to learn, change, adapt."

That was precisely one of the reasons Thone was given when he asked others in the party why Warner would not have received wholehearted support from the GOP. Some people came right out and said Warner was too nonpartisan. Others, Thone said, alluded to the fact that Warner is not a forceful platform speaker.

"He gets kidded in the Unicameral for mumbling," Thone says, "but there they know him so well and trust him." Warner's speaking style may not have played as well on the campaign trail, Thone says, and it may have contributed to his detractors' belief that the senator should stay where he was.

Warner himself says, "I would have been a lousy campaigner," probably too quiet to have an influence on voters and too unwilling to promote himself for governor. He likes to advocate his positions—but not himself.

Even Warner's close friends and supporters recognize the problem.

"He's clearly self-effacing and modest," U.S. Representative Doug Bereuter says. "That's not what one usually sees in a person going for a statewide office."

Warner doesn't like campaigning even for the Legislature. It would have been worse if he had run for a statewide office. In fact, Warner probably would have been uncomfortable with many parts of the governor's job. He's not comfortable being fawned over.

Warner once told Hannibal, the former state senator, he would enjoy the business of state administration—being the chief executive officer—but not the ceremonial parts of the governor's duties. "I'd be very happy being CEO."

Besides not enjoying the political spotlight—either before or after an election—Warner would have a hard time organizing a campaign organization. He hates to ask people for help.

"It doesn't bother me to help someone else, but I don't like to ask for myself," he says. That reticence is a drawback to anyone wanting to run for statewide office in an era when such a campaign requires hundreds of thousands of dollars for advertising and travel.

Warner's son Jamie thinks the prospect of raising campaign funds was a big factor in his father's decision not to run for governor in 1986. A gubernatorial candidate must ask lots of people for lots of money, and the senator, his son says, "didn't want to be beholden to anybody."

Warner has never been comfortable accepting either time or money from other people. He has disliked it from the start, from his first campaign for the Legislature. And he hadn't taken any contributions for that first campaign. "But when I voted differently from the people who had really made an effort to help me with campaign work, it was a trying experience." All of that would be multiplied hugely in a statewide campaign.

Warner is the kind of person most anyone would want as governor, but getting elected involves posturing and talking about issues that push buttons with the public. It is not about the pressing issues of the day.

Warner is not known as an orator, either on the stump or in the Legislature. To be blunt, he mumbles. And sometimes he rambles.

"His mumbling is legendary," says Lee Rupp, former senator. "Sometimes even when he's not mumbling I have trouble following him."

However, most senators learn early on that when Warner speaks clearly, it would be wise to listen. It means the senior senator feels strongly about an issue and wants the Legislature to understand his position.

Some of Warner's mumbling, Moore says, is by design, intended to ward off too much probing into what he means. "But when he needs to, he can look you straight in the eye and say what he has to say *very* clearly," Moore says.

"He is articulate in direct proportion to his passion for something."

Warner admits that he's not known for being a rousing speaker. And he admits that he can speak very clearly when he's provoked. When he's annoyed or irritated about something, he says, everyone knows exactly what he's saying.

While those within government know and chuckle about Warner's speaking style, the voters of the state to whom Warner would have had to pitch his campaign may not have been so willing to put up with a candidate they would have trouble understanding.

All that said, Warner's decision not to run for governor in 1986 may have been most influenced by his commitment to and love of the Legislature. He had told the World-Herald that January that he was concerned about taking time away from the legislature to campaign. As chairman of the Appropriations Committee, he had legislative duties on his mind during the session and said, "I would not, under any circumstances, choose to abdicate those responsibilities" to go out and campaign.

That point of view met with editorial approval from the Lincoln Journal: "The Journal submits there is no more universally respected state political figure today than the unassuming Waverly farmer/stockman. A central reason for that respect is found in Warner's restatement of a basic philosophy—first chores first. ...

"Respect for the Legislature as a responsive and responsible policy-making institution, not a cockpit for raw bargaining by self-serving interests, always has been a Warner family trademark."

The senator himself says the Legislature is the place to be if a person wants to make a difference: "What intrigues me about the Legislature is that you deal with the issues. Issues are what I like, and it's in the detail of the issues that you have an impact. If you're on the executive side ... you can initiate and you can sign and you can veto, but you don't have the same kind of opportunity in between to participate in the discussion and the drafting."

Ron Withem, current speaker of the Unicameral, says he can relate to Warner's love of the Legislature. "You can have a huge impact on public policy," Withem says, "and see your beliefs actually placed into the law of the state." And yet, the job is not one that demands a person's full-time attention every day of the year, Withem says.

Not officially, anyway. But Jack Pittman from the Department of Roads says, "It's full time for him," Pittman also remarks on how Warner has created a balance between being a senator, a farmer and a husband and father.

"I'd go talk to him in the cornfield," Pittman remembers, to discuss potential roads legislation. "He was always thinking" about his legislative responsibilities even while he plowed, planted or harvested. "He had that family-farming-legislative thing down," Pittman says. "It absorbed every minute of his day." Occupying the governor's office or a seat in Congress "would have taken him away from the things he loved."

It also may have reduced his political influence.

Warner understands the power of the Legislature over against the governor in Nebraska, both structurally and in terms of accountability.

Structurally, the nonpartisan Unicameral includes no political party apparatus, so Nebraska's governors have no legislative clout through political channels the way governors of other states do. As a result, the

Legislature is free to be relatively independent of the governor, a fact Warner understands well. As chairman of the Appropriations Committee, for instance, he made it clear that it would be the Legislature that made budget decisions for the state. In Warner's book, the governor proposes; the Legislature disposes.

When it comes to accountability, too, the Legislature has an advantage. The governor in Nebraska, particularly an activist governor, seems to serve as a lightning rod for voter frustration. Nebraskans tend to get rid of governors who take strong positions.

Much of the weakness of the executive branch can be attributed to the Legislature's nonpartisan nature. The governor has no party apparatus within the Unicameral through which he or she can advance a program and exert discipline over individual senators. It puts the governor at a distinct disadvantage.

Senator Dave Landis says he believes Warner is sincere in his belief about the power of the Legislature.

Furthermore, Landis says, "Take a look at his list of accomplishments. They dwarf those of any governor in my lifetime. There isn't a governor who's done as much as Jerry Warner."

While Warner sounds now as if the decision to forgo the gubernatorial race was an easy one to make, he told reporters at the time that he made it "with regret." Perhaps the regret arose from setting aside the excitement of a statewide campaign and possible statewide office and from not fulfilling the wishes of the friends and supporters who had encouraged him to run. But the decision to stay in the Legislature was also strategic; it allowed Warner to maintain and build on his considerable influence.

Both before and since his 14 years as Appropriations chairman, Warner has had plenty of clout. Yet it was probably when he led that powerful committee that he truly enhanced his influence and had an opportunity to lead the state in the direction he thought it should go.

"If you're here to make an impact, being chair is a major assistance," Warner says. "But it's not the position, it's what you do with it. ...You have to be able to handle yourself in controversial areas and have respect for other views."

More specifically, being chairman of Appropriations is a particularly effective position. "The chairmanship is helpful. It's one ingredient that helps you be more effective. It didn't make any difference what the issue, I was still associated with chairmanship of Appropriations."

DiAnna Schimek, a member of the Unicameral since 1989, says, "Being chair of any committee increases your influence in the Legislature, but the Appropriations chair is the most powerful. He is nearly as powerful as the speaker because all our policy is guided by the money available. The Appropriations chair, through the process, can help determine what gets approved in the final analysis."

But even at the height of his influence—developing the state's budget, leading fights to override gubernatorial vetoes, being sought for advice and support—Warner consistently and characteristically downplayed his power. A 1986 incident provides a good example:

Bill Barrett, then a state senator, "who was sitting off to the side of the legislative chamber," was asked by a reporter the generic question "What's going on?" just as Warner came strolling by.

Rather than respond, Barrett quickly said, "I don't know; let's ask Warner. If anybody knows what's going on he does.'

To which Warner replied, 'Don't ask me. All I do is figure out which way the Legislature is going, then jump out in front so I look like a leader.'"[8]

It's the same kind of self-deprecation Peggy Brown of Waverly associates with her senator. A native of Waverly, Brown remembers asking Warner during his term as speaker what he did in that august position.

"Just look important," the senator said.

[8]Lincoln Star, April 1986

Taking the Lead in Controversies

Warner has done a lot more than just look important during his years of service in the Legislature, and his leadership has consisted of a lot more than just jumping in front of the parade as it goes by.

Warner's reputation as a consistently honest, trustworthy senator continued to grow. And it meant he sometimes took the lead in touchy matters involving his fellow legislators. His colleagues believed they could trust him to do the right thing without regard to his own personal or political advantage.

As early as 1972, well before the senator had been in office long enough to be the chamber's senior member, Warner initiated and led a legislative investigation into attempted bribery of a fellow senator. It was the first—but certainly not the last—major ethics controversy he helped investigate during his years in office, he says.

On his way to the Capitol one morning, Warner heard then-Senator John DeCamp on the radio, announcing that a banker in northeast Nebraska had attempted to bribe him for his vote on a personal property tax exemption bill Warner was working on.

When DeCamp made an announcement like that, Warner says, one could never be sure whether it was cold, hard fact or had been "glamoured" up a bit. But if the allegation were true, the attempted bribe was certainly illegal. Particularly since the bill in question was one he had sponsored, Warner decided something needed to be done.

A resolution Warner introduced was approved, and an investigative committee was formed. Warner was chairman.

As the investigation proceeded, the committee became convinced that

DeCamp was telling the truth: The bribe had been offered. So the committee recommended to the county attorney that he file charges against the businessman. Ultimately, the banker was found guilty and fined.

Warner's 1972 investigation into DeCamp's charge may have been relatively straightforward. The next one wasn't.

In 1975, Warner found himself knee deep in a controversy involving his old nemesis, Terry Carpenter. In 1974, Carpenter didn't file for re-election to the Unicameral in time for his name to appear on the ballot, but he apparently decided he wasn't ready to retire from public life and launched a write-in campaign. "Terrible Terry" had been popular in his district, and it wasn't unreasonable to think he could succeed as a write-in candidate.

He almost did. Bill Nichol, whose name was actually on the ballot, won the election—but not by much.

Carpenter asked for a recount. In 1974, that meant the Legislature needed to establish a committee to investigate the matter. Plenty of state senators were not sorry that Carpenter had lost his fight to return to the Legislature, and some suspected that a special committee appointed by the speaker or chairman of the Executive Board might be prejudiced against Carpenter. To avoid the perception of bias, the committee members and chairman were elected by the entire Legislature.

Richard Marvel, chairman of the Appropriations Committee, one of the most respected members of the Unicameral of that day, received the highest number of votes to chair the committee but declined to accept the job. Warner had the next highest number of votes, so he was named chairman.

That could hardly have made Carpenter comfortable. It had been only a few years before, when Carpenter was seeking the chairmanship of the Executive Board, that Warner had taken a strong, if symbolic, stand against the Scottsbluff senator.

Carpenter was the only nominee for the position, and the standard procedure in a case like that was for a senator to move to cast a unanimous ballot in favor of Senator Carpenter. Warner rose and asked that the legislative journal show him as not voting on the motion.

"Politically that probably wasn't a very bright thing to do ... but I felt very strongly, and so I did it."

Warner did not appreciate Carpenter's style. Carpenter expected lobbyists and his fellow legislators to consult him on every major bill. If that didn't happen, "he'd work against it and fight it." Eventually, it became a practice that those in favor of a piece of legislation would get Carpenter's blessing before trying to move it through the Legislature. Warner believed Carpenter was using power politics simply to build his own image and influence.

Carpenter seemed to care far more about that influence than about any particular public policy. "He'd carry any amendment for anybody," Warner says. "The only thing was that they had to assure him there were 25 votes to adopt it." If a senator can do that often enough, Warner says, "it gives the perception that he's a leader because people are following him" even though he may have had nothing to do with gathering the support for the measure.

It's a method of acquiring influence for which Warner has no use, and his refusal to go along with the unanimous ballot for Carpenter put that sentiment on record.

Still, Warner was elected to chair the committee that would look into Carpenter's disputed election.

"It was a terrible mess," he says of the case.

To begin with, the committee could not determine whether the punch card ballots were marked correctly. For some reason, the Scottsbluff County clerk had, after the election, punched out the names of both candidates on several hundred ballots. So evidence that might have been used to establish the final outcome had been destroyed.

In addition, at the committee's hearings, a number of senators testified in support of Carpenter and accused the committee of being biased, adding to an already tense situation.

After the hearings had been under way for a while, the state attorney general informed the committee that Carpenter's attorney had not filed a bond for a recount. At that point the committee recommended to the Legislature that Carpenter's request for a recount not be considered. The Legislature could simply have dropped the whole thing.

Warner, however, was not willing simply to ignore the question Carpenter had raised, although it would have been a quick way to dispatch his nemesis to political oblivion. Warner believed the Legislature had to be even more precise about the letter of the law than a court would be, believing that a court has more experience and latitude to interpret the law.

"I didn't think we should say, 'Close enough,'" Warner says.

The Legislature followed Warner's lead and granted the request for a recount. There is, of course, no quantitative way to measure how much Warner's stand affected his fellow senators when the matter was debated on the floor. But when the Legislature voted, the senators did not settle for "close enough." Once the recount was completed, Nichol was seated, and Carpenter's legislative career was permanently ended.

More than 10 years later, Warner found himself investigating the biggest and worst scandal of his career. It was the Nov. 1, 1983, insolvency of Commonwealth Savings Company.

The issue involved far more than the failure of one so-called thrift institution. It also involved the fate of the depositors whose money was lost, questions of wrong-doing or neglect on the part of the state banking department and the 1984 impeachment of Paul Douglas, who had been attorney general since 1977.

The problem started long before the actual bank failure. State laws at the time did not allow the banking department to work with a troubled institution to take corrective action. "About the only thing the department could do was close a firm down," Warner says.

In the Commonwealth case, the department suspected two sets of books were being kept. "But they couldn't prove it." And as long as they had no proof, they could take no action.

At root, Warner believes, the fault was the Legislature's. The Legislature had passed the laws that allowed the Commonwealth fiasco to develop.

Warner was serving on the Legislature's Banking Committee when the process that created the laws was begun. The legislation was designed to provide state-guaranteed deposit insurance only for small credit unions, the largest of which had about $4 million in deposits, and the reserves that were established were adequate for that size.

Two years later, industrial banks—like Commonwealth—were added to the system. Commonwealth's deposits alone were close to $68 million, far greater than the state's reserves. Warner thinks the Legislature should have realized when it expanded the insurance system that it was setting the stage for disaster.

Warner was no longer on the Banking Committee at that time, but he remembers the legislative action that added industrial banks to the Nebraska Depositors Insurance Guaranty Corporation. His instincts told him the action was not wise.

"That was one of the votes I remember very well—voting yes on that bill with this feeling in my stomach that there was something wrong."

The failure of the institution itself was bad enough, Warner says. But Paul Douglas's involvement made it even worse. Douglas and Warner had been friends for many years.

Despite his friendship with Douglas, Warner was appointed to serve on the committee investigating the Commonwealth failure and surrounding problems.

The Legislature first proposed John DeCamp, chairman of the Banking Committee, to lead the investigation. But after further consideration, the senators decided DeCamp might not be the best choice. DeCamp's own ethics had been questioned not long before, and the flamboyant senator had been known to turn ordinary issues into dramatic situations.

So Vard Johnson, chairman of the Executive Board, was named to lead the investigative committee. It was a logical choice, Warner says, although it was an example of the Legislature's working backwards, deciding first on the end result and then coming up with the rationale to justify it.

Under Johnson's leadership the committee worked with special counsel Richard Kopf, who Warner remembers as an excellent attorney. Despite that, the investigation was not easy.

"The Legislature is not a good body for investigative responsibility," Warner says, because its business is done almost totally in public. Ordinarily that openness is a good thing. But when the Legislature publicly investigates potential wrong-doing, many people are questioned purely to provide background. Their names become part of the public record and the public may assume they are part of the scandal.

"Rumors fly. It's an exceedingly poor setting for investigative responsibility."

One of the most difficult parts of the matter for Warner was the vote to impeach or condemn Douglas for his role in the whole banking fiasco. "I ended up voting to impeach," Warner says. "I hated that a lot." But based on the evidence turned up in the investigation, Warner believed it was what he had to do.

All the Lincoln senators were at least tangentially involved in the Commonwealth investigation because so many of their constituents had been Commonwealth depositors. After the institution failed, those depositors wanted the state to pay up on the insurance money they thought they had been guaranteed. The money for the guarantee fund, of course, had never been appropriated.

Unfortunately for Nebraska depositors and the Legislature, the banking-related problems did not stop with Commonwealth. Other thrift institutions were also in trouble in the early to mid-1980s, notably State Security Savings. The failure of that institution still rankles many former depositors, including Dolores Schiebinger of Lincoln.

A special legislative subcommittee of the committee investigating the Commonwealth matter wrote a letter in May 1986 to James Barbee, then director of the Nebraska Banking Department. The letter outlined the subcommittee's concerns about matters surrounding the closing of State Security Savings Company in 1983. The subcommittee, of which Warner was a member, urged Barbee to "consult immediately with the appropriate law enforcement authorities to determine whether criminal prosecution is warranted." The Banking Department did not follow that recommendation.

Schiebinger complained that the letter was never made public. Had it been made public, Schiebinger believes public pressure would have caused the authorities to file charges against the owners of State Securities and its parent company and would have allowed depositors to recover some or all of their losses.

Warner says he remembers the letter and Schiebinger's complaint but doesn't know what the Legislature could have done. The letter from the subcommittee raised questions about the legality of some actions taken by State Securities' owners. But no proof of illegality could be found, only proof of poor judgment on the part of the institution's officers. "For poor judgment, you can't be prosecuted."

As had been true in the Commonwealth debacle, the banking department could do little to solve State Securities' problems short of shutting down the institution. Furthermore, until the Commonwealth and State Security collapses demonstrated the need for a more effective regulatory system, the financial community would have opposed any such changes and the Legislature would have been unlikely to pass them.

Not only would the Legislature have had trouble opposing the wishes of the banking lobby, but it would have seemed silly to worry about potential problems with Commonwealth. S.E. Copple, Commonwealth president, was presumed to be a financially stable and sound person.

However, people making that presumption were ignoring history, Warner says.

Warner knew the history. Copple had owned a bank in Walton, just east of Lincoln, that failed in 1929. "I still have neighbors whose folks were stockholders in that bank. They looked on S.E. Copple with considerable suspicion," Warner says.

It's not that Copple was downright dishonest, but he seemed to be all too willing to take big risks and operate on the fringe of responsible banking practices. When the bank failed, Copple didn't suffer much, but many stockholders and customers were in a different boat. People felt they had been taken in.

Forty-five years later, circumstances were similar. "Some of what was done at Commonwealth was of the same nature as what had been done at the Walton bank."

When the whole mess came crashing down, the investigators' initial interests seemed to be more in finding someone to blame—"to nail someone's hide to the barn door"—than in recovering protection for the depositors or, technically, investors. Warner thinks that was a mistake. "Those people who were investors had every reason to feel they were misled, because they certainly were."

The next major controversy Warner helped investigate also involved a financial institution—or, at least, its name. The Franklin Federal Credit Union in Omaha went under in 1988. But this time the insolvency was only the beginning of a series of events the senator describes as "bizarre." It included allegations of a child abuse or pornography ring that was said to involve a number of powerful, well-known Nebraskans. "I have no idea if it occurred or not," Warner says of the alleged child abuse.

The problems were brought to the Legislature's attention by Senators John DeCamp and Loran Schmit. Schmit was named chairman of the investigative committee, chosen by the Legislature's Executive Board. Warner was a member of the committee.

The legislative committee met early on with people in law enforcement to find out why no criminal or legal investigation was under way. Essentially, the senators were told the accusations could not be substantiated, but the Legislature proceeded with its own investigation anyway.

The committee hired legal counsel and special investigators, and tried to piece the facts together. "There were so many stories" about what was alleged to have happened. "The allegations just boggled my mind."

"We sat through meeting after meeting," the senator recalls, but results were minimal. He began to wonder how much of the investigation was being driven "by a vindictive attitude," some senator or senators enticed by the idea of bringing down a big-name Nebraskan.

Regardless, it became clear that the Legislature was not capable of handling the intricate investigation.

The matter was finally referred to a grand jury, and none of the accusations were substantiated. The upshot was that "a lot of people's reputations were hurt, damaged, that shouldn't have been," Warner says. If the investigation had been handled by the law enforcement system and the courts instead of the Legislature, many of the allegations would never have been made public unless and until they had been proven true.

"There were bits and pieces of truth," and that tended to make people believe that all the stories were true. The implications made it harder for the public to sort out fact from fiction.

Warner thinks much of what was raised in the Franklin case was fiction. Very seldom does a conspiracy theory prove out, he says. "It just happened. It's a series of unrelated, unplanned, unconnected circumstances."

Whatever the outcome of the investigation, Warner says the whole process reinforced his belief that he would never be part of another one of these investigative committees unless he were chairman. "You're too vulnerable if you're just on the committee" and don't have all the details about what's going on.

But he adds, "People were good about telling me things to help me keep out of trouble." For instance, a State Patrol officer told him, before the fact became public, that many of the young people who had made the original allegations of abuse were recanting their stories. Warner didn't tell anyone what the officer had said was happening, but eventually the accusations were dropped. In the meantime, Warner became more vocal, he says, about easing off on the investigation.

"That has happened many times," the senator says. "People told me what I needed to know. I didn't repeat it, and I didn't use it as an excuse. But it enabled me to make a better decision."

Warner was a member of yet another special committee before he left Appropriations. This one did not involve criminal allegations but did serve to put Warner in what he calls an awkward position. Like the Carpenter matter, this case involved elections and election laws—and their interpretation.

In 1988 Jerry Conway of Wayne had defeated Tore Nelson for the 18th District legislative seat vacated when Bob Murphy, the incumbent, declined to stand for re-election. Nelson filed a protest against Conway's election, pointing out that Conway was on the faculty at Wayne State College. Murphy backed Nelson's contention that an employee of a state institution could not be elected to the legislature. The state colleges are part of the executive branch of government, Murphy contended; a person working in the executive branch should not hold office in the legislative branch.

Warner believes Murphy took the action not so much out of a concern for electoral propriety but because he didn't like Conway. Whatever the reason behind Murphy's protest, the Legislature was forced to deal with it.

The Legislature had established a tradition of forming a credentials committee that would meet at the start of each new biennium to certify that the candidates elected in November were eligible to be seated. The five senior members of the Unicameral make up the credentials committee, so of course, Warner was among the five.

The credentials committee was charged with settling the protest against Conway's election. The committee dug through a lot of case history both within and outside Nebraska, trying to come up with something that resembled a legal determination.

When the committee's investigation was complete, Warner believed Conway met all the constitutional requirements to be a member of the Legislature and was eligible to be seated. But the committee's report suggested that Conway might not be able to remain on the faculty at Wayne State if he were to take his seat in the Unicameral.

It was something of a fine point, Warner admits. Many people could not see the difference between saying that Conway was eligible to be seated but may have to give up his faculty position at a state school and saying that he was not eligible because he held a faculty position.

"The Legislature is not a good place to make judicial-type decisions," the senator says. "They're bound to be political in many respects. The Legislature is always accused of protecting itself or the members protecting each other from the outside while they cuss each other strenuously inside. There's no question there's an element of that all the time.

"But the basis, it seemed to me, was a strict interpretation that he was, in fact, eligible (to serve in the Legislature) and that the proper place to determine his eligibility to be faculty was in the court system," which is where the case went after the Legislature made its decision. The court eventually ruled that Conway could not remain on the faculty while serving in the Unicameral.

Warner had a chance to apply his thinking about disputed elections again in 1991. This time questions of partisanship clearly came into play.

Incumbent senator Dennis Byars of Beatrice, a Republican, and challenger Paul Korslund, a Democrat, ran an extremely close race; the election's outcome hinged on absentee ballots. Then authorities discovered that 508 of the absentee ballots had been initialed on the front rather than signed on the back by Gage County election officials. Technically, the ballots should have been disqualified as not meeting election law standards.

If the ballots were deemed legal and counted, Byars would win by 40 votes. If the ballots were discarded, Korslund would win by 14 votes. The matter went to the Legislature for resolution.

In name and usually also in practice, the Nebraska Unicameral is a nonpartisan body. But, although they are not elected under party labels, the senators are almost all either Republicans or Democrats. In the case of the Gage County election, that made a difference.

"This one was partisan," Warner says, of the dispute. The Democrats supported Korslund and the Republicans Byars.

But Warner, the Republican, again came down on the side of strict compliance with the statutes. Ballots that did not meet the specific requirements laid out in the law should not be counted, he concluded. "So I came down on Korslund's side." So did a 6-5 majority of the Executive Board conducting the investigation. They recommended that Korslund be declared the winner of the election.

However, the full Legislature seated Byars on a 25-24 vote. The only two senators who did not vote the party line were Scott Moore and Warner.

The next day Korslund withdrew his contest of the election, and the committee's minority report, recommending that Byars be seated, was

162

adopted. Warner moved on the floor that the Legislature certify Byars as having won the election; the motion passed, 44-1.

"It was difficult for me," Warner says. "I liked Byars" and had actually helped him campaign for re-election. "I was on his side as an individual, but I had to come down on the other side with our interpretation." He did what he believed to be right.

Warner told the World-Herald at the time that he was bothered that the improperly marked ballots could not be counted since it seemed to penalize innocent voters. However, he was even more concerned that accepting the ballots would undermine the integrity of the election process.

"It may be the law, but it is not justice," Warner said of his and the Executive Board's decision. "I desire to come down on the side of justice, but I feel compelled to come down on the side of the law as I see the law."

Supporting the University

Warner's leadership in controversial matters has contributed to the integrity of the Unicameral, but it is not the thing most people think of first when they assess the senator's career. Most people would probably mention highways first and Appropriations second.

But the far-thinking senator has also had a consistent and consequential influence on higher education in Nebraska.

Himself a graduate of the University of Nebraska-Lincoln, Warner has exhibited a deep and abiding interest in the state's system of postsecondary education ever since he entered the Legislature more than 30 years ago.

"He has a sweet tooth for the university," says Warner's friend, former senator Gary Hannibal. "He always has."

Warner believes, though, that his support for the university simply reflects the views of the people of Nebraska. "I think the people of the state take a lot of pride in the university," Warner says. That support may not be applied uniformly, however: architects tend to value the College of Architecture, lawyers the Law College, agriculture interests the College of Agriculture, and so on.

"About the only college that doesn't have a constituency in the way of alumni is the College of Arts and Sciences, which is the nuts and bolts for everything," Warner says. Nonetheless, he believes support for the total institution, not just an individual piece or two, is what makes a great university.

Warner's support for the university springs from a familiar source: his family.

"I grew up in a home where education was important," the senator says. His father supported all levels of education during his years in the Legislature, and his mother also was a big proponent of education.

His mother skipped two grades in elementary school, went on to high school and then attended Nebraska Wesleyan. She was the only one of the seven children in her family to attend college.

When Warner was a child, he heard his parents talk frequently about college faculty members and programs. He simply accepted higher education as an essential part of life. Once elected to the Legislature, he was in a position to do something directly to benefit higher education and, especially, the University of Nebraska.

Lee Rupp, the only registered lobbyist for the NU system, says Warner is intimately acquainted with the history of the university. "How do you lobby a person who knows more than you?" Rupp asks.

Before joining the university administration in 1988, Rupp was a member of the Unicameral for five years. During his time in the Legislature, Rupp sat behind Warner and "enjoyed being a Warner student."

The university is one of Warner's "pet areas," Rupp says. "But that doesn't mean he automatically agrees with everything the university wants to do. If he thinks our ideas are foolish, he tells us."

On the other hand, if he thinks the Legislature's ideas about the university are foolish, he will tell his fellow lawmakers, too. Warner has little patience with politicians who automatically attack postsecondary education in an apparent effort to build their political fortunes. The strategy appeals to some voters, Warner admits, but hasn't usually helped state legislators' careers in the long run.

Generally, Warner says, the state has done well by the university, although more vigorous support at times could have made a big long-term difference. He remembers a time in the late 1960s when NU was ahead of the pack on a lot of computer technology. Increased funding would have moved the program ahead, but the Appropriations Committee of the time—well before he was the chairman—balked, and the lead dissipated.

Had the Legislature supported the fledgling technology program with adequate funding, Warner believes Nebraska might have become a little Silicon Valley.

Had Warner been at the helm of the Appropriations Committee at the time, things might have turned out differently. A decade later, he used his influence as Appropriations chairman to help guide the university to as much success as possible with the Unicameral.

Ron Roskens, president of the University of Nebraska system from

1977-89, remembers how closely university officials worked with Warner during those years. In fact, both Jerry and Betty Warner would meet with university administrators at 7 a.m. several days a week during the session for coffee, doughnuts and 30 minutes of discussion, Roskens says. The discussions were candid.

It was a close, productive, comfortable relationship, but it caused a major fight between Warner and his Appropriations Committee in 1979.

Roskens had told Warner during the previous fall, well before the legislative session began, that the chiller that provided air conditioning for much of UNL's East Campus was inadequate and needed to be replaced. The administrators had a $2 million bid on a new chiller, which they said was substantially less than they had expected. If they accepted the bid during the fall, they said, the university could save several hundred thousand dollars.

The UNL officials asked Warner whether he thought the Legislature would approve the purchase. "I never made a commitment for the committee," Warner says. But he agreed to hold a special hearing on the matter in January because, by Feb. 1, the university needed either to accept or reject the bid. While the committee's approval would not have been a guarantee of final approval by the entire body, "it might have been worth the gamble," Warner says.

So he convened a special hearing in January. "I could not get the committee to take any action. They would not say yes or no."

After the meeting, Warner told the university officials they should go ahead and take the bid for the chiller because it was such a good deal. Although the committee was not acting on the proposal, he was convinced approval would soon be forthcoming.

As the weeks went on, the committee continued to drag its feet. It's a fact of group dynamics in the Legislature that, if one or two members of a committee say they don't want to vote on a matter, something like "senatorial courtesy" sets in, and the rest of the committee will not force the issue.

The committee followed its regular hearings schedule during the next few months, which meant the university's capital construction bill came at the end of the procedure. When the committee considered the university's capital construction proposal, Warner could not get the five votes he needed to add the $2 million for the chiller. In the meantime, other committee members had added some budget items with which

Warner took issue. The disagreement led to what Warner calls "the biggest fight I ever had with the Appropriations Committee."

Warner actually voted against the appropriations bill that was reported out of committee, a rare situation for the chairman of the cohesive Appropriations Committee.

The chiller was still not included in the bill, and senators and citizens were accusing the university of underhanded dealings. That simply was not true, Warner says: "What was true was that the Appropriations Committee wouldn't act."

What bothered Warner was not that his proposal had been voted down but that the committee had refused even to consider it in a timely manner. "Had they said no in January, that would have been the end of it."

He planted his feet. When the bill reached general file on the legislative floor, he argued—and voted—against advancing the bill. The measure became so controversial that it couldn't move one way or the other on the floor—not without the blessing of the Appropriations chairman.

"A lot of people followed my vote," Warner says.

The Legislature recessed for a few days, and Warner met other legislative leaders to figure out how to resolve the dilemma. "I remember Frank Lewis said to me, 'What is it you want?' and I said, 'I want the chiller.'"

The chiller found its way into the bill. And the bill passed at the very end of the legislative session.

Warner says he would not have fought as hard for the chiller if the common perception had not been that the university had done something wrong.

Warner's first love among the state's institutions of higher education is probably still the University of Nebraska-Lincoln, his alma mater, but he is also unquestionably committed to higher education in general. Throughout his decades in the Legislature, he has spent a great deal of time, effort and political capital trying to enhance the state's system of postsecondary education.

Specifically, he led the campaign to increase the coordination of postsecondary education in Nebraska. It was another complex and controversial issue—like state aid to education and the Nebraska highway system. Once again Warner was willing to jump into the fray and encourage, cajole and nudge his colleagues into looking at the long-term implications of a solution to what had become an ongoing concern.

The concern centered on a belief in many quarters that Nebraska's system of postsecondary institutions had, like Topsy, "just growed." Individual state colleges and universities acted independently of one another. Sometimes several schools offered similar programs and competed against each other. Sometimes no school offered a needed program, leaving gaps in the state's educational opportunities. Many legislators and state leaders believed more statewide coordination of the postsecondary institutions would help solve both problems.

The topic had come up in the Legislature regularly since at least the late 1930s, but it moved to a front burner in the early 1970s. Governor Exon had established a study group after congressional measures enabled each state to set up a permanent coordinating commission. A bill to that effect—but giving the commission strictly limited authority—was introduced in 1974.

Warner didn't like it.

In 1975 the Legislature created its own interim study committee, chaired by Warner and Senator Frank Lewis, then chairman of the Education Committee. The study committee spent months gathering information from other states about how they coordinated postsecondary education.

"It became apparent to me there was no system," Warner says. If a state seemed to be successful at coordinating its institutions of higher learning, it was because the people involved were effective, not because a particular system was necessarily superior.

The senator says that came as no surprise to him. In almost everything, he says, the way a system is organized is not the key to success. "It's who you put in there." Effective people can make a poorly organized system work, but the wrong people can kill even the best-organized one.

So the interim study committee found no magic formula to be applied to Nebraska's postsecondary needs. Instead, committee members tried to discover what was happening in Nebraska and what kinds of changes the people of the state believed would improve the situation.

The interim study committee held hearings all over the state, Warner recalls. He remembers one especially, held at Kearney. The study committee was represented by three senators: Warner, a farmer from Waverly; a Grand Island businessman who sold plumbing fixtures; and a farmer from Alliance.

One of the first people to testify at the hearing was the president of the Kearney State College faculty senate. "He started out saying he was a little nervous because he'd never appeared before a group of state senators."

"Think of us as two farmers and a plumber," Warner said.

"Now, that really makes me nervous," the faculty member said.

Warner chuckles at the recollection.

"I thought, yeah, two farmers and a plumber really ought not to be out here trying to establish postsecondary policy for the State of Nebraska."

But Warner says the hearings and the other work of the committee were good preparation for his later work as chairman of the Appropriations Committee. Many of the concerns raised at those hearings were later raised before the Appropriations Committee and continue to be raised today.

For instance, at a hearing in Norfolk, one of the speakers said every Nebraskan should be no more than 20 miles from a site where postsecondary courses were offered. "In a state like Nebraska, that obviously was impossible at that time," the senator says. Today, however, access is far better thanks to telecommunications, "which I believe very strongly that the state needs to expand more rapidly."

He says he can't understand the flat-out opposition to teaching by telecommunications that he has often encountered. Part of the problem is the money needed to finance distance learning, he says, but another part is "the perception—depending on your age—that you have to have a teacher in the room to effectively learn."

That's simply not the case, Warner says. Young people today grow up using computers and other non-traditional learning methods. Taking classes at a distance by satellite is acceptable to most students and is a way a geographically large state like Nebraska can provide reasonable access to higher education for all its citizens.

But that solution was not available when the study committee was holding hearings in the mid-1970s, and it wasn't until 1976 that any coordinating legislation was actually passed. When Warner became chairman of the Appropriations Committee in 1978, he found himself involved in a move to strengthen the supervision and coordination of higher education.

It was an idea he originally did not approve of.

"The first 25 or 27 years I was in here, I was unalterably opposed to a coordinating commission" for postsecondary education, Warner recalls. He believed the authority for higher education should remain with the Legislature. But he also believed something needed to be done to clarify and define the relationship among the state's postsecondary institutions.

In 1977 the Legislature tried to accomplish that goal by enacting a number of bills to establish the role and mission of each public institution of higher learning. Then-Governor James Exon vetoed the bills.

Warner says he remembers being annoyed with Exon's strongly worded veto.

It was part of a running disagreement between the two men regarding higher education.

In the early 1970s, Exon had appointed a so-called 1202 Commission, an out-growth of federal legislation, that served as a precursor to a coordinating commission. Warner didn't like the 1202 Commission; he was still opposed to any kind of coordinating body.

While Warner was chairman of the Education Committee in 1973-74, Senator Frank Lewis had introduced, at Exon's request, a bill to move beyond the 1202 Commission and establish a permanent coordinating commission. A Warner staff member who attended a meeting about the proposed bill reported that supporters claimed they had lined up 30 votes in favor of the measure.

Warner found out later that supporters had simply *talked* to 30 senators and that support was not nearly as solid as it sounded. At the time, though, he assumed he could not get the bill killed on the floor.

So he proposed amendments to make every section inoperable.

The amendments passed easily with no opposition from Lewis, who didn't much care what happened to the original bill. Then the bill itself passed, but the attached amendment made it utterly worthless.

Undoubtedly, the maneuver did not endear Warner to Exon.

In the ensuing years, Warner came to believe the state needed better coordination of higher education, and the result was the role and mission bills. At that point, Warner says, he believed the Legislature should establish role and mission and approve proposed new programs on the various campuses. "I was told repeatedly that was not going to work, but I didn't believe it," he says.

The bills would have, in a sense, made the Legislature itself the coordinating body, something Warner now believes would have been a mistake. Exon may have vetoed the bills for that reason. Or the veto may have been simply another skirmish in the ongoing battle between the governor and the senator.

Exon's vetoes were usually strongly worded, Warner recalls. The governor liked to condemn the Legislature for actions with which he didn't agree. The senator took offense at that, and in the case of the role and mission bills, he voiced his unhappiness on the legislative floor.

"I was wound up," he remembers. And when he is wound up and angry, no one has trouble understanding what he's saying, despite his reputation for mumbling under ordinary circumstances.

He doesn't remember exactly what he said.

"It probably wasn't too dramatic, but it seemed so at the time. I did my pitch to override, and Frank Lewis moved to cease debate. He figured we'd hit our peak. And we had it all over within a few minutes after it came back from the governor."

One of the goals of the 1977 bills—and another batch of bills in 1978—was to avoid unnecessary duplication among programs. One result was that only the University of Nebraska-Lincoln was allowed to offer graduate programs—except for advanced degrees in education. However, UNL was directed to sponsor cooperative graduate programs with all the other institutions.

Warner thought assigning one institution primary responsibility for the graduate programs would be the best way to avoid duplication and still provide access to students in all parts of the state.

The Legislature provided funding for UNL to operate a master of business administration program at Kearney. Warner and others responsible for the role and mission legislation assumed UNL would allow faculty at Kearney who were already teaching MBA courses to become part of the university's graduate faculty under UNL's auspices.

"As it turned out, they wouldn't accept anybody," Warner says. UNL's College of Business Administration started flying faculty members to Kearney to teach classes. Only several years later was one Kearney professor finally admitted to the graduate faculty.

"There was probably fault on both sides," Warner says. The faculty at

Kearney resented not being allowed to have their own graduate program, and the faculty at Lincoln thought only they should be allowed to teach graduate students.

With those kinds of attitudes on both sides, the cooperative program failed.

About 10 years after the role and mission bills were passed in the late 1970s, the Legislature gave back to Kearney the right to its own MBA program. "I was opposed to it," Warner says. "But there wasn't a soul left in the Legislature other than myself who had been involved" in the original legislation. "All the changes sounded reasonable because they (the senators) had no background as to what had been done over time."

The legislative flip-flop was one of the major reasons, Warner says, that he changed his 25-year opposition to a coordinating commission with constitutional authority.

He came to believe that the Legislature is simply unable to make decisions about higher education on the basis of what is educationally sound. Instead, the decisions would always be political—at least in part because "there is no such thing as a bad educational opportunity. They all sound good." Especially to people who have no institutional memory to help them understand why things are as they are.

So Warner did an about-face and, in the late 1980s, became a proponent of a postsecondary coordinating commission. The body was designed to take the politics out of higher education planning much the way the highway legislation had taken the politics out of roads planning.

Before the commission actually came into being, though, Warner came up with another idea, something he thought of while he was farming. "A lot of things I've done I've thought of when I'm sitting on a tractor planting corn."

It became so common for him to return to the Capitol with an idea he'd had while working in the fields that staff started teasing him: "If we were working on something and having trouble trying to think of a solution, somebody would say, 'Why don't you go sit on a tractor for a while?'"

In the spring of 1989, one of those tractor-induced ideas was to introduce a bill that would make Kearney State College part of the university system. Warner had been pondering a proposal to designate KSC a separate university. He didn't want two university systems in the state, so he decided to pre-empt the movement and try, instead, to absorb KSC into the existing system.

The senator asked his staff to see whether the change could be made through legislation or would require a constitutional amendment.

In the meantime, he told Roskens, then president of the university system, what he was pondering. At that point, Warner had said nothing publicly about the proposition.

Later that summer, he found out that the senator from Kearney, Lorraine Langford, planned to introduce legislation in the next session changing the names of all the state colleges to universities. Warner decided the time had come to float his proposal as an alternative to Langford's idea.

He let Henry Cordes, an Omaha World-Herald reporter, know what he had in mind. As he researched the story, Cordes also asked people in Kearney for their reactions to Warner's proposal, and he quoted Senator Langford's response: "Over my dead body!" That didn't surprise Warner.

Later that fall Bill Nestor, then chancellor of Kearney State, stopped by Warner's Capitol office. Nestor asked whether Warner was sincere about bringing KSC into the university system. Warner said he had been taught, when he arrived at the Legislature, that a senator should not introduce a bill he did not support.

Nestor told the senator he thought there was a lot of support in Kearney for such a move, including from the KSC faculty. "That surprised me no end," Warner says. He continued to pursue the merger.

The NU Board of Regents was officially neutral, but individual members of the board privately spoke against the bill. The State College Board of Trustees was officially against the bill, although the board allowed Nestor and others from KSC to speak on behalf of the measure.

Once the 1990 session began, the bill was referred to the Education Committee, where it looked as if it might languish. "We couldn't get five votes to get it out of committee. I think it might have had more to do with me than the issue," Warner says, implying that some of his colleagues resented his influence on higher education.

Regardless of the reason, the bill was not going to make legislative progress under its own steam. So Warner and Ron Withem, then chairman of the Education Committee, found an alternate mode of transportation. Withem agreed to amend the Kearney State measure to his own bill pertaining to higher education. Warner's name was not attached to the bill, but he says he worked as hard to get it passed as if he had been listed as a sponsor.

What Warner wants to do is make good public policy. Having his name associated with the Kearney State bill "wasn't something I needed ... another gold star behind my name—or a black mark, whichever the case may be. I was just interested in getting it done."

The bill passed that spring, 36-11. It had a lot of help from Doug Kristensen, then a new senator from Minden, and Withem as well as from KSC Chancellor Nestor and a citizens group from Kearney.

Nonetheless, it was Warner's backing that made the bill a success. Warner had long been regarded as the "staunchest protector" of the university system in general and UNL in particular. Other senators seemed to assume that his support for the merger meant the university system would not be hurt by the move. Had Warner not proposed the idea, the measure would undoubtedly have failed.

Later that year the bill survived a challenge from the Attorney General, who said making KSC part of the university system would require a constitutional amendment. Ultimately, the matter went to the Nebraska Supreme Court, which, on a split vote, upheld the Legislature's right to change Kearney State's status.

It seems fitting somehow that it would be Warner who would shepherd Kearney State into the university system because it was his father who, as a member of the Nebraska Legislature, sponsored the bill in 1903 to create one additional "normal school" at a place that turned out to be Kearney. A normal school was already in place at Peru, and others were established at Wayne in 1910 and Chadron in 1911. The "normal schools"—including what was to become Kearney State College—started out as teachers colleges.

But Warner didn't bring up his family history regarding the Kearney school when he was leading the charge to make the state college part of the university system. He was afraid too many people would have assumed he was making the move for sentimental reasons instead of policy reasons.

"I do think it was the right decision," Warner says of the legislative action. "Kearney didn't really fit very well with the other three state colleges. It was so much bigger and obviously should have a broader role and mission."

Warner thinks part of Roskens' later difficulties with the NU Board of Regents arose from the Kearney situation. Officially, Roskens, then president of the university, took no position on the question and did not promote the bill.

However, if asked, Roskens would tell people he thought that it was good educational policy to make KSC part of the university. That offended some Regents who thought the president was not supposed to have an opinion separate from the board's official stand.

But as Warner indicates, the conflict over the Kearney merger was probably only one factor in Roskens' eventual demise as president of the NU system.

Warner doesn't know for sure what initiated the unrest, but he knows the Regents had an unofficial meeting at one of the Nebraska bowl games in the late 1980s at which some of them expressed unhappiness with Roskens.

"I always thought it was kind of a personality thing," the senator says.

Another contributing factor was an incident that occurred at the public hearing on the university's budget in 1989. The usual procedure was that a Regent would speak first about the budget, followed by the system president and then the chancellors of the various campuses. Members of the Appropriations Committee would ask questions along the way.

That year, Scott Moore, a member of the committee, had some questions for Nancy Hoch, chairman of the Regents. When she looked to Roskens to help provide answers, he was not where she expected him to be.

Later, Hoch alleged that Roskens hadn't backed her, had actually left the proceedings. He may have stepped out of the room for a moment, Warner says, "but I know he had not left the hearing."

Furthermore, Warner doesn't think Roskens should have taken the blame for whatever misunderstanding Hoch had with the Appropriations Committee. "She either didn't know the answer or didn't respond very well" to Moore's questions, Warner says. "It was nobody else's fault."

Yet another factor in Roskens' situation was related to Hoch's charge that the university had ordered a mainframe computer before the purchase had been approved by the Regents or Appropriations Committee. "That, too, was not accurate," Warner says.

He had talked to Roskens about the computer before the session that year. Roskens told him the university had a chance to buy a mainframe at a significantly reduced price because the original purchaser had canceled the order while the equipment was enroute. The distributor asked that the equipment be stored on the campus, pending legislative funding for the purchase, and agreed to take the computer back if funding did not materialize.

"It made sense to me," Warner says. "It was something we knew we were going to be doing anyway."

But it didn't make sense to Hoch. "Somebody led Nancy to believe that Roskens ... had made a commitment for the equipment." Actually, a staff member at the university's Central Administration had agreed to the storage before Roskens even found out the computer was in Lincoln. Furthermore, no commitment had been made.

"It was nothing but a set of circumstances," Warner says, and nothing inappropriate had been done.

But Hoch portrayed the incident in news stories as mismanagement on the part of Roskens and his administration, and it increased the tension between the president and the board.

Once the dealings to bring Kearney State into the system were added to the mix, the situation deteriorated further. That summer, the Regents dismissed Roskens.

Warner believes Roskens would probably have left the university within a few years anyway, but the senator does not approve of the way the president was dismissed.

Warner and a number of other legislators got involved in the matter when reporters asked for their responses to the situation. Most of the senators questioned said they did not approve of the way the Regents went about the dismissal. Furthermore, Warner says, many of the allegations against Roskens "simply were not true."

"Once it became obvious that some of us were highly critical of what the Regents were doing and how they were doing it, that invited more questions."

The Regents handled the matter poorly, Warner believes. Both the way they dismissed Roskens and the way they hired Martin Massengale as the next president had an adverse effect on the university, he says. Massengale, the chancellor at UNL, originally had not been in the running as Roskens' successor. But after the search committee had narrowed its list of candidates to three, the Regents added Massengale's name and, eventually, hired him as president.

A process like that, Warner says, makes the university look bad among academic communities throughout the nation and makes it difficult to attract quality people.

Whatever its role in the Roskens situation, the bill that made Kearney State College part of the NU system was definitely related to another major change in higher education, the establishment of a postsecondary coordinating commission.

The relationship arises out of Senator Ron Withem's bill to which the KSC move was amended. That measure established another study of postsecondary education, 15 years after the Unicameral's own study had resulted in no action.

By the time the Legislature met for its 1990 session, Widmayer and Associates, the consultants hired by the study committee, had made a recommendation.

The proposal would have established a statewide board of regents with six members elected by the public and five appointed by the governor. The board would have submitted a budget for all seven state schools to the Legislature, which would have continued to appropriate funds for the individual campuses and continued to approve or eliminate academic programs on all campuses. Individual boards of regents for each institution would have set specific tuition rates for the respective campuses, but the overall board of regents would have set general tuition policies to guide them.

Warner and Withem introduced the resolution proposing a constitutional amendment to establish the new structure, but it was not immediately popular. "There was a lot of opposition," Warner says, not the least of which was from the University of Nebraska. The senators had to work hard to move the bill through the legislative process.

The bill did get first round approval on March 14, 1990, on a 26-19 vote and advanced to final reading on April 2 on a 25-14 vote. But its fate was still far from certain. At that point, Warner told the Lincoln Journal, "I've reached the conclusion that coordination is like the weather. Everybody talks about it. Nobody does anything. We simply are not going to address the issue."

With the end of the session looming, Warner and Withem knew they didn't have the 30 votes required to place an amendment on the ballot for voter approval. However, an amendment by then-Senator Gerald Conway of Wayne added technical community colleges to the bill and seemed able to attract enough additional votes that the bill might pass after all.

That possibility prompted university officials to do some negotiating. On Saturday, April 7, Warner and Withem met with NU Regents Don Blank and Kermit Hansen to talk about ways to make the proposed constitutional amendment more palatable to everyone involved.

After the meeting, Warner and Withem decided to simplify their plan and eliminate from the proposal the separate boards of trustees for the individual campuses. They wrote a second amendment, this time proposing a Nebraska Coordinating Commission for Postsecondary Education.

The new proposal wasn't exactly a shoo-in, either. Blank, who had been at the meeting that initiated the new plan, told reporters he was confused and not sure what was actually being proposed. An Omaha World-Herald editorial said the new proposal had come up too fast and advised the Legislature not to put either of the amendments on the ballot that year.

A delay, however, was not what Warner and Withem had in mind. They did not want to see the proposal tabled, and they brought it to a vote.

"We had one argument—or one discussion, I should say—on the floor and passed it on the last day" of the session, April 9, 1990.

It was a monumental change, accomplished in record time and under unusual circumstances. "Looking back, I suppose had we had a lot of time to do it, we probably couldn't have got it done."

The voters of Nebraska approved the amendment that fall, and a coordinating commission stronger than anything the state ever had tried before became a reality. Warner told the Omaha World-Herald in August 1991 that the primary responsibility of the commission approved by the voters the previous fall "is going to be to say no. ... We've had all the groups we needed say yes. We don't have the financial resources to have a virtual feast in higher education in Nebraska and retain quality."

Warner had achieved his goal of taking at least some of the politics and short-sightedness out of higher education policy in the state. Creation of the commission meant, he hoped, that those responsible for such policy would have a statewide perspective on higher education's needs.

Creation of the postsecondary commission was vintage Warner strategy, another instance in which the senator led the legislature into concrete action that helped advance his long-term goals.

This particular theme had not yet been completely played out by the mid 1990s. Warner believes it will be at least another decade before Nebraskans will know whether the new arrangement works. Its biggest test will be to withstand political pressure that is bound to come to bear on any controversial decisions.

If the commission assures that decisions about postsecondary education are made for educational instead of political reasons, Warner will be satisfied. It will fit right in with his long-term vision for the good of the state.

Although much of Warner's influence on education in the last decade has been on the years after high school, kindergarten-grade 12 schooling and its financing have also stayed close to his heart.

During the last of his 14 years as chairman of Appropriations, Warner had an opportunity once again to be involved in state aid to schools, the issue he had addressed in the first bill he had introduced in 1963. This time he was not leading the charge, but those who were sought his opinion and influence.

In 1990 the Legislature considered passage of LB 1059, a measure designed to do two things: to provide more state income tax dollars to schools in order to ease the burden on property tax; and to distribute more state aid to the poorer school districts in the state, the places the aid was most needed. Both had also been goals of earlier, Warner-sponsored legislation.

Ron Withem, then chairman of the Legislature's Education Committee, says Warner was not involved in developing LB 1059 but "was the key to its passing." Once the senior senator was convinced that the measure would continue to move state aid to education in the direction he had been advocating, he threw his support behind it.

Perhaps that's why he was courted by the head of ConAgra, the food-processing giant based in Omaha.

Sometime during the 1990 session, Warner remembers, he was invited to have breakfast with Mike Harper, ConAgra CEO, to "talk about 1059." The meeting was to take place at a Duncan Aviation building at the Lincoln airport.

In an aside, Warner explains that he has always called the ConAgra executive "Mr. Harper." Warner says Harper told him on several occasions to call him Mike, but "if I wasn't in the Legislature, I assumed I would be calling him Mr. Harper." So he says, with a bit of sarcasm in his voice, he thought it was more appropriate just to keep on using the formal term.

Warner was there at 7 a.m. the day of the meeting and watched Harper land in his private plane. The two men had an elaborate breakfast in Duncan's meeting room and talked for an hour-and-a-half. Neither was converted to the other's point of view.

"It was a good discussion," Warner remembers. "I didn't change Mr. Harper's mind, and he didn't change mine. In fact, we disagreed. I almost always disagreed with Mr. Harper, but we always seemed to get along pretty well."

The conversation may have been pleasant, but it accomplished little. Warner tried to explain how important it was to the state to have educational financing on solid footing. But Harper wasn't much interested.

"What he knew was that he didn't want any higher sales or income tax because it would adversely affect the stockholders of ConAgra."

That position may have been appropriate for Harper, the senator says, "but it was not a position I could take. We had different stockholders."

On behalf of his stockholders, Warner supported 1059—from the sidelines. He says many people thought the measure would not pass the Legislature. Or that Governor Kay Orr would veto it and the Legislature would not be able to override the veto. Or that it would make it to the November ballot but be voted down.

Instead, the bill survived at every one of those steps: It was approved by the Legislature, which also overrode the governor's veto, and was adopted by the voters in the November election.

PART FIVE
PRACTICING STATESMANSHIP

Leaving Appropriations

During his 14 years as head of the Appropriations Committee, Warner's influence in the Legislature continued to grow. Part of it was structure: As a committee chairman, he was in an ideal position to gain and use power. As chairman of Appropriations, he could exercise influence in all parts of state government.

Part of it was circumstances: The financial crises of the early 1980s opened the door for strong leadership. Nebraskans looked to their Legislature to help them deal with their problems, and the members of the Legislature looked to Warner for the experience and wisdom to lead them through difficult times.

Part of it was commitment: Warner came into the Legislature wanting to serve, wanting to be active, wanting to accomplish things. And he did. By the time he had served as Appropriations Committee chairman for 13 years, he could take credit for dozens of pieces of major legislation.

Eventually, though, he began to feel the need for a change. In 1990, he announced he would not run for re-election to the Appropriations chairmanship in January 1991.

The Appropriations process was wearing him down, Warner says, and—even worse—was becoming too routine. And he thought he was beginning to be part of the controversy surrounding budget negotiations. It was time to move on to something else. A lot of the trick to being effective in the Legislature, Warner says, is "knowing when to hold 'em and knowing when to fold 'em."

Besides losing interest in Appropriations, Warner was gaining interest in the Revenue Committee. "If I wanted to have an impact on what programs could be financed, the clout was there," at Revenue.

The Revenue Committee is widely regarded by Nebraska state senators as second only to Appropriations in power and prestige, and a 1984 change in the way Nebraska sets its tax levies amplified the Revenue Committee's influence. From the time the state had instituted income taxes in 1967 until 1984, Nebraskans' state income taxes had been figured as a percentage of their federal income tax liability. The state income tax levies were set by the State Board of Equalization, which would divide the state's budget by the anticipated yield from sales and income tax and set the tax rates accordingly.

Warner believes the system worked well, but he admits it was hard for the public to understand. People began to think that when their state tax rates went up, it was because the Legislature had somehow voted to raise taxes.

That was not the case. It was just a matter of circumstances. Nebraska's income tax levy always had been a percentage of the federal levy. When the federal levy went down, the state had to increase its percentage just to take in the same amount of money in the following fiscal year.

"It wasn't long before it was in ill repute," Warner says of the system, "and it was going to die."

It did. Now the Legislature sets the rates.

The change came in 1984, as a direct result of the budget crises of 1982 and 1983 and after years of encouragement from Governor Exon and then Governor Thone. The governors thought it was too easy for the Legislature to increase the budget and hide behind the Board of Equalization—of which the governor was a member—when tax rates went up. They believed the Legislature would be more likely to cut the budget if the senators were the ones who had to change the rate.

People forgot the other side of the formula, that rates automatically went down when times were good. Once the responsibility was shifted to the Legislature, "that put an end to that side of the equation." If the state raised more money than it had anticipated, it just "blew the money," Warner says.

The outcome, he believes, is appalling. If government uses windfall money—one-time money—to expand its budget, the entire system will suffer badly the next time the economy turns sour. Programs should not be built on dollars that will not be available on a long-term basis; it just sets the state up for another fiscal crisis.

Warner did not let go of the Board of Equalization's rate-setting authority without a fight. When the Legislature debated the matter in 1983, he proposed what was described as a "hybrid plan" that involved both the Legislature and the Board of Equalization. The Legislature would set base rates during its session, and the Board of Equalization would make changes in the rates during the year if the economic picture changed.

But Warner's proposal failed, and the responsibility for setting tax rates has been back in the Legislature's hands since 1984. The change made Revenue a "ways and means" committee, which was one reason the Revenue Committee looked appealing to Senator Warner.

Furthermore, Warner was beginning to feel he'd stayed long enough at Appropriations. Too many people had begun to believe that he dominated the committee's processes.

With the possibilities of the Revenue Committee pulling him and the baggage he'd accumulated at Appropriations pushing, Warner made the decision to move.

He had almost made the move in 1988, when Vard Johnson, then Revenue Committee chairman, announced on the floor that he would retire from the Legislature. Warner remembers that he had just walked downstairs to his office when a reporter asked him if he were going to run for Revenue. Annoyed that he was being pushed to make an immediate response, Warner said no.

Although that comment was made on the spur of the moment, Warner tends to take seriously any commitment he makes. "If I'd had a couple of days to think about it, I might have done it," Warner says.

Beside that, the 1988 session was full of activity, Warner says, full of issues he was interested and involved in. He didn't really have time to give a lot of thought to the possibility of a different leadership position. And his off-hand decision was thoroughly reinforced when Senator Tim Hall of Omaha decided he wanted to run for the vacant position.

Warner refused to run against Hall. Although he occasionally disagreed with Hall's political philosophy, Warner thought Hall was easy to work with and could see no good reason to try to keep Hall from the Revenue chairmanship.

Warner's 1990 announcement that he would depart from Appropriations was greeted with regret in the press. The Lincoln Star editorialized that Warner's power as Appropriations chairman had come "as much from his reputation for fairness and integrity as from his careful attention to detail or his personal knowledge.

"Warner is a senator whose sincere desire to build a good life for

Nebraskans through a reasonable and responsive government is greater than any ambition for power or position.

"This sense of purpose will continue as he moves on to another chairmanship or to the quieter life of a regular senator."

There was to be no quieter life in 1991.

Warner had talked off and on for several months about how he was interested in being chairman of Revenue, but his decision not to challenge Hall laid that idea to rest. Instead, Warner announced in December of 1990 that he would challenge Senator Bernice Labedz of Omaha, chairwoman of the Legislature's Executive Board.

Warner told Henry Cordes of the World-Herald that his decision had nothing to do with whether it would be easier to oust Labedz than to defeat Hall. "I may have just as much difficulty with this," Warner said about his decision to challenge Labedz. He added that he had not polled his fellow senators to see whether he could have won in a race against Hall.

Labedz told reporters she was disappointed that Warner had waited until December before announcing his plans, and Warner said he understood her unhappiness. He also emphasized that he was running "for" the Executive Board, not "against" Labedz. However, it was the only time that he ran for a legislative leadership post against an incumbent.

The contest between Warner and Labedz got plenty of press and generated plenty of speculation among legislators and the public. On Jan. 9, 1991, though, Warner was elected to lead the Executive Board. He also was named a member of the Revenue Committee.

Two years later, he was elected its chairman, and Hall became chairman of the Exec Board. In essence, "Tim and I exchanged positions," Warner says. By that time Hall was ready to leave Revenue, and Warner was still interested in leading the committee.

"We had a brief conversation about it one day, and that was all there was to it." The two principal actors had agreed on a course of action, and no one seriously questioned their decision. The senators' legislative colleagues approved the switch, and Warner became chairman of the Revenue Committee.

With a break of only two years at the Executive Board, Warner moved from one side of the state's ledger to the other. After 14 years at the helm of the committee that plotted the course for the state's spending, Warner moved to the committee that must raise the money to be spent.

The Appropriations and Revenue committees are closely related; Revenue always has an impact on what Appropriations can do.

The two committees work fairly closely, and Warner's experience at Appropriations makes the process easier. "In some respects, when I see what they're doing (the Appropriations Committee), I know what we've got to do. It's because I was there so long myself. Most things are highly predictable."

When he first took over at Revenue, Warner says, and Scott Moore was chairman of Appropriations, they scheduled Revenue bills to be dealt with on the floor in the morning and Appropriations bills in the afternoon. "We had everything moving across at the same time, and we knew between us what had to pass or what had to be taken out to keep things balanced."

That system the senators devised remains in place and is likely to be standard procedure from now on, Warner says. It makes it easier for all the legislators to see the relationship between spending and income. "It keeps everything together, and that helps a lot."

When he moved from Appropriations to Revenue, some of Warner's strategies remained remarkably similar. For instance, during his years on Appropriations, Warner would introduce a bill to abolish a program when he really just intended to review it. Of course, any threat of abolition met with outcries of opposition, and the committee got a lot of help examining various programs to be sure they were functioning as intended.

In Revenue, Warner automatically introduces a "shell bill" each year to change sales and income tax rates. It's a plan-ahead scheme made necessary by the fact that the Legislature, not the Board of Equalization, must set tax rates. "In the event that you need a vehicle (to raise tax rates)—and you never know till the end—we put the bill in."

But that's only part of Warner's strategy. He also plans ahead so that the Legislature can be prepared to accommodate the results of political maneuvering. Warner knows that, at every session, senators are likely to introduce bills to broaden the sales tax base in return for specific property tax exemptions. Warner tries to stay ahead of that game by introducing bills that aren't tied to any specific program. That way, if the Legislature needs more revenue for something approved during the session, a vehicle is available to raise the revenue.

Warner always explains that he has introduced the bills simply as contingency measures, but other senators or interest groups often oppose them anyway. And that's OK with him. Should the bills actually be adopted by the entire Legislature, it's good to have had a hearing at which opposition was voiced. The same kind of thing occurred when he introduced appropriations measures on a just-in-case basis. It is another similarity between the two committees.

On the other hand, Warner's move from Appropriations to Revenue required a shift in perspective. At Appropriations, a senator could profess to be in favor of a program but lament that he could not vote for it because the money was simply not available. Or he could be against a bill for the same reason.

Things are different at Revenue. When he led the Appropriations Committee, Warner could tell a program's supporters the state would not be able to fund a program without raising taxes, and people would take that to mean he was against raising taxes. If he says the same thing at Revenue, people think he is in favor of raising taxes.

The change in perceptions surprised Warner at first, but he admits it's logical.

Despite the general public's aversion to increasing taxes, Warner has never been adamantly opposed to doing so. If the Legislature votes for a new or expanded program, it should also vote to raise the revenue to fund it, he believes.

"There's nothing that annoys me more ... than people who vote yes on appropriations and no on the revenue to do it." And it does happen.

Warner himself has tried to maintain consistency when it comes to finding adequate revenue to support approved spending, but he has never developed a reputation as a senator who is always in favor of cutting the budget rather than increasing taxes. He has led plenty of fights to increase spending and plenty of fights to cut it.

"I've got more scars from cuts than I do from spending."

While it has become customary for legislators at all levels of government to oppose increased spending and higher taxes almost automatically, Warner's decisions depend on the purpose the money is to serve. For example, he has seldom favored increasing state aid to governmental subdivisions—except for schools, of course. He has consistently favored increased aid for K-12 education.

In 1993, Warner's dedication to improving the quality of schools by equalizing the funds available to them led him to take another position opposite his usual inclination. He asserts that he is opposed to ear-marking funds for specific purposes because that reduces the Legislature's options. Yet he introduced a bill that year to ear-mark a third of the state's annual budget for local educational purposes. He said the proposal was way to provide relative income stability for Nebraska's schools.

The proposal—which was not adopted—flies in the face of most of Warner's record on state spending, but it does parallel the plan he pushed to fund Nebraska's roads, the variable gasoline tax. While he defends that plan as "dedicating" funds rather than "ear-marking," he admits the distinction is probably artificial. But the fact that, for both roads and education, he's willing to surrender the Legislature's control over spending underlines his commitment to those two public policy responsibilities.

In nearly every other case, though, Warner believes the state should fund its programs and local governments should fund theirs. Even when the trend has been to return dollars to local subdivisions, Warner has insisted on protecting the base for the state.

He has also tried to protect the state's financial base when the Legislature has tried to hand out tax incentives to lure businesses to locate or expand in Nebraska. He opposed the three bills—LB 773, 774 and 775—the Legislature passed in 1987 to do exactly that.

"I dislike tax incentives with a passion," Warner says, because what they give away to businesses and corporations must be made up by the rest of the taxpayers. He believes the best tax system is one with a broad base and a low rate. "That's healthy for everybody."

Always one to see both sides of an argument, though, he realizes the state may not be competitive in attracting business if it fails to offer incentives. However, he's afraid that once the incentives start to trickle out, they may become a torrent impossible to stanch.

After the Legislature approved the 1987 legislation, Warner was quoted in the next day's Lincoln Journal: "If tax breaks were fast food, there'd be golden arches over this chamber."

Loran Schmit, another opponent of the 1987 legislation, says Warner opposed the measures and spoke against them. And yet, Schmit says, "he would not go for the jugular."

Ultimately, Schmit says, Warner ended up voting for LB 773. Schmit asked him why.

"Because 775 is going to pass, and we're going to need the money." LB 773 raised taxes on individual taxpayers to make up for what would be lost thanks to LB 775's exemptions for corporations, exactly the kind of shift Warner dislikes.

Yet, Warner is a practical man. As chairman of Appropriations, he was aware what the loss of revenue offered by LB 775 would do to the state's budget. So he voted for the tax increase that would help keep state government solvent.

He didn't change his philosophical opposition to tax give-aways, though. In 1995, Warner found himself involved in helping to put together a tax package to try to lure Micron, a manufacturer of computer chips, to Nebraska. Before long, he realized he was "helping to put through a public policy I did not believe in," so he backed out of the effort.

"I slept good that night."

While Warner may consistently fight efforts to give one sector of the economy a tax break at the expense of others, he has voted to increase taxes when he sees the Legislature voting to expand programs, even some he opposes, if he thinks existing programs will suffer by having revenue siphoned off for new undertakings.

He can be blunt about the tax situation even where he knows his message will be unpopular. He told the Lincoln Chamber of Commerce in May 1989 that the state would need a tax increase in the 1990 session. But he predicted that, in an election year, many candidates would be promising not to raise taxes. The only alternative would be cuts in state services, the senator told the Chamber members.

That attitude is the exact opposite of the "no new taxes" mantra that has become commonplace among politicians.

Not that the mantra is all that new. Warner has good evidence that politicians have been railing against taxes for decades.

Early in 1995, one of Warner's neighbors sent him something he had found among the belongings of an elderly relative who had died. It was a brochure from Charles Warner's campaign for governor in 1938.

The brochure promoted more efficient government, vowed not to increase taxes, promised better roads—the same kinds of promises Nebraska politicians campaign on today.

"It is ironic, though," Warner says. "Anyone who says he will increase taxes is off the horse before he gets out of the chute."

The major overhaul of taxes that the state undertook in the 1960s might be an exception, but at that time many citizens bought the government's pitch that it was broadening the tax base in order to provide alternative sources of revenue, not to increase spending.

"You wouldn't get by with that argument nowadays," Warner says.

During the 1996 session, he and the Legislature put the matter to the test, passing a set of bills to restructure the state's tax system—and some other parts of state government, too. The Legislature was prompted to take on the project by threats of constitutional amendments from other fronts. Those amendments had been prompted largely by discontent with the state's continued heavy reliance on property taxes to fund education and local government.

When asked, Warner can and does summarize the history of property tax discontent in Nebraska. He cites the percentage of personal income that went to property taxes in 1968 as compared to 1995, the amount that goes to support schools and a handful of other figures.

"I remember numbers better than I do words," he says.

Most of the facts he uses to make his case pertain to legislation that has been proposed or adopted during his tenure in the Unicameral. His extensive experience and institutional memory help him prepare for what he thinks will happen next.

Knowing that several groups were planning to place constitutional amendments to limit or even eliminate property taxes on the 1996 ballot, Warner nudged his legislative colleagues into developing their own plan. During the 1995 session, the Legislature proposed its own tax restructuring amendment. Public hearings on the proposal began that fall.

Lee Rupp says the plan Warner and his colleagues developed could have saved the state a lot of agony.

"He's the one person who could get us out of this alive," Rupp says. The carefully structured plan developed by Warner and the Legislature could prevent the other groups from "throwing out the baby with the bathwater."

The Legislature's plan was designed to go far beyond simply changing the tax structure. Warner also hoped a constitutional amendment would allow for restructuring of local and state government. And he wanted to find a way to combine the tax levying authority of a variety of small subdivisions such as cemetery districts and fire protection districts under the county board. That would allow a dozen or so tax requests to be dealt with in a single public hearing.

The committee wanted a plan that would not mandate a reduction in the number of counties but would provide incentives for more cooperation among counties and cities—especially between Douglas County and the City of Omaha—in such things as prosecution and defense of criminal cases. It's in urban areas that the biggest savings would be possible, Warner points out.

And, of course, the legislative portion of the plan was also to deal with taxes and valuations. But the senator believes simple tax shifts that don't also include changes in the structure and delivery of services would not be enough to satisfy the citizens.

"Perception is more real than fact when it comes to public policy," the senator says.

He knew the plan would not be an easy sell, and he was right. On Nov. 5, 1996, the voters of Nebraska declined to approve the constitutional amendment that would have put the Legislature's plan into place.

"Somebody will be opposed to everything you do," Warner says. "We have to find a balance so that there's a little bit you don't like but a whole lot that seems reasonable."

It reminds him a bit of how it felt to be on Appropriations. "It wasn't bad as long as you understood that whatever you did was wrong," he says with sarcasm coloring his voice. "The total was always too much, and the individual parts were always too little.

"This tax issue is the about the same caliber. Nobody likes what we have. The only thing they like less is to change to something else."

Despite the voters' rejection of the constitutional amendment, the 1996 Legislature was surprisingly united in passing the bills proposed by Warner's Revenue Committee. Warner says that means a lot of senators believed the Legislature needed to take the lead on tax matters.

The state's special interests, on the other hand, were unable to unite to fight any particular part of the plan as it made its way through the legislative process. The extent of disagreement among the various lobbying interests made them less effective than they might otherwise have been, Warner says.

Perhaps another factor in getting the legislation passed was the fact that every member of the Revenue Committee also happened, in 1996, to be the chairman of another standing committee. The members were chairs of the Banking, Transportation, Urban Affairs, Rules, General Affairs and Retirement committees and the chairman of the Executive Board. Since committee chairmen provide much of the leadership for the Unicameral, the make-up of the Revenue Committee meant that the plan devised there would get an extra boost of support from many legislative leaders.

Warner is pleased with the success of the legislation, believing it makes good changes in the law, changes that will allow institutions and people to improve their own efficiency and their cooperation with each other.

In many quarters, Warner gets primary credit for the plan—and for Nebraska's tax policy in general. John Jordison, head of the privately-funded Nebraska Tax Research Council, Inc., says, "Nebraska's tax policy is whatever Jerry Warner wants it to be. Here's a guy who's been doing it for 34 years."[9]

Warner says Jordison's assertion is an overstatement. But there's no question one of the major reasons the veteran senator decided to run for re-election again in 1996 was to continue to clean up the details of the tax policy crafted earlier that year. Warner gets more satisfaction from that kind of long-term planning for the state than he does from short-term legislative victories, the prestige of leadership or the admiration of his constituents.

Warner came into the Legislature with an eye to the future, and it didn't take long before he had developed a reputation for thinking and planning for the long term. From the beginning of his legislative career, his primary goal has been to help establish programs and procedures that will serve the state well for decades to come. He also wants to be sure that the Legislature's actions accomplish what they are supposed to accomplish.

"He looks long term and peripherally," Lee Rupp says. "He sees the unintended consequences."

And he loves the challenge of trying to anticipate those consequences. The potential tax crisis was one reason Warner wanted to move from Appropriations to Revenue. "I saw it coming," he says. "I knew it was going to be the intriguing issue."

During the fall of 1995, as hearings about the new plan were getting under way, Warner went to meetings not with volumes of information and documentation but with the tax plan on a single sheet of paper in his pocket. Traveling light is nothing new for the senator.

His pockets are his portable office, Warner says. He admits he regu-

---

[9]Omaha World Herald, July 21, 1996

larly carries envelopes or single sheets of paper on which complex matters are summarized. "If I really think it's important, it's in my pocket," he says.

In fact, he adds, when he buys clothes, he takes papers along with him to be sure the coat will fit with its pockets full.

Carrying the tax plan in his pocket makes the matter sound simple. Looking at how many people and groups were part of the process makes it sound hard.

Eight different legislative committees were involved with various parts of the subject matter to be considered, and an overall steering committee included the chairmen of each of those committees plus the speaker and chairman of the Executive Committee.

The size of the group of legislators—and the number of individuals and groups outside the Legislature who had a stake in the outcome—required some careful handling.

"This orchestra is getting very big, and it's awfully hard to keep everybody on the same song sheet," Warner said during the 1996 planning stages.

Warner himself conducted the orchestra. He instigated the planning and served as the unofficial chairman because he was acceptable to the various factions involved. Like any other group of people, the Legislature includes some folks whose chemistry doesn't mix, Warner says. In the midst of that volatile situation, he is often chosen to lead the competing interests to a satisfactory conclusion.

The reason may be that Warner has a reputation for being fair, for trying to be sure all sides of an issue are represented at the debate, that all interested parties have their say, that no one is shut out of the process.

Besides that, Warner says, "I'm highly predictable." People know he won't flit from one side of an issue to the other.

That doesn't mean, though, that he never changes his mind. He believes he can be wrong on an issue, and he can eventually be persuaded to take a different stand—even on a major policy issue. He says he gradually comes to see things differently and, finally, has to start voting differently.

"My old biases finally just won't withstand the facts anymore."

Any politician who changes his mind leaves himself open to charges of vacillation, of blowing with the prevailing winds of public opinion. Warner tries to avoid that by being sure that changes in his policy positions don't conflict with his underlying principles. It's not an easy balancing act. Sometimes, the senator says, he doesn't like the results of living up to his principles.

Citizens will sometimes tell Warner they disagreed with his vote on a particular matter. "My usual response is 'You ought to be in my shoes. I don't agree with my vote all the time, either—and I'm pushing the button." Warner's commitment to legislative integrity may require that he vote a certain way even when, as an individual, he may not agree with that position at all.

Sometimes, in fact, the way Warner the state senator felt bound to vote has actually been costly to Warner the individual. One such incident occurred in 1984 when the Legislature voted in special session to place an amendment on the November ballot to give tax preferences to owners of farm land. Thanks to an increase in land valuations, taxes on agricultural land were going to rise severely if the amendment were not adopted.

Warner was one of only 16 senators to vote against the measure. Representing a largely rural district and being a farmer himself, Warner stood to lose if the amendment failed. However, he continued to believe that, with rare exception, all property should be valued on the same basis and said the amendment would advance improper and dangerous tax policy.

"Once again, principle was the highest determinant for the veteran state legislator," the World-Herald said in a Sept. 2 editorial. The amendment passed, amidst considerable controversy.

Confrontation and argument over tax matters is an ongoing part of legislative life, of course. However, Warner often finds a way to keep the mood from getting too gloomy.

In 1995, when senators were examining the Revenue Committee's handout on the major tax restructuring proposal, Senator Carol Pirsch asked Warner how the panel had arrived at its figures that projected tax reductions.

"Arbitrary," Warner deadpanned, getting off what he called a good one-liner.[10]

Regardless of how much of a struggle the current state government

---

[10]Lincoln Star, April 14, 1995

overhaul may be, Warner finds real satisfaction in the process. He likes dealing with difficult, complex and controversial issues.

"That's why I ran for the Legislature," he says.

Warner revels in the complexity of issues because he believes problems can be solved only by admitting that quick and easy fixes don't usually fix much of anything. He told a meeting of the Southwest County Officials Association in McCook in 1979 that government should avoid the temptation to oversimplify:

"There is an old saying that every complex problem has solutions that are simple, easy—and wrong." Everyone is better served by admitting that problems are complex and solutions are not simple.

Dave Landis, a state senator since 1977, calls Warner "one of the few strategic thinkers in the Legislature." Landis defines strategic thinkers as those who examine current problems with an eye firmly fixed on future ramifications. Effective strategy in the Legislature also requires knowing whether something can be done and having the patience and determination to change conditions and opinions to allow it to happen. Warner is a master at that kind of strategic planning, Landis says.

The 1995-96 restructuring effort is an example of that kind of planning. And many of its goals can still be accomplished, Warner believes, even though the necessary amendment failed at the polls. The Unicameral will do what it can by means of legislation and then "come back with another amendment," he said a week after the November election. That next proposal will probably be on the 1998 ballot.

Having built a successful career, Warner can take the lead on complex issues like the tax restructuring out of sheer interest and desire to serve. "What subject of interest is not available to Jerome Warner if he wants it?" asks Kermit Brashear, elected to the Unicameral in 1984.

And, in fact, Warner has had an opportunity in the last few years to take on a wider variety of topics once again. Because of the intense work load at Appropriations and the focus on the specifics of the state's budget, he had backed way from involvement in other parts of government.

Before he became chairman of Appropriations, he says, "I used to have amendments galore in my desk for about everything." If the appropriate situation arose, he would pull out an amendment and introduce it. While he served on Appropriations, though, he simply didn't have time to create potential future amendments.

At Revenue the issues may be equally complex, but the concentrated hours of budget hearings and planning are absent, and Warner has been able to turn his attention back to the variety of issues that really interest him. Senator Doug Kristensen, who sits next to Warner on the floor, says Warner's drawer is once again full of amendments.

It is likely to remain so for another term. Warner garnered about 75 percent of the votes against his one opponent in the May primary election; results in the general election were nearly identical. On Nov. 5, 1996, Jerome Warner won his 10th election to the Nebraska Legislature.

Term Limits

Running for re-election in 1996 almost became a moot point for Warner because of a term limits initiative approved by the Nebraska voters in 1994. The measure amended the Nebraska Constitution to allow state senators to serve no more than two four-year terms in office.

Contrary to what many people thought, the term limits amendment would have taken effect immediately; no "grandfather clause" would have allowed senators who had already served at least two terms to run again. Warner and a number of other senators would have been gone at the end of 1996.

However, the Nebraska Supreme Court subsequently ruled the term limits amendment unconstitutional, and no limits are currently in effect. The matter is far from settled, though. Term limits proponents took a slightly different approach in a successful measure on the 1996 ballot, but they haven't given up the fight.

Personally, Warner takes a philosophical attitude toward term limits. Even when he thought he might be prevented for running for another term, he was not personally alarmed. The thought of returning to private life after 34 years of public service had its appeal, he says.

"My attitude is the worst you can do to me is make me stay home and make money—or at least not lose as much, and that's OK with me."

On principle, though, Warner is opposed to term limits. He believes they are a big put-down to the citizens. Term limit laws are based on the assumption that the voters aren't bright enough to make the right decisions at the polls.

One of the most drastic results of limiting legislators to two terms would be the impact on institutional memory. If none of the senators could serve more than eight years, the only people with long-term experience would be the staff and the lobbyists. The people's elected representatives, the folks most likely to be responsive to the wishes of the citizens, would not be allowed to stay long enough to develop real institutional memory.

Warner admits that simple staying power does not equal quality in a legislative official. He says he can think of senators in the past who stayed a long time but contributed very little.

But rapid turnover does not necessarily guarantee quality, either, and turnover is plenty rapid without legal limits on terms.

During the decades Warner has served in the Unicameral, about half the body—or more—has served four years or fewer. The Lincoln Journal reported in November 1994 that almost half of the senators then in office had served fewer than four years; 75 percent had served fewer than eight.

If senators were limited to two terms, everyone in the Legislature would be either a freshman, serving a first term, or a lame duck, serving a second and last term. "Neither one is desirable. It takes at least four years to get oriented if you're really going to be active," Warner believes.

Newly-elected legislators see the system only as it is when they enter it and have little understanding of how the present situation developed. They have no historic viewpoint, no familiarity with the gradual changes that may have taken place over a 10- or 20-year period.

"Part of the benefit of being here a long time is seeing similar situations," Warner says. "You recall a process that was used, and sometimes what you recall is that it didn't work. So you don't try that again."

Experience also helps legislators plan for the future, Warner says. Those making laws must think as far ahead as they can, must try to foresee consequences of the potential legislation. That kind of foresight can be difficult for inexperienced people.

"While I'm getting educated, the public pays the tuition for my education," Warner says. "It can be fairly expensive."

Warner's years of experience have saved the people of Nebraska a bundle on that kind of tuition. The senator has been deeply involved for so long that he remembers when issues arose in previous decades and how they were dealt with then—or why they weren't dealt with. Most of the issues before the Legislature today are simply new versions of the same things the senators dealt with in the 1960s: tax policy, education policy, roads, public employees, public works.

Dave Maurstad, a senator elected in 1994, says, "The only things recycled more than aluminum are legislative issues." Maurstad says he appreciates Warner's wealth of institutional knowledge that can give the more junior senators a lot of background about recycled issues.

But, despite his longevity, Warner has not become entrenched or stagnant and unwilling to change.

"He doesn't close his mind," Vard Johnson says. After 34 years in office, Warner is not likely to find any issue brand new. But Johnson admires Warner's willingness to reexamine issues in the light of current circumstances.

So does Scott Moore. "He's not opposed to new ideas," Moore says. "A lot of people won't let you get to the future." But that's not true of Warner.

Warner seems to have found a middle ground between clinging obstinately to the past and rushing willy-nilly into the future. By doing so, he has brought stability to the legislative process.

Ben Nelson, governor since 1990, points particularly to the stability Warner has brought to the state's appropriations process by his insistence on a professional approach to budgeting.

Nebraska editorial writers have praised Warner for the same achievements. An editorial in the Dec. 18, 1990, Lincoln Star said Warner, who was leaving Appropriations after 14 years, had designed a budget process "that blends thoughtful review of spending with a careful consideration of future needs" and "provides the key to planned, orderly spending."

A Lincoln Journal editorial endorsing Warner for re-election in 1992 said the senator should be respected for more than just his longevity in office. In addition to his institutional memory, the editorial said, Warner also has a masterful grasp of fiscal affairs and the relationships between various state programs.

The Omaha World-Herald endorsed Warner's 10th bid for the Unicameral: "Every institution, be it a school, family, parish or legislative body, needs continuity. It needs keepers of the institution's memory who can be counted on to provide perspective in crunch times. Warner is such a person for the Legislature."[11]

Loran Schmit says, "He has that history. It's just there. It's like a computer. He understands how the pieces fall into place."

[11]Omaha World-Herald, Oct. 27, 1996

Maurstad compares Warner to major league baseball player Cal Ripken, who set a record in 1995 for consecutive number of games played during his career. Warner is the Cal Ripken of the Legislature, Maurstad says. "He has served so long, we know we can count on him as a teammate, a captain, a mentor—someone to look to who won't steer you in the wrong direction."

Warner has been described as a living argument against term limits.[12]

Jack Rodgers says, "Some people probably shouldn't serve five minutes in the Legislature." But Warner has come back term after term out of a desire to serve. "Supposedly that's what a citizen legislator should be."

Warner's respected standing in the Legislature was confirmed by a 1994 skirmish involving Senator Kate Witek of Omaha. Warner had announced he planned to seek re-election to the Revenue Committee chairmanship at the beginning of the 1995 session, and Witek wrote to him, asking him to drop out of the race. Her plan was to open the Revenue chairmanship for another senator and uncomplicate the anticipated battle for chairmanship of Appropriations.

"You do not need this position for your ego or your political career," Witek wrote, implying that Warner had already had plenty of opportunity to enhance both.

Warner politely declined to do as Witek asked, and he was re-elected to the Revenue position without much contest in January 1995. With tax restructuring looming on the horizon, many senators apparently wanted Warner to stay where he was, ready to lead the state through the labyrinth that was sure to come.

Commenting on Witek's request, Speaker Ron Withem told the Lincoln Journal, "She is correct that Jerry Warner doesn't need another chairmanship, but the body needs Jerry Warner."

Even a term limits proponent like Charlie Thone says Warner is a shining exception to the kind of politician the measure is designed to get rid of. "Jerry Warner, I suppose, comes as close as any person who has had such tenure—34 years—who has not become arrogant," Thone says. "You couldn't accuse him of that. It's not his personality or style. And that's why he's remained as popular and effective as he has."

Warner did not think, in 1962, that he'd serve the next 34 years in the

---

[12]Lincoln Journal, Nov. 2, 1994

Legislature. He just figured he would "run until I got beat." That phenomenon has yet to happen. In fact, at most elections, it hasn't even been a serious possibility. Warner has seldom had to do more than minimal campaigning to keep his legislative seat.

But his 1992 opponent came closer to beating him than anyone else had—and closer than most people expected. It may even have startled Warner himself.

Mary Wickenkamp, a Lincoln attorney, had filed for election to the Unicameral, believing she would oppose incumbent LaVon Crosby. However, district lines had been redrawn following the 1990 census, and Wickenkamp ended up running against Warner.

"She got more votes than people thought she would get because people thought that Senator Warner was an institution," Vard Johnson says. "Of course, Senator Warner didn't want to lose his seat. ... So he was galvanized into some action."

That year Warner did hire people to help with his campaign. He expected a closer race than usual because he never ran as well in a newly-drawn district. He says he thinks citizens "tend to resent it when they're moved to a new district. If there's an incumbent involved, they feel he's being imposed on them." Furthermore, his wife, Betty, was very ill in 1992, and he himself was too distracted to be able to run a campaign alone.

For all those reasons, Warner and his supporters campaigned more that year than in many a previous election season, accepting contributions and spending between $27,000 and $28,000.

Wickenkamp got 42 percent of the vote, not enough to defeat the incumbent but enough to come closer than anyone had since Warner was elected the first time in 1962.

Warner does not like having to raise money, put up yard signs and attend campaign functions. But Vard Johnson says that reticence could also separate Warner somewhat from his constituents.

Although Warner has always attended candidate forums during campaigns, Johnson says Warner has not had to spend time "teaching and preaching" to his constituents and so has also missed out on the opportunity to find out how the constituents think and feel. That may make it difficult for a senator to sense the "hopes and fears in the people the legislator is serving," Johnson says.

Charlie Thone, former governor, agrees. "He's been involved with the Unicameral for so long, he might not be totally objective anymore from the citizen point of view," Thone says. "He's so enmeshed in it, he might not see a fresh, different viewpoint an ordinary citizen might see."

If Warner has begun to lose touch with his constituents, it has not been reflected at the polls. He took 59 percent of the vote when he was elected in 1962. Since then, he has averaged 67 percent, excluding the 1988 election in which he ran unopposed.

Art Althouse, who has known Warner since they were in high school together, says, "People in this community feel he's represented us very well." Althouse farms near the Warner place and, now, rents crop ground from the Warners.

"He's in the same kind of business the rest of us are in this community," Althouse says, which helps keep Warner in touch with his constituents. Although Warner is concerned with issues all over the state, he is also aware of and knowledgeable about the issues his own constituents care about, Althouse says.

Peggy Brown, a Waverly native, is business manager at the Waverly News. She says although she is a Democrat and Warner a Republican, she agrees with the philosophy she learned from her father: "As long as Jerry is there, there's nothing to worry about."

"I know he cares about the people," Brown says, and she's willing to trust him to do what's right. "If Jerry says that's the way it's going to be, then that's the way it's going to be."

Brown tells how Warner, like his father before him, is never too busy to stop and talk with a constituent. She remembers driving past the Warner farm one summer when the senator was moving a center pivot irrigation system. Someone had driven out and parked alongside the field, and Warner had gotten off the tractor and was talking to the visitor. "You *know* they weren't talking about the crops," Brown says with a laugh.

Warner's son Jamie tells a similar story from the days when he was still at home, helping his dad with farm work. A young man came out to the field to talk to Warner about putting a warning light at a rural intersection where the man's brother had recently been killed in a collision. Despite the time it took away from his farming, "Dad talked to him 45 minutes to an hour," Jamie says. "He did that kind of thing all the time. He always tried to help people."

Art Althouse confirms that notion. As farm neighbors often do, the Althouses and Warners have helped each other with farm work over the years. Althouse remembers many occasions when he would be helping the Warners work with their cattle and the senator would get a phone call and disappear to take care of the business at hand.

All the Warners have been known for putting their own interests behind those of the people they represent, Althouse says. "There could be farm work that needed to be done, but if something else needed attention, the farm work probably suffered." Or, at least, more of it was done by hired help than would otherwise have been necessary.

Althouse says that fact has made it expensive for Warner to serve in the Legislature, but it's a price the senator has not complained about. "He's taken on this job and is dedicated to it."

Betty Schlaphoff of Waverly, Warner's high school science teacher, thinks the senator has been very responsive to his constituents. "We've called on him automatically," she says. "He's been very good to Waverly" in terms of helping the community work with state government."

For instance, in the mid-1970s, Waverly wanted a rescue squad for the area. The city declined to get involved, so the matter was handed to the rural fire district. Brown, whose father was president of the district, says the board wasn't sure how to finance a rescue squad without "blowing taxes out of the water."

Brown's father called Warner, who "took the ball, and within months Waverly had a rescue squad."

Schlaphoff says it was thanks to Warner's knowledge of the system. The community was able to use all the state contacts and help available and get the job done.

Actually, both women say it was not only the senator but also his wife, Betty, who helped with the project. Betty understood the system, too, and was able to help the community get in touch with people and programs they needed to meet their goal.

The same kind of thing happened when Waverly tried to establish a nursing home in the community in the late 1980s. Again, the community turned to Warner for advice, and the project became a reality.

"If we have a problem here in Waverly ... a call to Jerry Warner pays off," Brown says. People remember those kinds of things.

Warner has done so well by his district that he has seldom had serious opposition for re-election. It's difficult to find an issue to use against Warner in a campaign, Althouse says. "They have very little to get a hold of."

Warner himself says he is fortunate to represent the kind of legislative district he does. "No single economic interest is dominant in my district. I've got agricultural, urban, affluent, low-income, small towns, labor, management—it's the kind of district that lets you be a state legislator. You don't have to vote with a narrow constituent viewpoint."

It is important to Warner that he be a state senator, responsible not just to his district but to all the people of Nebraska. That feeling of responsibility, that sense of duty, has come at personal cost.

In fact, Dave Landis, a current state senator, remembers asking Warner one summer what he was raising on his farm.

"Debt," was the answer.

While many who know him point out that the Warner family is financially well off, the time the senator has devoted to his legislative duties has undoubtedly kept him from being as successful on the farm as he might otherwise have been.

One year in the early 1970s, Warner says he lost 300 acres of milo because he never had time to get out and harvest the crop. A state aid to education bill, which he had sponsored, was under attack from opponents seeking to put its repeal on the November ballot. "I felt obligated to go out and defend it across the state," he says.

He planned carefully, accepting speaking obligations so that he could be gone a week, then home a week to do some harvesting.

"As it turned out, the only nice weather we had was the weeks I was gone, and the weeks I was home it would be muddy or raining. Then the first part of November we had a big snow storm and everything went flat. ...

"It was a fairly significant loss—and besides that the state aid bill was overturned at the election," so he had nothing to show for the time spent and the crop lost.

Long-term service in state government is costly. Warner estimates his career in the Legislature has cost him $30-50,000 a year. "I can pretty well document it."

His $12,000 a year legislative salary is a drop in the bucket compared to the income he's lost and the expenses he's incurred from having to hire extra help for the farm.

"But I volunteered, so I don't complain."

Despite the low pay and the difficulties of juggling legislative duties with another job, Warner does not favor higher salaries for legislators.

"Since I've been here 34 years, I suppose I'm a professional politician, but I still view myself as a citizen legislator. I'm opposed to offering a salary that will attract people to the Legislature. If they need the income, they're more likely to succumb to something inappropriate" to stay in office.

That means, of course, that service in the Unicameral is most attractive to people who are at or near retirement or who have further political plans or are in business for themselves and want to earn some publicity and name-recognition, Warner admits. But even those people often have trouble making a living while serving in the Legislature.

However, the well-known Warner humor applies to this dilemma, too. Ron Withem, speaker of the Unicameral, says Warner has told him he keeps returning to the Legislature because "it beats feeding cattle in January."

More seriously, Warner simply says of his legislative career, "I like it." He likes the process, the intricacy, the opportunity to influence the state's future. Despite the financial loss, he has kept coming back for more. And the voters of his district have said the equivalent of "Amen" to his decisions to run again, re-electing him by comfortable margins.

The only significant exceptions to that rule may be in the years after those pesky reapportionments made necessary by each census count of Nebraska's population.

The reorganization that made the Nebraska Legislature a one-house nonpartisan body in 1937 included a thorough redistricting. The mandate for equal apportionment was actually included in the amendment that established the Unicameral. So the last bicameral session, in 1935, drew the boundaries for the new districts in accord with the amendment's mandate. The resulting one-person-one-vote districts put Nebraska well ahead of many other states at the time.

However, the situation didn't last. Somehow, between the 1935 reapportionment and the time Warner was elected in 1962, the state had fallen off the one-person-one-vote wagon. Nebraska had not once redrawn its legislative district lines despite population shifts that made the districts increasingly disproportionate. Politically, the Nebraska state senators just could not bring themselves to reapportion. The same thing was true throughout the nation, and the states' intransigence eventually drove the issue to the federal level.

A 1962 U.S. Supreme Court decision, Baker v. Carr, ordered every state to return to drawing its legislative districts on the basis of equal population. The process had just begun in Nebraska when Warner came to the Legislature.

His district that year had the third largest population in the state, the senator recalls, but he had no desire to hold onto that lopsided advantage. He always favored one-person-one-vote apportionment.

The Nebraska Legislature had made a move in that direction by placing a constitutional amendment on the November 1962 ballot to apportion by means of a formula that rested 80 percent on population and 20 percent on geographic area. It was designed to give some advantage to the sparsely populated parts of the state.

"I never did quite understand how that was supposed to work," Warner says. But the formula was approved.

During Warner's first year in the Legislature, the body passed a bill to implement the concept, combined with the legislation that increased the size of the Unicameral from 43 to the current 49 members. But, because of the formula's dependence on geographic area as well as population, the plan did not go far enough toward equalizing the population among districts. "The disparity was pretty high," Warner says. The matter went to court, and the whole apportionment formula was thrown out.

A new plan, proposed in 1965, came closer to the Supreme Court's mandated ideal and was based purely on population. This plan was upheld by the district court. Warner's future wife, Betty, drew the maps for the new districts. She also was the principal witness when the plan was tested in the U.S. District Court.

Further changes in apportionment came more gradually, and by the time the Legislature was dealing with redistricting after the 1970 census, "we were in pretty good shape," Warner remembers.

Many observers say the redistricting contortions of the 1960s were a rural-urban fight. However, Warner argues that, in Nebraska's case, the battle was "the last gasp of the county vs. municipal government conflict" and the last gasp of the struggle between the political factions that divided along the Platte River and had dominated the state throughout its history.

Warner says he doesn't understand why anyone would be opposed to the one-person-one-vote concept. "I can't see why it's any different for the person who lives in Valentine than the person who lives in Lincoln."

Despite the fact that one individual lives in a rural and the other in an urban area, their interests are not significantly different.

But many people from rural Nebraska were afraid of what Lincoln and, particularly, Omaha might do to the rest of the state if those population centers gained increased representation. "There was a lack of trust ... and there still is."

However, Warner says, "Nebraska's problem is no different from any other state that is dominated by one city. ... It's going to have a certain impact that's inescapable," sometimes providing big benefits to the part of the state with a relatively small geographic area but the largest concentration of population.

Omaha has done well economically, sometimes as a result of breaks the rest of the state has not received. The city has benefited as its legislative delegation has become more cohesive and aggressive.

"But I don't think it's reached a detrimental level. Well, it may have been detrimental from time to time, but there's not been irrevocable harm done. It's been more of a temporary harm," Warner says.

No matter how Omaha's influence may have affected state politics, there was no getting around the one-person-one-vote mandate handed down by the Supreme Court, and the Legislature was forced to reapportion accordingly.

Many times during those years of arguing about how the state should be divided, someone would suggest that the Unicameral revert to a two-house body. Many of those who advocated that idea did so because they thought a state senate's districts could be drawn on the basis of geographic area. When they found out that state senates cannot be apportioned in the same way as the U.S. Senate, they usually lost interest in the project. Warner says a return to two houses was never seriously considered.

Although the Legislature eventually resigned itself to the one-person-one-vote principle, that was not the end of the story. At the beginning of each new decade, the Unicameral must actually redraw its districts on the basis of the population shifts discovered by the census count.

The process begins in the corners of the state, "and you keep pushing your problems ahead of you," Warner says. "You're going to end up at some point in the state where you have kind of screwy boundaries." Those odd looking districts have traditionally occurred in the southeast part of the state.

Much of the problem is caused by simple circumstances rather than by gerrymandering. However, Warner admits it is difficult for a small group of people like the Legislature to be forced to draw districts that will put one of their own out of office.

As Nebraska's population has shifted toward the metropolitan areas, the legislators knew that, each time they took on reapportionment, they would be losing representatives from the rural areas and adding them in the urban areas. "It was always a bit of a problem for the club—the Legislature—to pick somebody to be gone," Warner says.

If an incumbent indicated he or she was thinking about not running for re-election, that district would automatically become one that would be divided in the reapportionment.

If the redistricting would mean that two incumbents were destined to face each other at the next election, the senator with the weaker record in office usually would be the one whose district would be eliminated in reapportionment. Some people might call that gerrymandering, he says, but "putting two strong people against each other wouldn't serve any purpose. ... It was no better representation."

Warner remembers only one time that the senators clearly tried to draw a district on the basis of politics rather than logic. Senator James Waldron from Callaway in Custer County would have had difficulty being re-elected in the existing district, so he asked that his district be redrawn to include North Platte and, primarily, Lincoln County with only a small "hook" into Custer County. The political maneuvering was probably obvious to the voters, and it didn't work. Waldron was not re-elected.

In Lancaster County reapportionment has, purposely, never pitted two incumbents against each other. However, Warner contends reapportionment has never resulted in distorted boundaries, either. Some would criticize the preservation of incumbents, the senator admits, "and I suppose there's truth to that. But nobody's been able to show me where there was any harm from it."

The 1980 reapportionment in the county certainly seemed to divide fairly in terms of partisanship. Two of the newly-drawn districts included predominantly Republican voters, two included mostly Democrats "and two were kind of a toss up." If the Legislature had tried to be sure that each district included an equal number of Republican and Democrat voters, the result would have been distorted districts with odd-looking boundaries.

The last time the Legislature went through reapportionment, following the 1990 census, Warner paid hardly any attention. He made it known that, if possible, he'd like his district to include southeast Lincoln and then walked away from the redistricting process. When it was over, he had what he'd asked for.

Earlier in his tenure as a senator, Warner argued that all of rural Lancaster County should be in one district. "I argued that for 30 years." But by 1991, the population had grown too much to allow the entire county—outside Lincoln—to be included in a single district.

So this farmer whose address is Waverly, represents part of rural Lancaster County and part of the City of Lincoln.

"As long as I've been in the Legislature, I've had people in Lincoln ask why they're represented by someone who has an address of Waverly." But Warner lives almost as close to Lincoln as he does to Waverly. If his house were three-eighths of a mile farther south, he would have both a Lincoln address and a Lincoln telephone number.

As for representing both rural and urban voters, Warner thinks that's actually a big advantage to him. The broader the cross-section of people a legislator represents, the broader his or her viewpoint is likely to be. The make-up of his district allows him to take middle-of-the-road positions between competing rural and urban interests.

Devotion to the Institution

In an era when the citizenry's opinion of politicians and elected officials ranges from mild dissatisfaction to downright disrespect, Warner continues to look forward to being part of government. He is proud of the Legislature in which he serves and on which he has had so much influence. He believes in the Unicameral's ability to do good for the people of Nebraska.

"Jerry really does believe in the institution," says Speaker Ron Withem. "It's been his whole life." Warner is an advocate for the Legislature, defending it against those who would erode its responsibilities and influence. That includes the many new senators who arrive as critics, having run against the system.

Doug Kristensen, elected in 1988, does not fall into the category. Instead, he attests to the positive side of the equation: Warner's willingness to explain to new senators how things work in the Unicameral.

On the advice of friends, Kristensen chose to sit next to Warner when he came to the Legislature. He believes it was an excellent decision and says he would never move.

On the first day of the 1989 session, Kristensen told Warner, "You'll have to tell me how to vote."

Warner replied, "Vote like me until I tell you not to."

Sometimes Kristensen voted as Warner did; sometimes he didn't. Even when the two senators disagreed, Kristen says he never felt Warner was angry with him.

Warner does not conduct a personal program of welcoming new senators into the Legislature, but he's happy to provide information and advice to those who ask for it. Many do, Kristensen says.

Peter Hoagland, a member of the Legislature from 1980-86 and a U.S. Representative from 1986-94, served his first two years in the Unicameral as a member of the Appropriations Committee. Chairman Warner was generous with his time, Hoagland says, helping educate the new senator on the basic nuts and bolts of state government.

Warner told Hoagland the safest thing to do is vote no on a major bill that passes. Then, if one's constituents disapprove of the legislation, a senator can wash his hands of it. The second safest thing is to vote yes on a bill that fails—for the same reason.

Warner would tell those stories with a smile, Hoagland says, and then get down to the real advice: make a decision early, announce what it is and stick with it. It is advice Warner himself has followed successfully through the years, Hoagland points out.

As the senator with the most seniority, Warner does what he can to teach new senators about the issues—and to teach a respect for the Legislature as an institution.

Reporter Henry Cordes says Warner truly believes in the Legislature and its processes.

Cordes covered the Legislature long enough to see patterns of behavior emerge. Often, when the body would get bogged down in a debate that seemed to be going nowhere, many senators would lose interest and wander off the floor. Not Warner. Rather than being bored by the proceedings, Warner enjoys the process itself.

"He's a student of the process," Lee Rupp says. "His dad was, too." And so was Betty, who Rupp describes as "his soul-mate on legislative stuff" as well as in his personal life.

However, Warner can also turn his wry wit on the very institution he loves. People may think that the democratic system means the voters carefully elect 49 individuals with broad backgrounds to represent the state's specific needs and concerns. But that picture is far too idealistic.

"I suspect 95 percent of the bills would pass if those 49 people were selected out of the phone book," Warner says.

Be that as it may, Warner leaves little doubt that he respects and loves the institution. Dick Herman, retired editor of the Lincoln Journal, tells a story that illustrates Warner's jealousy for the reputation of the Legislature.

Many years ago, Herman says, a senator who was a good friend of Warner's was so frustrated by what was going on in the Unicameral that he arrived on the floor one day wearing a clown suit. The costume was designed to illustrate the senator's irritation with colleagues he thought were acting like a bunch of clowns.

"That really outraged Jerry," Herman says. Some senators and members of the press saw that incident and others like it as just good fun. Warner saw it as degrading to the institution.

Some believe, though, that Warner's love for and trust in the institution may occasionally interfere with his effectiveness.

For instance, Warner often does not use the help and influence of lobbyists as effectively as he could, says Dave Landis, a current state senator. Warner believes so strongly in the Legislature's own procedures that he wants to see the 49 senators handle their own affairs without interference from outside interests.

That means, says Landis, that Warner is pleased when the Legislature doesn't follow the course of action laid out by the interest groups. "At the times when we fall into chaos, Jerry loves it—because we have returned the body to its own possession."

Warner sees those days as opportunities for the body to rise above itself, Landis says, and to act appropriately. "He likes to see fights on the floor" rather than in the rotunda. "He likes to see value judgments made by the Legislature rather than negotiated off the floor."

Doug Kristensen, who has sat next to Warner in the Legislature for the last eight years, has noticed the same thing. Kristensen recalls a time when he was frustrated over lengthy debate that was preventing the Unicameral from moving on and taking action. Warner told him, "Yes, but the scariest part of the Legislature isn't when there's a bitter debate but when people don't disagree and there's no debate." Warner believes the system ultimately accomplishes what is best for the people.

That love for the pure legislative process means Warner will sometimes simply offer an idea on the floor without having lined up support and worked out questions and conflicts ahead of time.

Ron Withem, the current speaker, thinks personality may be as much the cause as deference to the institution.

"In many ways Jerry is not a naturally outgoing individual," Withem says. "He could have been even more effective if he had taken the initiative in more cases to initiate coalitions with other senators." At times, Warner seems to put an issue forward and let it stand or fall on its own merits rather than trying to build support before the matter reaches the stage of formal action.

Of course, that is not always the case. Warner has not survived more than three decades in the Unicameral simply by hoping that the system will prevail on its own. Many is the time that he has used the system to his advantage.

Landis says as much: "It's much easier to have Jerry Warner on your side. He's a very effective floor general. He knows the rules, knows the system, and he's just tough as a boot to beat."

Warner's nonpartisan nature has helped him learn how to make the nonpartisan Legislature function to what he sees as the state's best advantage. But the fact that Warner is not partisan certainly doesn't imply that he's not political. The practice of politics is, after all, what makes representative government work. Any elected official who pretends he is somehow above politics is probably forgetting who put him in office in the first place. That's not true of Warner.

"You survive 34 years only by being political," Rupp says. "He still has to face elections. He still has to look over his shoulder and feel the hot breath of what his constituency is thinking."

On the other hand, Warner usually puts politics aside when it comes to setting a budget or meeting a tax crisis. Rupp says the senator tends to resist the temptation to "put his finger in the wind and pander to the gallery," promising tax cuts or restructurings that might play well to the voters but do the state a disservice in the long run.

However, Rupp cites Warner's reaction to Initiative 300 as one instance of the senator's political instincts at work. Initiative 300 was a measure placed on the ballot via citizen petition in 1982. It was designed to ban corporate ownership of Nebraska farmland, and it generated plenty of controversy before it was approved at the ballot box.

During the public debate on the measure, Rupp spoke out against cluttering the Nebraska Constitution "with 1300 ill-advised words that nobody could understand about outlawing corporate farming." Privately, Warner agreed with that point of view. Publicly, though, he supported the initiative.

As Warner recalls the situation, he didn't have much to say about the measure one way or the other.

While the initiative was intended to protect family farmers, the language of the amendment was so restrictive that the measure is, in some ways, an economic deterrent to farmers.

"Overall, I suspect it's not good public policy," Warner says. "It restricts the market for those who want to sell or need to sell. ... In retrospect, I agree it was a mistake."

In 1982, though, Warner did not publicly label Initiative 300 a mistake. Rupp sees that as a political decision. Farmers all over Nebraska were suffering an economic depression, and corporate farming took a lot of the blame for small farmers' problems. No doubt Warner heard plenty of complaints from his neighbors and constituents about how they couldn't compete with the big guys.

Rupp says he can understand Warner's decision not to take a stand against Initiative 300. "It's a hard thing to tell people corporate farming is not the bogeyman everybody makes it out to be. And I can understand that he has to think politically at times. ...You can offend 49 percent of the people, but you'd better not offend 51 percent."

Scott Moore thinks Warner is sometimes as political as the next elected official. Warner admits some votes he makes are politically safe. However, in many cases, Warner understands the potential political consequences of his actions but simply chooses to ignore them.

On high-profile issues with long-term implications, Moore believes Warner makes up his mind on the basis of principle and what he sees as good public policy. Political fallout doesn't seem to be a problem because people have come to expect Warner to take a principled stand on major issues. "He's done that so many times over the years it's not a political detriment," Moore says.

Warner doesn't like to play political games, says Sandy Myers Sostad, and has little patience with politicians who do.

Former Governor Exon played a lot of those games. Most of them involved the budget. The governor would consistently propose inadequate funding for state programs. The Appropriations Committee would have to ask for more money, and Warner would take the blame for increased spending.

Exon built himself up by attacking the Legislature, Warner says.

"It's easy enough to do." The governor speaks with one voice, the Legislature with 49. If the governor can get just one senator to join him in criticizing the Unicameral, his jibes begin to look credible, and his power increases. In a state with a strong nonpartisan legislature, a governor may be tempted to use any opportunity to gain influence.

The senator himself has plenty of influence to be an effective legislator. His years of experience have taught him the best way to work within the Legislature to accomplish his goals. He understands the system and knows how to use it.

Sometimes that means simply knowing and using the Legislature's own procedures to maximum effect. Sometimes it means knowing how to get help from one's fellow senators. Vard Johnson, a senator during the 1980s, felt the full effect of Warner's finesse in that regard.

It happened in 1980 when Johnson was on the Revenue Committee, and it involved the gasoline tax structure. To that point, the Legislature had set the tax each year. But during the 1980 session, Warner's bill to create the variable gasoline tax was making its way through the legislative process.

Johnson remembers the incident this way:

"One day Senator Warner came to me. He got down on his knees and leaned his arms on my desk, and he said to me, 'Vard, I have a bill that's going to be before the Revenue Committee in a couple of days. It's the variable gas tax bill. Have you heard of that bill at all?'"

Johnson said he knew little about the bill.

"He said, 'I need your help with that bill. You are the smartest member on the Revenue Committee, and you're the only person on the committee that I think can understand that bill and how it works. That's why I'm calling on you for your help on this bill.'"

Warner asked if Johnson would meet with a lobbyist in the next day or two to learn about the bill so he could help get it through committee.

"I said, 'I'm sure I could, Jerry. I'm sure I could.'

"'Thank you so much,' he said. 'You're such a help,' he said. And he walked away.

"Well, that son of a gun hit me in my vanity point. I'd only been there (a few) years, and he came to me, this veteran legislator, and he said I was the smartest and ablest man on that committee. And because of that, he was looking to me to carry his bill."

It made Johnson feel great at the time. It made him feel awful once he realized what the bill was designed to do. It took away from the Legislature the authority to set the gasoline tax and, instead, arranged for a tax that would vary automatically to raise whatever amount of money was needed to fund the roads budget the Legislature adopted each year.

"That bill was anathema to my way of thinking, absolutely anathema," Johnson says. "I have always believed that the Legislature should set the tax directly. ...

"But I had promised Senator Warner that I would help him with this bill, and I was too young and too green to go back to the senator and tell him that I was going to change my point of view."

Johnson kept his word, and the bill was advanced from the Revenue Committee with five votes. " I was the fifth vote, the necessary vote," he says ruefully.

Tempering his discomfort was his surprise that another committee member, Senator Dave Newell, had also voted for the bill. Johnson went to Newell and said, "I was stunned. Why did you vote for that bill? That bill is totally contrary to what you and I believe."

Newell told Johnson, "Oh, I promised Senator Warner I'd vote for the bill." Johnson has a good laugh now as he remembers how he and Newell found themselves voting against their own convictions thanks to some very effective persuasion from Senator Warner.

Johnson went on to oppose the bill during floor debate, but it did pass and remains Nebraska law.

"I went back to Warner after that and said, 'Jerry, I allowed myself to be conned by flattery. And that's a comment on me, not on you. But it won't happen again.'

"And if I was lucky, it didn't happen again."

The incident was out of the ordinary, Johnson says. "You didn't see Warner work legislation much on the floor. He didn't do what he did to me very often—it didn't seem—but obviously when he did it, he did it with considerable finesse."

Dave Maurstad, elected to the Legislature in 1994, was also flattered when Warner asked for his support on a measure. But in Maurstad's case, the support did not turn out to be a problem.

Maurstad sits in the front row on the floor of the Legislature, in a high profile spot that doesn't entice a lot of his fellow senators to stop by just to chat. When they come, they come with a purpose.

Warner came to Maurstad's seat one day, the younger senator recalls, and began explaining a bill he was supporting.

"He must have thought the vote would be close," Maurstad says. "When he started to leave, I asked him what he wanted me to do. He said, 'Vote for it.'"

Maurstad says he realized Warner was trying, through explanation and discussion, to convince him to support the bill in question. "But he didn't pontificate," Maurstad says, nor did he ask for speeches or arm-twisting to help the bill along.

"He just simply wanted me to know my vote would help—and that he needed it," Maurstad says. "He had enough respect for a new member to say, 'Your vote is important.'"

Warner sometimes has words with rookie senators after votes are taken, too. Kermit Brashear, also elected in 1994, remembers Warner's questioning a vote after the fact. It was a matter about which Brashear had had plenty of doubts, and being a freshman legislator made matters worse.

The vote he finally cast was against Warner's position on the bill. Warner told Brashear he was surprised by the Omaha senator's vote and tried to explain his own position further. Ultimately, Brasher changed his position out of respect for Warner's reasoning.

But Brashear, too, says Warner is not flashy on the floor. "He doesn't stand up on every issue and use his accumulated seniority, age, experience, wisdom and personal clout to persuade you. Sometimes you have to literally go ask him what he thinks."

Ron Roskens, former NU president, also notes Warner's inclination not to take the lead in debate and discussion. "I'd like to see him, on occasion, more aggressive," Roskens says. "He is so reluctant to move onto the floor to say things unless it's something he feels very strongly about."

Sometimes, though, Warner uses that very reticence to accomplish his goals, according to Senator Dave Landis. "His chief tool is silence — and elliptical answers." But his second tool is "clear speech when it matters," Landis adds. Warner is not afraid to confront his fellow senators when they differ on issues that are important to him.

Warner is known for spending a lot of time on the floor of the Legislature during debate, something that may have been ingrained in him when senators did not have offices to which to retreat. Frequently, though, Warner simply listens to the flow of the discussion, often without participating. He is careful to speak only when he believes the timing is right.

"He picks his fights intelligently," current Speaker Ron Withem says.

However, when he does engage in legislative battle, Landis says, "he conducts himself in an honorable way that permits differences to be conducted at a policy and not a personal level. He has few enemies ... because while he's beaten people—me included—he doesn't do dirt."

He doesn't throw temper tantrums, either, Lee Rupp points out.

"But that's not to say he's a good loser. He doesn't hold a grudge. But he doesn't like to lose."

Rupp sat behind Warner during his days in the Legislature and recalls how the back of Warner's neck would get red when the senator came out on the short end of a vote or an issue.

He recalls one particular occasion in the mid-1980s when then-Senator John DeCamp offered an amendment to cut $6 million from the University of Nebraska budget. "The back of Jerry's neck was almost crimson," Rupp remembers, but Warner didn't blow up. Instead, he tried to correct the damage slowly and methodically.

Doug Bereuter also recalls Warner's tendency to turn red when he is angry. "If he got red, people would watch out," Bereuter says. But, he adds, Warner was always courteous, even to senators with whom he was doing battle.

"He disagrees without being disagreeable," Sandy Scofield says.

Furthermore, "when he beats you, he beats you fair and square," Landis says. And the absence of malice and manipulation "makes the next day livable." Warner uses the system effectively but fairly—and consistently.

"Warner has established a standard of conduct and behavior, and his conformance to that is admirable. ... He does to you what you would like a colleague to do," Landis says.

Governor Ben Nelson says, "If we had more like him, the state would do even better."

Lee Rupp agrees: "He's good. It's too bad there aren't more Jerry Warners."

The kind of faithfulness and consistency his colleagues attribute to Warner is something many politicians have trouble maintaining over the course of a long career. But it's not the only way Warner differs from what might be expected.

Political scientists have identified a number of common traits among members of the U.S. Congress, and many of those traits also surface among state legislators. One is credit-claiming, the tendency for elected officials to tell their constituents—and as many other people as possible—what they have accomplished: legislation passed, changes made, dollars saved.

It's something Warner seldom does. In fact, he is known for his modesty, his unwillingness to blow his own horn.

Jim Joyce, former legislative reporter for the Lincoln Star, says he thinks Warner exhibits "almost no ego," almost never wants credit or publicity for his accomplishments.

Someone who has been elected term after term for more than 30 years and who has been behind some of the most comprehensive and important changes the state has made during that time "has every right to have developed an ego," Ron Roskens says. "But he's modest and humble—and it's real."

Charlie Thone, former governor, also praises Warner's modesty. As someone who has been around policy-makers on the state and national level for 30 to 40 years, Thone says, "I've noticed a lot of fine, good people become arrogant. ... After a while, it's hard to keep one's proper perspective. That has never happened to Jerry Warner."

Warner seldom promotes his achievements. About all the senator will allow himself is a wry smile that tells those who pay attention that he is delighted at the way matters turned out.

Perhaps Warner's unwillingness to seek publicity is one reason he has gotten what he calls "exceptionally good press" during his career. He contends he doesn't know why that has been the case.

Henry Cordes of the Omaha World-Herald has an explanation: "He shoots very straight and wouldn't try to mislead you. If he knows something, he'll tell you. ... He's a great person for reporters" to work with.

Jim Joyce also likes the fact that Warner doesn't seek out publicity. Reporters become wary of people who are always trying to get their names in the paper or on the air.

Cordes says Warner understands the role the press plays in the governmental process as a conduit to let the public know what's happening.

Warner also understands another traditional role of the American press, the role of critic.

The media are not generally kind to politicians, he says, "nor should they be. They are, in fact, the watchdog. Even the most minor impropriety that any public official does should be blown up big as a deterrent."

However, he thinks inappropriate activity among Nebraska politicians is relatively minor. "People have dumb ideas, but that's not the same thing."

Warner's ideas and opinions have attracted mostly positive attention from the press during his career. The press has recognized Warner's achievements even when he has not sought that recognition.

It has also recognized his even-handedness. An October 1972 editorial in the Lincoln Star says, "Within the Legislature he has gained a reputation for freely discussing the pros and cons of all legislation, including the bills he has sponsored. In short, he is a fair, reasonable man who works well with other senators."

The senator understands there are several sides to every issue and doesn't try to pretend his point of view is the only one possible. So the nonpartisan nature of Nebraska's Unicameral is right up Jerome Warner's alley. Warner does not believe issues can or should be neatly divided according to party ideology. Instead, they should be sorted out as to how much good they can accomplish for the people of Nebraska.

"He never let political affiliation get in the way of what he thought should be done," says Jim Exon, a strongly partisan Democrat.

Warner delights in the nonpartisan nature of the Unicameral. "I get terribly annoyed with partisan politics," he says.

His antipathy toward partisan politics is almost the same as what he feels toward radio talk shows: "Whatever viewpoint they're trying to promote, they absolutely will not acknowledge more than one position—which is theirs. ... I learned a long time ago that simply is not how it is."

In national politics, where partisanship holds sway, a politician usually must argue as if his or her position were the only possible answer or be accused of being wishy-washy. Warner shakes his head: "It's a wonder the system works as well as it does."

And it's not just the partisan loyalty to one-sided positions that bothers Warner. He also dislikes the idea of party discipline. He admits the U.S. Congress is probably too big to function without partisanship and party discipline. But for himself, he says, "I just don't like it. I don't do it much."

In his younger years he was more active in Republican politics, Warner says, but even then partisanship had begun to bother him. As he learned more about the issues, he saw more sides to them and became less critical of those who disagreed with his position. Had he been serving in a partisan body, he would have had trouble maintaining the party line.

Although the Unicameral is officially nonpartisan, many observers have said party politics does come into play in legislative deliberations. Warner disagrees and cites history to support his claim that the body is nonpartisan in fact as well as in theory.

When the state moved from the two-house partisan system to the current one-house nonpartisan arrangement in 1935, he says, the membership included 22 Democrats and 21 Republicans. Yet his father, a Republican, was elected the first speaker, not a likely outcome if the vote had been along partisan lines.

Charles Warner was a proponent of the move to the one-house legislature. He had been elected to the lower chamber of the two-house body in 1901, 1903 and 1905. Then he served in the Senate from 1919-35 before spending two years as speaker of the new one-house institution.

Warner has known others who served under both the bicameral and the unicameral arrangements. "Without exception, there was a profound preference for the Unicameral," he says.

Furthermore, Warner says, moves to return the Unicameral to a partisan body have been overwhelmingly defeated, despite the efforts of both major political parties to convince senators and voters to do otherwise.

Governors sometimes have tried to use party loyalty to influence legislators, but few have been successful. Thone may have tried most often in recent years, but the number of senators who felt a loyalty to the Republican party and the Republican governor was too few to make much difference in legislative decisions.

Thone would be the first to admit that he would like to see a partisan Nebraska Legislature. "It would bring added responsibility into the process," Thone says. As it is, he believes, too many state senators act as if they are totally independent of any responsibility.

Thone admits, though, that neither he nor anyone else is likely to convince Warner the Legislature should go back to a partisan system. "He is totally institutionalized," Thone says. Warner has bought into the nonpartisan ideal and constantly tries to keep partisanship out of his decision-making.

Party authorities, Warner says, have a hard time understanding legislators' positions. "They don't look at the issues broadly enough." A partisan viewpoint is a narrow viewpoint, he says, at least partly out of necessity.

However, experience in a nonpartisan body has converted many an elected official who had been clearly partisan before arriving in the Unicameral, Warner believes. Most people who arrived as partisans have been converted to fans of the nonpartisan Legislature.

Some questions the Unicameral faces, though, are traditionally partisan. Reapportionment probably tops the list, particularly when the Legislature must deal with Congressional, Public Service Commission and NU Board of Regents districts. Disputes regarding the Electoral College also become partisan. All those situations involve decisions that will influence action at a different level, not within the Legislature itself.

Most issues within the body are not partisan, Warner believes. Neither are the divisions. Legislative coalitions shift with the issues and can be rural vs. urban one day, county vs. city another and east vs. west the next. That can make life difficult for a governor who wants to influence the Legislature, but Warner likes the system and thinks others do, too.

He tells a story to back up his assertion. It happened during the fall of 1963 after the Nebraska Supreme Court had declared all purchases made on installment payments illegal, calling the practice usury. In response, the Legislature met in a six-week special session to try to resolve the problem. Lobbyists representing dozens of interests testified at public hearings, including a man who represented Sears, Roebuck and Co., the department store chain.

The Sears representative had testified in similar battles in other states, and he said he was impressed with Nebraska's system. In other states, he said, he would work just with the majority and minority leaders. In Nebraska he had to convince a majority of the 49 members. Despite the extra effort that required, the man said he thought Nebraska's nonpartisan system was better than the partisan systems in the other states. Warner believes Nebraskans generally agree with that assessment.

The Unicameral may look more partisan these days than it used to, and the senators often work more closely now with governors of their same party than was once the case. The trend started with Thone in 1978 and has continued, he says. "But it really is a mixture of partisanship and philosophy," Warner says.

At different times over the years, groups of Republicans or Democrats have been called together, usually by someone from outside the Legislature, to try to figure out a way to elect all standing committee chairmen from one party or the other. But the senators themselves have resisted such manipulations. "Efforts that are unsuccessful don't mean a whole lot."

Even so, Warner says it is becoming more difficult to maintain nonpartisanship in the form that was intended when the Unicameral was introduced in the 1930s. He recalls that when he first ran for election to the Legislature, he was invited to speak to the county conventions of both the Democratic and Republican parties. However, he has not been invited lately.

Although he has always been a registered Republican, Warner says, "I'm not too popular with the Republicans." He doesn't endorse candidates, is not publicly involved with party positions. He's disagreed with Republican governors and worked closely with Democratic governors, notably Bob Kerrey. "That's taboo for the real partisan people."

The coolness between Warner and the party has meant that he has not been elected as a delegate from his district to the state Republican conventions in recent years. "I don't have the right voting record on some issues." For one thing, he is seen as leaning toward pro-choice on the abortion issue.

Warner thinks that, in recent years, the Republican party generally has become "more exclusive and less inclusive." The handful of ardent partisans has managed to dominate and shape the party.

It has even kept him away from involvement with the party on the county level. He put his name up to be a delegate to the county convention in the summer of 1996 but ended up not going. "I thought I'd just get annoyed."

After 34 years in a nonpartisan Legislature, trying to consider issues on their merits instead of from a party-based perspective, Warner has become less and less partisan.

"The least persuasive argument I can imagine is 'That's the Republican position.'" He would feel the same way if someone argued an issue simply because it was the "Democratic" position. It's a philosophy Warner grew up with and which he has held since he arrived in the Unicameral in 1963.

Dedicated to the Unicameral's nonpartisan structure, Warner practices what he preaches. His leadership during the personal property tax crisis of 1992 is a prime example. The Republican senator worked with the state's Democratic governor for the benefit of the state—and nary a partisan word was uttered in the process.

PART SIX
PERFECTING STATESMANSHIP

Meeting Another Tax Crisis

T he problem arose when, in July of 1991, the Nebraska Supreme Court ruled that, thanks to a uniformity clause in the state's constitution, all income-producing personal property must be valued the same way for taxation purposes. That included farm machinery, livestock and farm and business inventories—all items that previous Legislatures had deliberately excluded from uniform valuation. No longer would such exclusions be permitted, the court said. Instead, the state would have to make a choice between returning to valuing all such property in the same way—or taxing none of it at all.

The amendment the 1992 Unicameral devised to meet the crisis got around the uniformity clause by changing the constitution to allow different systems of taxing real estate and personal property but applying uniformity within each classification.

Warner, then a member of the Revenue Committee, led the effort to write the amendment and accompanying legislation, working with his fellow senators and with governor Ben Nelson.

A headline in the Feb. 1, 1992, Lincoln Star says, "Warner promotes Nelson's tax solution," but Warner remembers things a bit differently. "I always looked upon it as the governor joining me."

The governor had appointed Warner to the special committee of legislators and administrative personnel that took on the situation, and Nelson did support and promote the plan the special committee wrote. But it was Warner who led the group through the thicket of practical and political considerations necessary to reach a conclusion.

He knew the potential pitfalls if all personal property had reverted to the tax roles. Taxes on Nebraska businesses would have risen and made it hard to compete with businesses in states that enjoyed exemptions for personal property. Before too long, that would also have had an impact on jobs in Nebraska.

The committee looked at a lot of alternatives presented by staff members. Although a proposed constitutional amendment requires only 30 votes by the Legislature to be placed on the general election ballot, an amendment to be considered at any other election requires 40 votes. Getting 40 of the Unicameral's 49 members to agree on anything is difficult; getting them to agree on an issue as contentious as this one was likely to be almost impossible.

Committee members knew they faced a tough battle, and it narrowed their choices considerably.

Once Warner had made up his mind what the alternative should be, he put the plan before the committee. Dave Landis was the only legislative member of the committee who voted with Warner. Tim Hall, the committee's co-chairman, voted against the plan. But most of the administrative people in the group supported Warner's proposal, and it became the committee's recommendation. The fact that the administrators liked the idea led Warner to believe the governor would also support it.

The governor's support had been open to question because, to that point, Nelson had not said much of anything about the problem. Instead, he appointed the special committee and waited for its recommendation. Warner calls that a smart political move, allowing the chief executive to "sit back and see what the repercussions are before he takes a position."

Warner talked to Sandy Scofield, then Nelson's chief of staff, and told her he would introduce the committee's proposal during the 1992 session if the governor wanted him to. As Warner had predicted, Nelson told him to go ahead.

Once the study had been completed, Warner was convinced the formula it proposed was the only workable solution to the problem. Once again, he found himself proposing legislation that did not necessarily benefit him personally:

"It was not Farmer Warner's preference, but it was State Senator Warner's conclusion it was the only thing that was going to fly—and to do nothing was the worst possible alternative."

Warner wrote a piece for the May 6, 1992, Lincoln Journal explaining and defending the proposal the committee had adopted. He admitted that farmers would have to pay more under the new plan, but he said all Nebraskans would be worse off if the amendment failed at the polls. If that were to happen, Warner wrote, all personal property would go on the tax roles at market value. The impact on the state's economy would be harsh.

The amendment, he said, would ease the impact by assuring that businesses, industries and large corporations would continue to pay their share of personal property taxes, preventing the burden from being shifted primarily to homeowners.

In that year's May primary election, voters approved the measure. As usual, Warner did not trumpet his leadership in solving the crisis, but, he says now, "I had my neck out long before he (Governor Nelson) did."

The fact that Nelson and Warner both backed the issue probably did help get the plan through the Legislature and onto the ballot. This was one time that the Unicameral's official nonpartisanship might have given way to partisan bickering. Some senators who are Democrats would not have supported it if a Democratic governor had not pushed it. And some Republican senators might have opposed it if Warner, a Republican, had not been so closely associated with the measure. "Eventually they all came aboard because of the realization that to do nothing was the worst possible thing."

On the same day the voters of Nebraska approved the amendment, the voters of the 25th District also gave Warner a primary victory and placed his name on the general election ballot for the fall.

Earlier that spring, on April 30, the Lincoln Journal had endorsed Warner for another term and given him much of the credit for solving the personal property tax problem: "Leadership and genuine responsibility are words which automatically define the 64-year-old Waverly farmer. Whether one likes or abhors the work product of the 1992 Legislature in proposing both a constitutional and statutory remedy for the state's personal property tax crisis, it can't be denied that Warner's knowledge, endurance, patience and multiple skills were pivotal."

Nebraska's nonpartisan legislative system probably made it easier for Warner to work with Nelson on a matter that might have divided people along party lines in other states. But the situation also underlines again Warner's allegiance to the people of Nebraska rather than to any political party or ideology.

Henry Cordes says Warner is probably just what George Norris, considered the father of the Unicameral, had in mind: a citizen legislator responsible and responsive to the state rather than to a party.

Cordes says Warner is a Republican who does not look at issues from a partisan standpoint. Instead, the senator looks to make policy he believes is right. "He'll work with a Democratic governor as much as a Republican," the reporter says, citing the 1992 tax crisis as a prime example. "The state comes first with him."

Governor Ben Nelson agrees: "He's been a good adviser to a lot of people. When he thinks your motives are pure and for the benefit of the state ... I have found him very open and very willing to share his thoughts when he agreed as well as when he disagreed."

Over the course of his 34 years in office, Warner has had plenty of time to develop and polish his stands on the issues, to learn on what basis he will agree or disagree and to find himself occasionally changing his mind. The result is a philosophy of government that puts the good of the whole above that of any part.

On Christmas Day of 1994, the Lincoln Journal printed Christmas greetings from various elected officials, including one from Senator Warner. His message included the following: "Nowadays we emphasize what divides us rather than what unites us. I hope that we can emphasize what we all share in common rather than things that separate us."

That belief in the need of people to emphasize what they share is a foundation of Warner's confidence in the need for and efficacy of government. He believes individuals are well served when they join together to meet the needs of the whole and that they can do that effectively through government. In an era in which many politicians run for office by running "against" government, Warner is an unabashed supporter of the system. He believes government serves a valid purpose.

But state government as Warner knew it when he arrived at the Unicameral in 1963 was a far cry from state government today in terms of size and range of responsibilities. Government in 1996 is bigger and more expensive—and is frequently criticized for both.

The common belief that government can be made cheaper simply by getting rid of waste, fraud and abuse doesn't impress Warner. He told a meeting of the Nebraska Association of Commerce and Industry in 1986 that the only way to make government dramatically cheaper is to make it dramatically smaller by eliminating entire programs. Simply scaling back won't have a significant effect, Warner believes, because the costs for most services are fixed.

He compares government to a waitress in a cafe who can handle only so many tables. If the number of tables increases, so must the number of waitresses. "That's just how it is."

Also, Warner disagrees with those who say government should be run like a business. It sounds like a good idea, but it's nearly impossible in a system of government that "is just full of checks and balances." The system demands that the different branches regulate each other and actually creates overlap. People may find that annoying, but in the long run, the public is protected by the required checks and balances, the senator believes.

Warner also disagrees with those who advocate competition as a cure for what ails government. If two publicly-funded entities are forced to compete, the government must provide ample funding for both. "That's sheer duplication." People are better served if government funds only one entity but then devises a method of oversight or review.

The senator admits his defense of government and spending doesn't sound like what many would expect of a typical Republican. Warner believes government serves a useful purpose. He does not apologize for its expanded size and reach.

"Somebody made a comment to me the other day that 40 years ago more of our time was spent in governing. Now government spends more of its time in providing. ... That's probably true," Warner says.

One reason behind the change, he says, is citizens' demanding more and more help from the government. Government responds by creating or expanding programs to meet the citizens' needs and demands.

But sheer size is not the only way government has changed since Warner was elected to the Legislature. The decision-making process has also changed, and computerization has had a major impact—not necessarily for the better.

"When I did my first state aid bills," Warner recalls, "you did a few hand calculations at night ... of selected school districts." Under those circumstances, senators would argue policy: whether proposed shifts in tax support for schools were philosophically wise and practically efficient.

Now that computers can calculate the specific effect of proposed legislation on all school districts in every senator's district, "it doesn't make any difference what the policy is. It's whether I'm getting more or less money than last year."

Warner says that actually may be another reason behind government growth. He offers an example. If, for some reason, a group of school districts is getting more than its fair share of aid and the Legislature wants to correct the problem, only one course of action is likely to succeed politically: continue to give the same amount to the districts receiving the larger amount of aid and give enough extra to the remaining districts to bring them to the same level. "You end up spending more."

Such situations arise more than occasionally, Warner points out. He doesn't believe the solution is necessarily a good one, but it's often the only one that's politically feasible.

Warner knows the public loves to criticize the Legislature for not slashing its budget, but he also recognizes how hard it is to make any cuts. Senators realize people don't want to pay more taxes, but the plea for more services never ends. Once a program is in place, it's especially hard to change it or eliminate it. Especially when, thanks to computers, all the senators—and all their constituents—can know instantly how the proposed change will affect them.

Even the language of government is different today from what it was 30 years ago. Warner notes it has become a habit to apply to governmental functions words that originated in business. For instance, "reorganization" or "consolidation" have given way to "restructuring" and "reengineering." Evaluation is now "performance-based" or "outcomes-based."

But language is a powerful force, and those who make public policy would do well to use it with care, Warner believes. He remembers a story his father tells about something that happened when Charles Warner was lieutenant governor.

It was about 1949, Warner thinks. The University of Nebraska had asked the state for $60,000 to build a new hog barn on the ag college campus. "Every good farmer knew you could build an A-frame hog house for $15 in those days." Charles Warner was convinced "there was no way they were going to get $60,000 for a hog barn. He said they'd have to come up with a different name.

"So then some bright person thought of asking for $60,000 to construct a swine research center."

The entire tone of the discussion changed. "Sixty thousand dollars for a swine research center made a whole lot of sense whereas $60,000 for a hog house was ridiculous. And it passed with no problem."

Changing His Mind

Government has changed plenty during the years Warner has been part of the Unicameral—and so has the senator himself. Although politicians are often criticized for changing their opinions, anyone who has been in office for more than three decades would surely be criticized if he hadn't grown and changed.

Warner has no problem admitting he has changed: "My thinking is much different than it was 34 years ago" on many subjects. "If you're not open to change, you're probably not doing your job." In part, that is simply a result of the learning process: more information about a particular issue may lead a person to revise his thinking.

Besides that, "times change, and you've got to be willing to adjust."

When he was elected in 1962, Warner thinks people considered his philosophy to be about in the middle of the road. He still considers himself a moderate.

But the middle of the road 34 years ago and the middle of the road today are not the same place. "The middle of the road has moved much to the left." Warner has moved with it.

Warner's changes of mind regarding the tax structure and coordination of higher education are well-known. However, his change of heart on another issue is less well-known because he has not taken the lead on the issue as he did on taxes and postsecondary ed. The issue is capital punishment.

When he was elected to the Legislature, Warner supported capital punishment. But he began to change his mind when a young girl, whose family he knew, started writing to him, telling him she opposed capital punishment and trying to persuade him to her opinion. Warner would write back to tell her why he favored capital punishment and why he thought she was wrong. The correspondence went on for a six-year period.

By the end of the six-year period, the senator had become an opponent of capital punishment.

Warner's opposition to the practice rests on two points. First, he doesn't like the idea of the state taking life. And second, he is especially concerned about what he believes is a vast inconsistency among cases in which someone has been sentenced to death.

The sentencing disparities seem to arise largely from which charge a county attorney chooses to file at the beginning of a case and on counties' willingness or unwillingness to pay for the cost of a trial.

Those may not have been the precise points Warner's young friend wrote to him about. But it didn't matter. "What she did was cause me to think about why I was on the side I was and think about it far more in depth than I otherwise would have."

In fact, Warner changed his mind to the point that he made what Vard Johnson remembers as a "wonderful speech" against the practice in 1980 when the Legislature voted to outlaw it. Despite Warner's support, the Unicameral did not have enough votes to override the subsequent Thone veto, and capital punishment remains the law of the land in Nebraska.

The questions raised by a young constituent drove Warner into a re-examination of his position on an issue. And to remain consistent in his belief that the state should be fair and objective, he changed his mind and his vote.

The same thing happened with his stand on banking laws. For his first 15 years in office he strongly believed in the local bank, local control. As bills were introduced to expand into what eventually became branch banking, Warner voted against them. "But then I started to think my historical position was totally out of step with financial reality, economic reality today." So he changed the way he voted.

Warner emphasizes that his changes of mind evolve slowly over the years. He says he usually knows a year or two before he actually begins to vote differently that he is gradually coming to that point.

Warner's belief in gradual change—for himself and for government—is not merely the product of advancing years; it's a belief he has held consistently throughout his career. A 1969 story in the Lincoln Star quotes Warner, who had been elected speaker for the coming term, describing legislative policy as "the policy of gradual change."

One way senators traditionally are influenced to change their minds, of course, is by lobbyists. And Warner says one result of the change to annual sessions in 1971 was a big change in lobbying.

Both the number of lobbyists and the intensity of their activity had increased. Before 1971, only a handful of lobbyists practiced their craft full time; most had other duties with the organizations they represented. Today, many associations and organizations hire full-time legislative lobbyists.

However, lobbying laws in past decades were considerably less strict. Today, any person who represents someone other than himself or herself must register as a lobbyist. And lobbyists must report what they spend on various legislators.

Warner has proposed the reverse: that senators be required to report what was spent on them by lobbyists. His proposal has never been seriously considered in the Legislature, but he still thinks the public would and should be more interested in what the senators do—from whom they accept gifts and invitations—than on what the lobbyists do.

Even then, it may not be easy to determine what constitutes a conflict of interest. What may be a conflict of interest for one person may not be for another, Warner says. But he understands the public's concern about the ethical standards of their elected officials. It's another of those lessons he learned at home.

He remembers a talk his mother had given to a group of high school girls about what it was like to be in public office. "The first line was that people who are in public office live in glass bowls, and the first thing they watch is the other fish in the bowl."

The reality of the glass bowl serves a good purpose, Warner believes, helping to prevent inappropriate activity by keeping public officials in the public eye. If legislators' constituents know their representatives may be up to something questionable and vote for them anyway, that's the voters' choice, Warner says.

He stops short of advocating complete disclosure, though. "There are some things the public is not entitled to know." One of those is the amount of income tax paid by an official—on the state or federal level. That kind of revelation is good for little other than political criticism, he believes.

"I think it's quite appropriate to know the sources of income but not the level." Some people may be influenced by a gift of $100 while others may not be influenced by $100,000, the senator says.

Like most laws, regulations governing campaign contributions or other ethics-related matters are passed because of misbehavior by "five percent of the people." So the entire group has to put up with additional regulations in order to keep the five percent in line.

Public perception has an effect on so-called ethics legislation, too, Warner believes. More than occasionally, aspiring politicians campaign for office by criticizing what they see as inappropriate conduct by elected officials. Once they've been in office for a while, the conduct no longer looks inappropriate.

For example, office-holders who campaigned against the influence of lobbyists may come to believe their votes are not at all affected by lobbying behavior. And they may be right. Most of the officials affected by the legislation honestly believe their opinion is not unduly influenced by a lobbyist who buys them lunch, Warner says.

"But they forget how it looks to the public." As Warner is fond of saying, perception is often stronger than reality when it comes to government and politics.

Thus, periodically, someone proposes that all elected officials be required to disclose their income, their campaign contributions and other financial information. Warner believes those demands cause resentment among office-holders, including the vast majority who try to do everything legally and ethically. They resent the implication that they are being accused of dishonesty.

Not that Warner is uncomfortable with the public looking over government's shoulder. A March 1983 World-Herald story quotes Warner as saying, "Open government is not a detriment to elected officials." That comment was made following failure of a bill he had introduced to require public disclosure of lobbying alliances formed to influence legislation. The following month, Warner opposed a bill to close senators' letters, memoranda and phone records to the public. His record has consistently been in favor of disclosure and openness to help insure ethical behavior by government officials at all levels.

That may become increasingly important if the trend continues to return more power to the states. Governors and state legislators promote the idea. Congress and the President pledge their allegiance to it. The Supreme Court rules frequently in favor of states' rights.

But not everyone thinks it's a good idea, even one whose influence could increase if more power is returned to the states.

As someone who been in office 34 years at the state level, Warner looks at the changes in the relationship between the federal government and states with less than wholehearted enthusiasm. Some argue that the federal government has usurped power that should belong to the states. Warner believes the federal government has often had to exert its power to get the states to do what is right.

In some cases, Warner says, "there's no question there are areas where things had to change," sometimes through judicial, sometimes through congressional action. Reapportionment is one case Warner cites on the judicial side: Until the Supreme Court made it mandatory, many states had refused to reapportion districts to comply with the one-person-one-vote principle.

Civil rights is a case on the legislative side. "The states had failed to do what should have been done for a hundred years." The federal civil rights legislation that required the states to uphold the civil rights guaranteed in the U.S. Constitution was both necessary and desirable, Warner believes.

While many proclaim the virtues of returning more responsibilities to the states, Warner has his doubts about the benefits of such a move. He's seen it happen before—and with mixed results.

"I've been here since before the federal programs started." One of the first power shifts was made by means of matching grants. The Nebraska Legislature's decision to participate in Medicaid bought into one of those matches: $2 of federal money for every $1 of state funds.

It would be nice to say that the Legislature decided to participate in Medicaid to provide services to Nebraskans, Warner says. But he suspects the real reason was to get the money.

Not many years later it became apparent that federal funds were often only seed money, available long enough to get programs started but not long enough to maintain them. Once the programs lost their federal financing, administrators and constituents would ask the Legislature for funding, adding to the state's burden.

By the late 1960s, block grants were being proclaimed as a way to make government more responsive. Proponents said states knew better than the federal government how to meet the needs of the nation's diverse citizenry. So the federal government gave the states—and smaller governmental units—blocks of money with which to fund programs previously funded directly by the federal government.

When the idea was tried during the Nixon administration, the states were allowed very little flexibility, Warner remembers. The money came with plenty of strings attached; he won't be surprised if the same thing is true this time around.

Politically, it makes sense to leave the strings in place. If he were a member of Congress, Warner says, he would not vote to give the states tax money for which he was responsible without plenty of direction about how the money was to be spent: "I don't expect Congress to send us money to use as we see fit."

Ever a supporter of equalization, Warner thinks federal grants to the states would make more sense if they were distributed to help equalize resources across the nation. In other words, poorer states with less tax capacity would receive more federal dollars than wealthier states. However, he thinks that's unlikely to happen.

Besides disliking the content of federal programs intended to transfer money and responsibility to the states, Warner also dislikes the procedure: The money goes to the governors' offices for distribution. The senator says he understands such a move makes it easier for the federal government to audit and monitor the use of the funds, but it puts the Legislature "out of the circle." That makes this staunch supporter of legislative governing uncomfortable.

Furthermore, Warner doesn't believe the shift will actually improve government services. Rather than getting bigger to accommodate additional duties, state government will likely get smaller, Warner predicts.

He is inclined to believe states should not be given more leeway because the states often will not act responsibly. If, as he suspects, Congress will be loath to increase funding for programs they no longer control, the states will be asked to pick up the difference. They may refuse to do so.

The prevailing mood of the voters is against expanded government, Warner points out. Elected officials hear over and over that people want less government and lower taxes. Generally, though, Warner thinks people are not in favor of cutting programs from which they benefit: only those that benefit somebody else.

Furthermore, it's harder for the state to expand its services than it is for the federal government because the states may not borrow money. In fact, Nebraska is constitutionally bound to produce a balanced budget.

That leads Warner to an aside about the federal budget system. He doesn't think much of it:

"I know how to play most of the games you play with budgets, because I've done a lot of it. Give me three bills, and I can make the general fund appropriation anything you want and still spend the same amount of money. But I can't hold a candle to what Congress does. The way they move money or count money makes absolutely no sense—other than it confuses everybody so nobody really knows what's happening."

The federal government's ability to borrow money has gotten it into deep debt, something Warner doesn't approve of. If the government is going to spend more, it should be willing to tax more, he believes. With mixed emotions, he favors a federal balanced budget amendment.

In theory, the senator says, a federal balanced budget amendment is unnecessary; the Congress should have the self-discipline to keep its budget balanced without constitutional mandate. During the last 30 years or so, though, Congress has not done that.

"It's such a screwy budget process," Warner says of Congressional procedures. Members of Congress talk about cutting $100 billion out of the budget, but it turns out to be over a five-year period based on projected costs. "And at the end of the $100 billion cut, you're still spending $100 billion more than you were when you put the $100 billion cut in. So I don't understand what they call cuts."

It's a matter of semantics, he admits. Leaders try to use words that are politically acceptable instead of explaining clearly just what's going on.

Warner admits it's not easy for a politician to find comfortable ground between being forthright and being politically palatable. "If you said what's really going to happen, you probably wouldn't get elected."

Once someone has served a while and compiled a respected record, he has a higher level of credibility and can make statements that might earlier have been considered politically unwise, says the senator who is living proof of the phenomenon.

Warner cites U.S. Senator Bob Kerrey as another good example. Both while Kerrey was Nebraska's governor and since he has moved to the Senate, "he has said some things that were exceedingly controversial ... and they seemed to wash right off."

Soon after Kerrey was elected governor, for instance, he spoke to the county officials' association and told them he would not support their proposal that the state take over 100 percent of the cost of Medicaid, relieving the counties of any responsibility for the funding. Kerrey told the county officials, point blank, that the state didn't have the money to take over the payments. Warner admires Kerrey's gutsy stand.

In the early 1990s, Kerrey and Republican Senator William Danforth put together a plan to revise the nation's entitlements program. Warner calls that another example of how Kerrey is still willing to take on tough issues and make unpopular proposals. While the plan was not adopted, its presentation didn't seem to diminish Kerrey's standing in national politics. Kerrey is willing to do things, move, make change.

It's more than charisma, Warner says. Something about Kerrey's conduct makes the public more willing to hear bad news from him than from someone else.

As one who has delivered his own share of politically unpopular news through the years concerning budgets and taxes and other high-profile issues—and has been re-elected 10 times—Warner should know.

One piece of news many in Nebraska do not like to hear these days is Warner's view on state-sponsored gambling. Legalized gambling has gradually expanded during the last 30 years, and the state initiated its own lottery after Ben Nelson became governor in 1991. Gambling has been touted as a way to keep taxes down and, at the same time, continue to provide government services.

Warner is not so sure.

"I simply don't like it."

Morally, personally, economically?

"All of the above.

"I don't like to think of gambling as a method of supporting government." If one legislative goal is to keep the cost of government down, "taxes should be painful and apparent when you pay them."

He uses taxes as an example. Sales tax is paid gradually, in small increments. Income tax is often withheld before a person receives a paycheck. People tend not to notice those taxes the way they do property tax, which is usually paid in large chunks. "It gets your attention," the senator says.

"Easy money, which you have in gambling, encourages easy spending."

Furthermore, Warner believes that gambling as a source of revenue is extremely regressive. A regressive tax is generally defined as one that falls more heavily on the poor than the rich.

And besides that, "As I recall, Rome burned—figuratively—because of deterioration of morals."

The pro-gambling forces argue that a lot of Nebraska money is going to purchase lottery tickets in neighboring states. That may be true, but it's like a child trying to convince his parents he should be allowed to do something because "all the other kids are doing it." Warner says he never won that kind of an argument with his parents. And he's never been convinced it is a persuasive argument.

"I don't think it's healthy for the people of the state to have outright gambling."

When Warner makes this argument, people ask him whether he's in favor of abolishing horse racing and the accompanying betting, practices that have been legal in Nebraska for more than 60 years. Warner knows the question is something of a trap because he serves on the Nebraska State Fair board, which sponsors horse racing.

"I say no—'cause you can't go back." But he probably would not have been in favor of expanding horse racing throughout the state if he had had a chance to vote on the matter in 1934, he adds.

He did vote in favor of a 1960s measure that permitted Bingo games and raffles sponsored by charitable organizations or civic groups—things people would likely donate to anyway. Since then, the courts have interpreted the measure to include a lot more than what Warner thought had been approved.

"I was thinking of the Bingo games they used to play in Waverly at the Firemen's Frolic in July," he says. "That was a totally different breed of cat than what we have now."

Warner can also enumerate a few other political changes he doesn't much like:

- the so-called motor voter bill. The bill allows people to register to vote at the same places they get and renew their driver's licenses in the hope that making registration easier will also improve voter turnout at elections. While he realizes that healthy voter turnouts are a reflection of a healthy democracy, Warner thinks people who invest the time and effort to go to the courthouse to register may also take the time and effort to find out about the issues and candidates before going to the polls and will, thus, make more informed voting choices.

- the errors that can result from the ease of getting an initiative petition on the ballot in Nebraska. Too many initiative petitions have been approved and then found to be defective or unconstitutional. Furthermore, Warner believes people seldom have enough information to make educated decisions about the petitions. He thinks public hearings should be scheduled on each petition, both to make it easier for the courts to divine the intent behind an initiative that may be challenged and to give people more information on which to base their votes. He is currently serving on two legislative groups that will probably recommend changes in the inititative process.

- paid petition gatherers. Warner has long been suspicious of the practice. However, the U.S. Supreme Court ruled the practice legal in 1988, and Nebraska has been forced to go along with the ruling. Warner's concerns about the pitfalls of paying people to get petition signatures were justified when several 1996 petitions included alleged signatures from people who turned out to have been dead before the petitions circulated.

No single official, no matter how respected, can always influence governmental matters to go his way, and Warner is no exception. He has had his share of legislative defeats.

And yet, when Senator Warner speaks, his colleagues do listen. So do people in other branches of government. So do people around the state who care about government.

Henry Cordes recalls covering the Legislature for the Omaha World-Herald. Reporters tend to pay attention to floor debate "with only half an ear," Cordes says, "but when Warner stood up, you'd want to listen."

Warner's record suggests it wasn't long after he arrived in the Unicameral that people began to value his opinion. Now that he's been there longer than anyone else, his opinion is valued all the more. Part of it may simply be respect for age and experience, but most of it is probably respect for an honorable and effective career as a legislative leader.

The senator says prominence in the Legislature is often mistaken for leadership but that the two are not the same. "Prominence is essentially determined by the media, and leadership is an internal matter." Leadership may shift with the issue and with a particular senator's expertise in an area. It may also depend on how reliable the other senators perceive him or her to be.

Prominence may not leave the long-term impact that leadership does, but it's not necessarily all bad. Even Warner admits that.

The senator remembers several times during his career when, after a redistricting, he would be welcomed by people new to his constituency. They would tell him they had nothing particularly against the senator who had previously represented them, but they just never heard about anything their former senator had done. At least they knew Warner was doing something, they said, because they read his name frequently in the newspapers.

"People prefer to be represented by someone thought of as an effective legislator," Warner says, and simple publicity can help in that regard.

But in some cases what the public perceives as leadership may be just prominence. Warner gives Terry Carpenter as one example: Most people considered him a leader, but Warner disagrees. "From my viewpoint he was more prominent."

Carpenter was more colorful than consistent, drawing attention and headlines for his attacks on issues and people. Warner likens Carpenter's activity to that of John Breslow, current state auditor: "He gets a headline every time he attacks somebody."

Another example of a prominent legislator, Warner says, is John DeCamp, who served from 1971-86. "He was willing to be on most any side of any issue. It's my observation that he would carry most any amendment that some lobbyist would want him to carry—provided they had 25 votes" so that the legislation would pass. After a senator's name is associated with successful legislation a number of times, the press, the people and other legislators start to believe the senator is a leader, Warner says. DeCamp used the process to his advantage.

Sometimes people gain prominence by opposing other senators' legislation, Warner says. DeCamp and Loran Schmit often worked together in the Legislature. In the 1970s, the two would often oppose certain legislation simply to oppose the senator who was carrying it. Then a few years later, they might come back with the same concept in a bill of their own.

Warner says he does not criticize senators who oppose legislation for ideological or policy reasons. That's legitimate opposition. But he doesn't approve of using legislative opposition simply to acquire power.

But Warner places that in context: "Most people in public office are highly competitive by nature." A competitive nature helps a person both run for office and acquire influence once elected.

Admitting that he wants to win somehow goes against Warner's innate modesty and unwillingness to push himself forward. Competitiveness is something he cannot deny, but he adds, "It's a fine line, I guess, when you cross over from being competitive to being obstructionist in order to win."

If that kind of behavior makes a person prominent, what makes one a leader? Part of it, the senator says, is that "people have confidence in the individual's judgment" and that the judgment is based more in objective reasoning about an issue than in a desire to get attention.

"Probably the most important thing," he adds, "is knowledge. ... There's no substitute for that." Also important is the willingness to admit that each issue has more than one side.

"Another thing that's tremendously important is that you never misuse leadership."

Warner doesn't like to declare himself either prominent or a leader, but he admits other people say he falls into both categories. After a long pause, he says quietly, "I suppose I would, too.

"But I don't think I'm prominent by doing exotic things."

The positions he's held have helped make him prominent. They have put him at the forefront of a great deal of legislative activity and helped get his name in the papers on a regular basis.

Another factor may be that, especially in the 1960s and early 1970s, "I was available. I was here a lot." He worked at the Capitol a lot, something far more convenient for a senator from Waverly than one from a district farther from Lincoln. As a result, reporters would call for his opinions and reactions, and government employees and other elected officials would stop by to talk.

Also, the Lincoln papers usually asked Lancaster County legislators for comments and opinions on legislation. Those papers had circulation well beyond the county, and that brought Warner and the other Lincoln senators additional publicity.

The Omaha World-Herald also has called frequently on Warner for information and opinions. In that case, the senator says, it was usually because he chaired a pivotal committee or carried important or controversial legislation. He says he still gets called if "a fuss" arises about state aid to schools, roads or sales and income taxes because he has been so deeply involved in those topics.

"And certainly it's been true the last dozen years that I'm probably the only one around who can talk background." Long conversations with reporters may result in his being mentioned only briefly in a story in those cases, but it still keeps his name before the public.

Warner has also gained prominence as the recipient of dozens of awards. Among the more prominent are the World-Herald's Midlands Man of the Year award in 1985, an award from the Nebraska Hall of Agricultural Achievement in 1986 (the same honor given his father in 1957) and induction into the Ak-Sar-Ben Court of Honor in 1994. Each award has added to Warner's name recognition among the people of Nebraska.

But sometimes both leadership and prominence come from the same source. The legislative offices Warner has held are a prime example. Speaker, chairman of the Executive Board and chairman of committees like Appropriations and Revenue are, as Jack Rodgers says, "plum positions that go to people held in great respect by their colleagues."

Warner says the issues that the person in those offices must deal with are major ones and, often, controversial. It requires a leader to steer his fellow senators through those issues successfully, something Warner has done for many a year.

It's something he plans to keep doing as long as his health allows.

Keeping On Keeping On

A lifetime of farm work has taken its toll on the senator. His son Jamie says Warner has been kicked many a time by cows and horses. And the senator himself talks about how he has rolled two tractors. One of those adventures probably could have been fatal.

He had been thrown from the tractor and "could hear that tractor behind me, and I was crawling like crazy. I can still remember hearing that thing."

The other time he rolled a tractor, "it just went over easy."

One of his other mishaps resulted in some fun in the Legislature, Warner remembers. He was planting corn with an air planter. He couldn't feel any air coming out of the bottom and didn't think the blades were working. Very deliberately, he says, "I put my fingers up there to see if it was turning. And it was."

He nearly cut the ends off several fingers. He called home from the farm lot where he had been checking out the corn planter and asked Betty if she was busy.

"I think you'd better run me to the hospital," he told her. "I got my fingers in the planter." Doctors sewed up the lacerations, and the fingers healed just fine.

But the sight of Senator Warner at his desk in the Legislature with his fingers bandaged led one of his fellow senators to hatch a scheme. The next day, all the senators had two bandaged fingers.

"In agriculture you have a lot of near misses, and almost all of them are pilot error, carelessness," Warner says.

The beating that farm work and accidents have given his body have led to serious arthritis, and Warner had a hip replaced in August 1993 and a knee in August 1994. "I wish I could have an ankle done," he says.

And he has prostate cancer. "But the doctors tell me 60 percent of

253

males over 65 do," he says. He is being treated for the disease but has not let it slow him down much. "The odds are there are 10 other things I could die from first," he says.

But probably as serious as his physical ailments are the losses he suffered in recent years. His wife, Betty, died March 21, 1994. His brother, Charlie, was killed in a tractor-train accident only a few months later, on June 1, 1994.

It has not been easy. "I worry about him," his son Jamie says. "It was tough when Mom died."

Betty had fought bone cancer for several years before becoming seriously ill and bed-ridden in 1993. The family had arranged for her to stay at home, and the senator took care of her himself as much as he could. Although her condition had turned critical that March, Warner continued to harbor a hope that she would recover.

"He never quite believed she would die," his daughter Liz says. "They were so close. She was his confidante and best friend."

Jamie says the same thing: "It was so hard for him to let her go, to lose her." The couple had been "so intertwined."

Jack Rodgers says the large attendance at Betty's funeral was a tribute to her influence in the state and to both her and her husband. "Very few people knew state government like Betty did," Rodgers says.

Many who know him have been touched by Warner's grief and loss. Henry Cordes, the World-Herald reporter, says he's sorry to see what the senator has gone through.

"You have to admire him personally," Cordes says. Despite the personal trauma Warner experienced, "he never missed a beat in terms of being responsive to the state and the public."

It is that concern for the entire state over the long haul that most observers of the Nebraska political scene cite when they talk about Jerome Warner. Asked to name Warner's specific programmatic contributions, they list roads, state aid to schools, higher education, the greenbelt laws, the appropriations and budgeting process and tax law.

Warner himself agrees those are the major legislative issues on which he has had an impact. But he says it's sometimes been the smaller, less obvious things that have brought the most personal satisfaction.

As an example he offers his priority bill in the 1995 session: It modified a bill passed the year before concerning purchase of prescription drugs by mail. The effect of that measure had been to increase significantly some people's bills for long-term prescriptions. The people affected were often those already in difficult financial straits because they suffered from chronic illnesses.

"There was no lobbyist to be on their side," Warner says. "The lobby force was all in opposition." So Warner took on the cause and got the legislation changed.

Another example happened in the early 1970s. That bill may have affected "only one person in the state: She happened to be my second grade teacher." The woman had taught outside Nebraska for a few years before returning to the state. As a result, she had missed a certain deadline for filing documentation for her retirement and was to receive less retirement pay than she was entitled to. Warner got the law changed to solve the problem.

The retired teacher had a legitimate case that simply couldn't be solved except through legislation, the senator says. Helping people in that way may ease citizens' perceptions of state government as rule-bound and aloof from the people it is supposed to serve.

Never comfortable tooting his own horn, Warner says, "This isn't going to sound very good, but I would like to think that I have had some impact on improving the image of the institution."

His legislative colleagues—current and former—other public officials and news reporters with whom he has worked as well as his constituents seem to agree: Not only has Warner left his mark on major and minor legislation, but he also has been and remains one of the most—if not the most—respected elected officials in Nebraska. In other words, he has met Abraham Lincoln's test of character.

"He's respected in every quarter," says Betty Schlaphoff, a constituent from Waverly.

Doug Bereuter says he doesn't think it's been hard for Warner to be both influential and respected. He has been able to wield power, Bereuter says, because he is well-prepared before he reaches a decision or speaks out on a matter. Others know that he has thought the matter through, and "his comments on the floor have impact."

Warner has built a reputation for hard work and careful study.

"There are other avenues to power," says reporter Don Walton: "bluster, threat, deal-making, pressure, going to the public with things that are misleading." The fact that Warner took the route of hard work may have been more difficult, but it means his influence has been longer-lasting.

Sometimes the hard legislative work has done actual physical damage. Doug Kristensen, who sits next to Warner in the Legislature, tells how he noticed in 1992 that Warner's hands were red and sore. Kristensen soon realized why.

The Legislature was in the midst of a tension-filled debate, trying to solve the personal property tax crisis. Warner was leading the way, standing for hours each day at a microphone to explain and defend his proposed amendment. Because the arthritis in his knee had become acute, the senator was using crutches, and he ground his hands on his crutches until they were nearly raw. Warner never quit, though, Kristensen says. "I marvel at his stamina."

Warner is know for putting the issues before his own convenience or any effect they might have on his own standing in the Legislature. He has a reputation for taking positions because he believes they reflect good public policy. Dave Maurstad, elected to the Unicameral in 1994, says, "When you do that consistently, there's no way it won't be successful."

Being open and straightforward about his ideas and goals has helped Warner, too. Tom Bergquist of the Legislature's research office observes that politicians are often tempted fudge the facts a bit in order to win a small victory at the expense of the larger goal. Warner resists the temptation, and it pays off. "If you're up front and straight, you my lose some battles, but in the long run, you'll win the war."

Kermit Brashear also points to Warner's commitment to the long view. "He won't compromise his long-term values ... for short-term gain."

A December 1990 Lincoln Star editorial says Warner's power as Appropriations chairman stemmed, in part, from his attention to detail and his vast knowledge about the budgeting process and state government in general. But most of his power, the editorial says, came from his reputation for fairness and integrity.

Scott Moore also notes that Warner sticks with his beliefs and speaks his mind, "even if it's not popular. ... People respect that." Warner is a realist who will adapt to changing circumstances, Moore says, but refuses simply to go along with what opinion polls indicate as the majority view.

Kay Orr, former governor, agrees. Warner has consistently adhered to his values, and that "builds a trust in those with whom you work."

Ron Roskens says Warner is "the same in the field talking to a fellow farmer as he is in the Legislature or at church. There are never any airs."

Henry Cordes, the reporter, says, "If he couldn't vote with his friends, he couldn't vote on anything. Everyone likes Senator Warner."

Shirley Marsh is one of Warner's friends. She says Warner is respected for the caliber of person he is. "You don't change from what you were" before being elected to office. "You just bring it in with you."

Dick Herman, retired editor, agrees. Warner has maintained both power and integrity "by functioning as Jerry Warner," he says.

Another quotation from Abraham Lincoln helps to illustrate what Herman means: "Character is like a tree and reputation like its shadow. The shadow is what we think of it; the tree is the real thing." In Warner's case, observers imply, the shadow—Warner's reputation for honesty, integrity and service—is a precision image of the tree, branch for branch and leaf for leaf.

Former Senator Jim Exon says of Warner's ability to combine influence and service, "It comes easy to him. It's just his nature."

In a column in the April 21, 1986, Lincoln Star, Don Walton wrote that Warner, then solidly in the midst of his leadership as chairman of the Appropriations Committee, was more powerful than the governor. Walton said leadership in the state's budget matters was not something that necessarily belonged to the Appropriations chairman. Instead, it was a byproduct of Warner's colleagues' admiration for and confidence in him. Warner had not abused the power he had been given or the trust placed in him.

In a piece printed the following February, Walton referred to Warner as the "voice of reason in the Legislature" and called him fair and politically courageous—"the consummate public servant."

James Joyce, former legislative reporter for the Lincoln Star, says once people have learned that a man can be trusted, that he's fair and that he knows what he's talking about, influence is his to lose. "He's never done anything to lose it," Joyce says of Warner.

Governor Ben Nelson says much the same thing: "He has never abused power. ... If he didn't have integrity, people wouldn't have confidence in him. If he abused power, he'd lose it."

Eleanor Stratton, who clerked for the Appropriations Committee in the 1980s, points to Warner's upbringing as the source of his integrity and desire to serve. "It was instilled in him as a child," she says.

Corliss Young agrees: "He was raised that way. ... He came by it naturally."

That's the same place Warner gives the credit. "When I was growing up, I was expected to behave, and I knew it," the senator says. He grew up in a Christian home, and he says he thinks his philosophy can be summed up by the Golden Rule: Do unto others as you would have them do unto you. "That's how I function, I guess."

Former Governor Charlie Thone says, "He truly means to serve. And he has served so well."

No one is perfect, of course, not even the dean of the Nebraska Legislature. However, no one speaking about Jerome Warner cites any character flaws. Yes, he may not always be as effective on the floor as he might be. Yes, he may be so devoted to the institution that he can't see it objectively. But no one questions his honesty, commitment, sense of duty or motivation for service.

Does he have any weaknesses? His aide Corliss Young cites one: "This office." She gestures around her at the piles of papers that cover Warner's desk, his bookcases and a conference table. "He doesn't throw anything away."

Yet he knows where everything is, Young says. She quotes a poster she has seen that says, "A messy desk is the sign of an organized mind." That is true of Warner, Young says.

Beyond the messy office, there's the matter of the senator's well-known love for scotch. No one has ever even hinted that Warner abuses alcohol, but his ability to hold his liquor is almost legendary. Scott Moore remembers, early in his years in the Legislature, going to lunch with Warner and trying to match him drink for drink.

"He'd get me sleepy and tired," Moore says, making it hard for him to be totally engaged in the afternoon's committee hearings. "I think it was a way to control me."

But those human foibles don't detract much from the picture of Warner as an honest public servant who finds deep satisfaction in serving.

Peter Hoagland, who served in the Legislature for eight years and in Congress for six, has watched a lot of legislators in action. Warner ranks at the top in terms of integrity, Hoagland says.

Furthermore, Warner is not just the legislative patriarch, sitting back and resting on his laurels. He's still in there pitching, trying to steer people toward what he sees as the long-term good of the state. That commitment to intense involvement may be another of the many things Warner learned from his father, who, at age 80, was serving as lieutenant governor when he died in 1955—and was still talking with his son about policy and the state's future during the months before his death.

After 34 years in the Unicameral, Warner is still talking about what needs to be done. A week after his 10th re-election, he had already begun to plan strategy for the 1997 session.

Ron Withem, legislative speaker, remembers a conversation he had with Warner in 1995. Withem told Warner that, after 12 years in the Unicameral, he was finding it difficult to stay intensely engaged in legislative business. But that doesn't seem to be a problem for Warner, who has been in office nearly three times as long.

"It seems to me as though he's just constantly renewed," Withem says of Warner. The senior senator is "still energized" by issues, willing to immerse himself in them and do his homework.

And Warner plans stay immersed and keep studying.

"I had no thought I'd be here this long," he says. "I wasn't elected the first time I ran, and I've always sort of assumed I would not be elected the last time I ran."

Warner is surprised he has survived at the polls in light of his involvement in so many controversial issues. "I've never shied away from controversy. As long as I feel right inside about the side I'm on, I'm comfortable."

Assuming that he would, at some point, be defeated at the polls, Warner has always reminded himself that he would feel better if defeat came because he had done what he thought was right instead of what was politically popular.

The job may not be easy, and it certainly is not financially rewarding, but Warner intends to keep at it because he likes it. Now that he has cut back on his farming operation, renting out all his land and keeping only the livestock, he has more time to spend on legislative duties. And he still finds issues like tax restructuring "intriguing."

"Lots of things are attractive about public office," Warner says, "ego, recognition. It's very easy to believe it's you getting all that attention. But it's not you, it's the office."

It's not the ego-building or the recognition that make the effort worthwhile. Instead, it's the opportunity to serve, to help, to improve things.

"Some nights I go home feeling like I made something a little better than the day before."

It's a point of view he learned from his father. "When you get all said and done, there's nothing there but that you feel you contributed something. You better assume you're going to do it just for that reason."